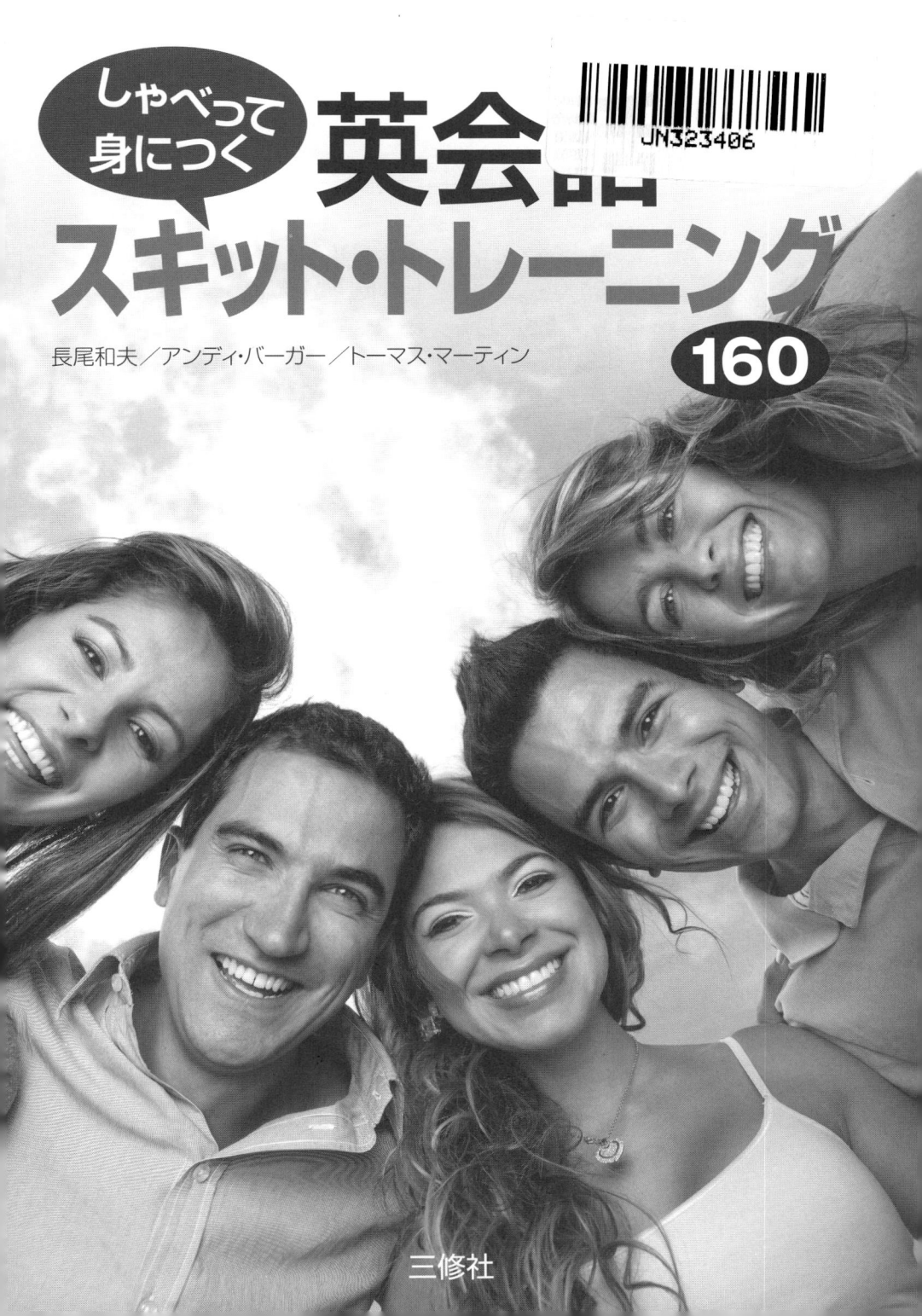

しゃべって身につく 英会話
スキット・トレーニング 160

長尾和夫／アンディ・バーガー／トーマス・マーティン

三修社

■はじめに

『しゃべって身につく 英会話スキット・トレーニング』は、**本格的に英語のロール・プレー・トレーニング（役割演技練習）ができる書籍**を目指して企画・制作されました。

ロール・プレーとはみなさん自身が**ネイティヴの役になりきって、ダイアローグのもうひとりのネイティヴ話者と会話しているかのように、スキット（寸劇；短いダイアローグ）の中で受け答えをする実戦的なトレーニング**です。ロール・プレー練習を数多く行えば、**ナチュラルな発音やイントネーション、タイミングで英語を口に出す**ことができるようになります。また練習を繰り返すことで、**英語らしい表現を知らず知らずのうちにカラダに染みこませる**ことが可能です。

本書では、ロール・プレー練習を通して本格的な日常会話を身につけていただくために、その素材として、**第1章の日常会話編、第2章の旅行会話編、第3章の異文化交流編**の3つの章立てで、**合計160ものネイティヴのスキットを用意**しました。三修社の既刊書籍『絶対「英語の口」になる！リアルな日常英会話で鍛える シャドーイング大特訓50』、『絶対「英語の口」になる！ネイティヴとの異文化トークで鍛える！シャドーイング大特訓50』、『絶対「英語の脳」になる！同時通訳方式（サイトラ）で鍛える ネイティヴ英語脳・育成大特訓50』の3タイトルの原稿の一部を改訂・再掲載するとともに、新たに書き起こした原稿を加え、**スキット（寸劇）内容のバリエーションを最大限に広げる**ことを心がけました。また、スキットはレベル別に★のマークを付してあります。★（初歩レベル）から、★★（中級レベル）、★★★（上級レベル）と難易度が高くなっていますので、自分のレベルにあったスキットで練習を進めていただくことが可能です。

ロール・プレー練習とは、スキットのふたりの話者の片方になりきって、ネイティヴさながらに英語を自分の言葉のように口に出す練習です。

ロール・プレー・トレーニングを行い、ネイティヴの会話をそのまま丸ごと口に出すことによって、より自然に英語がみなさんのカラダに染みこんでいき、みなさんの血となり肉となっていきます。

本書では、このロール・プレー練習の前段階として、まず、スキットのシャドーイング練習をステップ1と2として用意しました。

最初にシャドーイングを行うことで、**ネイティヴらしい発音やイントネーション、スピードなどを体得**していただき、その上で、ステップ3のロール・プレー練習に進んでいただきます。

　書籍タイトルにある「しゃべって身につく」という謳い文句には、もちろんこのシャドーイング練習とそれに続くロール・プレー練習の両方の意味が含まれています。

　まずは、**シャドーイングでネイティヴらしい英語の発話を身につけ、さらにその上で、ロール・プレーを行うことで、読者のみなさんのカラダに、きれいなネイティヴらしい英語をしっかりと染みこませていただこう**という意図があるのです。

　ステップ1と2のシャドーイングで、たっぷりとウォームアップしたら、そのあとには、本書の最大の特徴である**「ロール・プレー・トレーニング」**が待ち構えています。ロールとは**「役割」**という意味。本書では**最終的にスキットの片方の人物になりきっていただきます**。最初は書籍を見ながら、人物になりきって英語を発話してみましょう。さらに慣れてきたら、書籍をチラッと見る程度で英語を口に出せるようになる練習を行い、最後は、書籍を伏せて、**CD音声だけを頼りに、あたかも自分が話しているネイティヴであるかのように演技**していただきます。

　ロール・プレー・トレーニングは野球の千本ノックのように地道な練習ですが、練習量がそのまま実力となって身につく練習法でもあります。詳しい書籍の利用法は「本書の使い方」に譲りますが、ぜひ、本書でのトレーニングを最後まで、また繰り返し行って、ネイティヴ感覚の英語を体得していただければ幸いです。

　最後になりますが、本書の出版にご尽力いただいた三修社のスタッフのみなさんにお礼を申し上げます。

2014年8月末日
A+Café 代表　長尾和夫

はじめに

■本書の使い方

STEP 1

各センテンスをシャドーイングしよう。

ナチュラル・スピードで流れる音声に合わせて、スキット全体を通してシャドーイングしてみましょう。シャドーイングとは、流れてくる CD 音声にほんの少し（0.5 秒ほど）だけ遅れながら、音声をそのまままねて口に出すトレーニングです。シャドーイング・トレーニングを行うことで、ネイティヴらしい発音やイントネーション、音の連結や脱落などの特徴をつかみ取り、自分で口に出せるようになります。また、英語を繰り返しシャドーイングすれば、英語のつくりや考え方までもがカラダに染みこんできます。自力で英文を構成して口に出すときにも、シャドーイングで染みこんだ英語が自然と口から飛び出してくるようになり、英会話力の飛躍的な向上につながります。

最初はテキストを開き文字を見ながらシャドーイングを行いましょう。それが完全にできるようになれば、テキストを伏せ CD の音声だけを頼りにシャドーイング練習を行ってください。CD の音声だけでシャドーイングできるようになればステップ 1 は合格です。CD 音声だけでのシャドーイングは特に難しいので、くじけず忍耐強く練習を続けましょう。

STEP 2 テキストを見ながらスキットを演じてみよう。

シャドーイングでしっかりネイティヴの発音とイントネーションを身につけたら、CD に合わせて自分でスキットを演じる練習をしましょう。毎回、女性か男性のどちらかのパートになりきって片方の役を演じてください。慣れてきたら一人二役を同時にこなしてみてもいいでしょう。最初は、英文テキストをしっかり目で追いながら練習を行い、徐々に英文を見る頻度を落としていきましょう。最終的には、本の一部をチラッと見るだけで、あとは目を閉じてしまってもセンテンスがほぼ言える程度まで練習を行ってください。

STEP 3

日本語訳を見ながらスキットを演じてみよう。

　ステップ3は完全なロール・プレー（役割演技練習）です。まとめとして、ステップ3では、片方の人物の会話を演じていただきます。ここでは、演じていただく人物の会話を空欄にしてあります。日本語のヒントだけを頼りに、身につけた英文を口に出す練習をしましょう。難しければ、最初はCDをポーズ・ボタンでストップしながら、ロール・プレーしてもいいでしょう。

　CDでみなさんに発話していただく部分では、短い「ポン」という効果音が入っていますので、その音が聞こえたら、当該部分をロール・プレー練習してください。ステップ1と2のシャドーイングの音源でネイティヴが話したのと同じだけの長さのポーズを取ってありますので、そのポーズの間に発話を終えられるようにがんばりましょう。

　大学の英語部などいろいろな団体で、英語劇を演じて英語を身につけるような取り組みが長年行われています。完全に役になりきり演じることで、英語の世界にどっぷりと浸って英語を習得しようという取り組みで、イマージョン（言語文化に浸りきってその言語を学習する方法）の一種とも言えます。本書のステップ3では、擬似的に英語でドラマを演じ、その文化に浸ることが可能です。なりきればなりきるほど、身につけた表現が実際の英会話の場面でスッと口から飛び出すようになってきます。

　以上で、本書でのトレーニングの基本的な説明は終わりです。ステップ2や3が難しい場合は、まずステップ1の学習だけを最後のユニットまで進めてもいいでしょう。そのあとで、ステップ2を最後までトレーニングし、最終的にステップ3に取り組んでもいいでしょう。

　本書のトレーニングは、繰り返し英文をまねて口に出し続ける練習です。根気と努力が必要なトレーニングですが、やればやるほどに力がついてくることが実感できると思います。英語の基礎体力作りとして、徹底的に本書に取り組んでいただき、どんどん実力を向上させてください。

■もくじ

Chapter 1 日常会話

ユニット	レベル		ページ
1	★	朝の会話　Morning Conversation	11
2	★	出かける前の会話　Before Going Out	13
3	★	待ち合わせ場所を決める　Deciding a Meeting Place	15
4	★	慌てて出かける場面の会話　Rushing to Leave on Time	17
5	★	待ち合わせ場所での会話　Talking at the Meeting Place	19
6	★	久しぶりに会った相手と話す　Long Time No See!	21
7	★	人を紹介するときの会話　Introducing People	23
8	★	天気の話題で話をする　Complaining about the Weather	25
9	★	暇乞いするときの会話　Taking One's Leave	27
10	★	今夜は遅くなると連絡する　Calling to Say You'll Be Late	29
11	★	帰宅したときの会話　Talk After Arriving Home	31
12	★	就寝前の会話　Talk Before Sleeping	33
13	★	いっしょに料理を作る　Preparing a Meal Together	35
14	★	洋服を試着する　Trying On Clothes	37
15	★	値引きしてもらう　Asking for a Discount	39
16	★	カードで会計してもらう　Paying with a Credit Card	41
17	★	無料で配送してもらう　Getting Free Delivery	43
18	★	誕生日のプレゼント　Birthday Present	45
19	★	ゴミ出し　Chores	47
20	★	着替え　Getting Dressed	49
21	★	洗濯　Laundry	51
22	★	犬の散歩　Walking the Dog	53
23	★	手伝いを頼む　Getting Some Help	55
24	★	電球の調整　Adjusting a Light Bulb	57
25	★	買い物のリスト　Shopping List	59
26	★	荷物の配送　Package Delivery	61
27	★	子どもを叱る　Scolding a Child	63
28	★	子どもをほめる　Praising a Child	65
29	★	コーヒーをすすめる　Offering Coffee	67
30	★	メールを書く　Writing an email	69
31	★	ネット・サーフィン　Surfing the Net	71
32	★	ネット・ショッピング　Online Shopping	73
33	★	チャンネル　Changing the channel	75
34	★	気分が悪い　Not Feeling Well	77
35	★	道順　Directions	79
36	★	電車の乗り換え　Changing Trains	81
37	★	ドライブスルーの窓口　Ordering through a Drive-through Window	83
38	★★	朝食についての会話　At Breakfast	85
39	★★	今日の予定に関する会話　Today's Schedule	87
40	★★	今日の天気に関する会話　The Weather	89
41	★★	帰宅したときの会話　Arriving Home	91
42	★★	掃除についての会話　Cleaning/Housework	93
43	★★	スーパーでの会話　At the Supermarket	95
44	★★	帰りの時間を知らせる電話　Calling to Say When You'll Be Home	97
45	★★	夕食のメニューの相談　What's for Dinner	99
46	★★	料理中の会話　Cooking	101
47	★★	観たい番組についての会話　What to Watch	103
48	★★	就寝前のちょっとした会話　Before Bedtime	105
49	★★	旅行の計画に関する会話　Planning a Trip	107
50	★★	休暇の不満を漏らす会話　Having to Work on One's Day Off	109
51	★★	家計についての議論　Family Finances	111
52	★★	ガーデニングに関する会話　Gardening	113
53	★★	食事に招待する会話　Inviting Someone to Dinner	115

54	★★	初対面の人との会話　Meeting for the First Time	117
55	★★	待ち合わせの約束　Arranging to Meet	119
56	★★	外出準備中の会話　Getting Ready to Leave	121
57	★★	デパートでの会話　At the Department Store	123
58	★★	試着室での会話　In the Fitting Room	125
59	★★	レジでの支払い時の会話　At the Register	127
60	★★	返品する場面での会話　Returning an Item	129
61	★★	お酒を飲みながらの会話　Talking Over Drinks	131
62	★★	銀行での会話　At the Bank	133
63	★★	郵便局の窓口でのやりとり　At the Post Office	135
64	★★	病院での医者との会話　At the Hospital	137
65	★★	緊急通報の会話　Calling 911	139
66	★★	ファッションについての会話　Talking About Fashion	141
67	★★	旅の感想についての会話　Impressions of a Trip	143
68	★★	スポーツについての会話　Talking About Sports	145
69	★★	趣味についての会話　Talking About Hobbies/Interests	147
70	★★	書籍についての会話　Book Review	149
71	★★	映画についての会話　Movie Review	151
72	★★	携帯電話についての会話　Talking About Smart Phones	153
73	★★	季節についての会話　Talking About the Seasons	155
74	★★	ボランティアについての会話　Talking About Volunteer Work	157
75	★★	故郷についての会話　Hometown Talk	159
76	★★	人物についての会話　People	161
77	★★	消息についての会話　Long Time No See	163
78	★★	子供についての会話　Talking About the Kids	165
79	★★	婚約した人との会話　Significant Others	167
80	★★	仲直りするときの会話　Making Up	169

Chapter 2　旅行会話

81	★	レストランを予約する　Making a Restaurant Reservation	173
82	★	レストランに入店する　Entering a Restaurant	175
83	★	おすすめ料理をたずねる　Asking for Meal Recommendations	177
84	★	食事を注文する　Ordering at a Restaurant	179
85	★	お酒を注文する　Ordering Drinks with a Meal	181
86	★	デザートを注文する　Ordering Dessert	183
87	★	支払い時の会話　At the Cashier	185
88	★	アテンダントとの会話①　Talking with a Flight Attendant 1	187
89	★	アテンダントとの会話②　Talking with a Flight Attendant 2	189
90	★	入国審査　At the Immigration Counter	191
91	★	荷物の預け入れ　Checking In Luggage on a Flight	193
92	★	お金を両替する　Converting Currency	195
93	★	ホテルを予約する　Making Hotel Reservations	197
94	★	チェックイン時の会話　Checking In (to a Hotel)	199
95	★	ホテルで苦情を伝える　Making a Complaint (at a Hotel)	201
96	★	部屋を変更してもらう　Asking to Change Rooms	203
97	★	ルーム・サービスを頼む　Calling Room Service	205
98	★	コンシェルジェにたずねる　Getting Tips from a Hotel Concierge	207
99	★	チェックアウト時の会話　Checking Out (of a Hotel)	209
100	★	乗り換えについて聞く　Train Transfer	211
101	★	道順をたずねる　Asking for Directions	213
102	★	タクシーでの会話　Talking to a Taxi Driver	215
103	★	レンタカーを返却する　Returning a Rented Car	217
104	★	チケットを買う　Buying Tickets to a Performance	219
105	★	モールで店をたずねる　At a Mall Information Booth	221
106	★	品揃えをたずねる　Finding the Item You Wish to Purchase	223
107	★	お土産を買う　Choosing Souvenirs	225

108	★	医者との会話　Talking to a Doctor (About an Ailment)	227
109	★	警官との会話　Talking to a Police Officer (as a Crime Witness)	229
110	★★	駅への道を案内する会話　Giving Directions to the Station	231
111	★★	駅の構内を案内する会話　Giving Directions at the Station	233
112	★★	ホテルのチェックイン　Checking Into the Hotel	235
113	★★	ドライブスルーでの会話　At the Drive-thru	237
114	★★	レストランでの注文　Ordering at a Restaurant	239
115	★★	旅先でのスケジュール　Vacation Plans	241
116	★★	毛布を頼む　Asking for a Blanket	243
117	★★	荷物が出てこない　Luggage Doesn't Come	245
118	★★	苦情の電話　Calling with a Complaint	247
119	★★	おいしいレストランの推薦　Good Restaurant Recommendation	249
120	★★	バス・ツアーについてたずねる　Asking About a Bus Tour	251

Chapter 3　異文化交流

121	★★★	クリスマス　Christmas	255
122	★★★	バレンタイン・デー　Valentine's Day	257
123	★★★	祝祭日・休日　National Holidays	259
124	★★★	ライフ・ワーク・バランス　Life-work Balance	261
125	★★★	サラリーマンの生活　Salaryman Lifestyle	263
126	★★★	飲酒　Drinking	265
127	★★★	ラジオ体操　Radio Exercise	267
128	★★★	女性と仕事　Women in the Workplace	269
129	★★★	家事　Housework	271
130	★★★	大学生活　College Life	273
131	★★★	生涯教育　Adult Education	275
132	★★★	制服　Uniforms	277
133	★★★	公共交通機関　Public Transportation	279
134	★★★	自動車　Cars	281
135	★★★	街角の放送　Announcement	283
136	★★★	混雑と渋滞　Crowded Trains and Traffic Jams	285
137	★★★	街路　Streets	287
138	★★★	エアコンとヒーター　Home AC and Heating Devices	289
139	★★★	趣味　Hobbies	291
140	★★★	プロ・スポーツ　Pro Sports	293
141	★★★	アニメ　Animation	295
142	★★★	映画　Movies	297
143	★★★	ファッション　Fashion	299
144	★★★	サブカルチャー　Subcultures	301
145	★★★	観光スポット　Sightseeing Spots	303
146	★★★	コメディアン　Comedians	305
147	★★★	スターとアイドル　Stars and Idols	307
148	★★★	テレビ番組のスタイル　TV Styles	309
149	★★★	主食　Food Staples	311
150	★★★	麺類とパン　Noodles and Bread	313
151	★★★	子どもの好きな食べ物　Favorite Foods of Kids	315
152	★★★	肥満　Obesity	317
153	★★★	ファミレス　Family Restaurants	319
154	★★★	サービスのレベル　Service Standards	321
155	★★★	公衆トイレ　Public Toilets and Restrooms	323
156	★★★	チップ　Tipping	325
157	★★★	ハグとお辞儀　Hugging and Bowing	327
158	★★★	略語①　Shortened Phrases 1	329
159	★★★	略語②　Shortened Phrases 2	331
160	★★★	言葉の間違い　Getting Words Wrong	333

Chapter 1
日常会話

レベル 1 ★★★ ……… p. 11
レベル 2 ★★★ ……… p. 85

Unit 001 Morning Conversation 朝の会話

STEP 1 各センテンスをシャドーイングしよう。　CD 1-02

STEP 2 テキストを見ながらスキットを演じてみよう。　CD 1-02

M: Good morning! Did you have a good sleep?

おはよう！ よく眠れた？

F: Not really. I kept waking up in the middle of the night.

あまり。真夜中に何度も目覚めてしまって。

* not really は「ほんとうにではない」→「それほどでもない；そうでもない」ということ。

M: You need to stop drinking coffee after five pm. I keep telling you that!

夕方の5時以降にコーヒーを飲むのはやめなきゃね。ずっとそう言ってるでしょ！

F: Yeah, I know. I have to learn to break that habit.

うん、わかってる。その習慣はやめるようにしないとね。

* have to ... は「…しなければならない」という意味のフレーズ。

M: Anyway, what would you like for breakfast? Why don't I make us some French toast?

とにかく、朝食はなにがいい？ 僕がみんなにフレンチ・トーストを作るのはどうかな？

* would you like は do you like のていねいな言い方。
* Why don't I ...? は「私が…するのはどうですか？」という提案のフレーズとしてひとまとまりで理解しよう。

STEP 3 日本語訳を見ながらスキットを演じてみよう。　CD 1-02

M: Good morning! Did you have a good sleep?

F:

あまり。真夜中に何度も目覚めてしまって。

M: You need to stop drinking coffee after five pm. I keep telling you that!

F:

うん、わかってる。その習慣はやめるようにしないとね。

M: Anyway, what would you like for breakfast? Why don't I make us some French toast?

Unit 002 Before Going Out 出かける前の会話

STEP 1 各センテンスをシャドーイングしよう。　CD 1-03

STEP 2 テキストを見ながらスキットを演じてみよう。　CD 1-03

F : What time do you think you'll come back tonight?

あなた、今夜は何時に帰ってこられると思う？

M : Not sure. I have to finish up a report that I need to hand in tomorrow.

わからないよ。明日提出しなきゃならない報告書を仕上げないといけなくて。

F : Okay. I'll be home by seven, so I can make dinner.

わかったわ。7時までには帰ってるから、私が夕食を作れるわ。

＊ so は、前のセンテンスを受けて「…だから…」の意味をもつ。

M : There's a lot of stuff in the refrigerator. Why not just make a stir-fry?

冷蔵庫にたくさんものが入ってるよ。炒め物を作るだけにしたら？

＊ Why not ...? は「…したら？」という意味のフレーズとして理解しよう。

F : Yeah, that sounds easy. See you tonight.

ええ、それはかんたんそうね。また夜にね。

＊ See you. は I'll see you. という文が短くなったもの。

STEP 3 日本語訳を見ながらスキットを演じてみよう。 CD 1-03

F :

あなた、今夜は何時に帰ってこられると思う？

M : Not sure. I have to finish up a report that I need to hand in tomorrow.

F :

わかったわ。7時までには帰ってるから、私が夕食を作れるわ。

M : There's a lot of stuff in the refrigerator. Why not just make a stir-fry?

F :

ええ、それはかんたんそうね。また夜にね。

Unit 003　Deciding a Meeting Place　待ち合わせ場所を決める

STEP 1 　各センテンスをシャドーイングしよう。　CD 1-04

STEP 2 　テキストを見ながらスキットを演じてみよう。　CD 1-04

F : So, where should we meet? I don't know how to get there from the station.

じゃあ、どこで会うのがいい？ 駅からそこにどう行けばいいかわからないわ。

＊ how to get は「到着するための方法」が直訳。

M : Let's meet somewhere on the way. What train line will you be taking?

どこか途中で会おうよ。君はどの路線に乗るの？

F : The Inokashira Line. Should we meet in Shibuya?

井の頭線よ。渋谷で会いましょうか？

M : I hate meeting in Shibuya, because it's so crowded. How about Omotesando?

渋谷で会うのはいやなんだ。すごく混んでいるからね。表参道はどう？

＊ この it は「渋谷」を指す。
＊ How about ...? は「…はどうですか？」と提案するフレーズ。

F : Sure, that's no problem. Let's meet on the platform, close to the middle.

ええ、いいわよ。プラットホームで会いましょうよ、真ん中あたりで。

＊ problem は「問題」。no problem では「問題ない」という意味になる。
＊ close to the middle は「真ん中あたり」。

STEP 3　日本語訳を見ながらスキットを演じてみよう。　CD 1-04

F :

じゃあ、どこで会うのがいい？ 駅からそこにどう行けばいいかわからないわ。

M : Let's meet somewhere on the way. What train line will you be taking?

F :

井の頭線よ。渋谷で会いましょうか？

M : I hate meeting in Shibuya, because it's so crowded. How about Omotesando?

F :

ええ、いいわよ。プラットホームで会いましょうよ、真ん中あたりで。

Unit 004 慌てて出かける場面の会話

Rushing to Leave on Time

STEP 1 各センテンスをシャドーイングしよう。 CD 1-05

STEP 2 テキストを見ながらスキットを演じてみよう。 CD 1-05

F : Are you still at the computer? You're going to make us late for the show!

まだコンピューターの前なの？ あなたのせいで私たちショーに遅れちゃうわ。

M : Oh, sorry. I got busy with some emails. Let me just send this last one.

ああ、ごめんよ。ちょっとEメールでバタバタしちゃった。この最後のだけ、送信させてよ。

* Let me ... は「私に…させる」という意味の表現。
* this last one は「この最後のEメール」。one は email を繰り返さないために使用されている。

F : The kids have been waiting to go for ten minutes already!

子どもたちはもう10分も出かけるのを待ってるのよ！

* have been waiting は「(過去から現在まで)ずっと…している」という意味。

M : Okay, okay. There! I sent it! Just let me grab my jacket.

わかった、わかった。ほら、送ったよ！ ジャケットだけ取ってこさせて。

* Just let me … は「私に…だけさせる」という意味の表現。

F : Great! We should still be on time. I'll tell the kids to get in the car.

いいわ！ まだ時間には間に合うわね。子どもたちに車に乗るように言ってくる。

* should は「…のはずだ」という意味。

STEP 3 〉〉 日本語訳を見ながらスキットを演じてみよう。　　　CD 1-05

F : Are you still at the computer? You're going to make us late for the show!

M :

あぁ、ごめんよ。ちょっとEメールでバタバタしちゃった。この最後のだけ、送信させてよ。

F : The kids have been waiting to go for ten minutes already!

M :

わかった、わかった。ほら、送ったよ！ ジャケットだけ取ってこさせて。

F : Great! We should still be on time. I'll tell the kids to get in the car.

Unit 005 待ち合わせ場所での会話
Talking at the Meeting Place

STEP 1 各センテンスをシャドーイングしよう。　CD 1-06

STEP 2 テキストを見ながらスキットを演じてみよう。　CD 1-06

F : Hi, sorry I'm late! Were you waiting a long time?

ハ〜イ、遅れてごめんね！ 長い間、待ってた？

M : It's okay. You're not that late. I got here about ten minutes ago.

大丈夫。それほどは遅くないよ。僕は 10 分くらい前に来たんだ。

* that late の that は「それほど」という意味。

F : I'm sorry! Just as I was about to leave I got a couple urgent calls.

ごめんね！ ちょうど出かけようとしてたところで、急ぎの電話がいくつかかかってきたの。

* Just as ... は「ちょうど…のとき」と時間を表す言い方。

M : No worries. I thought maybe you were having trouble finding this place.

かまわないよ。ここを見つけるのに手こずってるのかもと思ってたんだ。

* have trouble -ing で「…するのに手間取る；手こずる」という意味。

F : Well, I did come out the wrong exit. But after that I was able to find my way.

ええ、実際、違う出口から出ちゃったわ。でも、そのあと道を見つけることはできたけどね。

* be able to ... は「…できる」という意味になるフレーズ。

STEP 3 日本語訳を見ながらスキットを演じてみよう。　CD 1-06

F :

ハ～イ、遅れてごめんね！ 長い間、待ってた？

M : It's okay. You're not that late. I got here about ten minutes ago.

F :

ごめんね！ ちょうど出かけようとしてたところで、急ぎの電話がいくつかかかってきたの。

M : No worries. I thought maybe you were having trouble finding this place.

F :

ええ、実際、違う出口から出ちゃったわ。でも、そのあと道を見つけることはできたけどね。

Unit 006 Long Time No See! 久しぶりに会った相手と話す

STEP 1 各センテンスをシャドーイングしよう。　CD 1-07

STEP 2 テキストを見ながらスキットを演じてみよう。　CD 1-07

M: Hey there, stranger! Don't I know you from somewhere?

ねえ、ちょっと、そこの人！ どこかでお会いしましたっけ？

＊ Hey there. は「ねえちょっと」という意味の呼びかけ表現。

F: Mark, hi! Long time, no see! You look great! You haven't changed a bit!

マーク、ハーイ！ 久しぶり！ 元気そうだね！ 全然、変わらないね！

＊ Long time, no see! は、「久しぶり」という意味になる慣用句。長い間会っていなかった相手に使う。

M: Ha, if only that were true! It's good to see you! How long has it been?

ハハ、それがほんとうならいいね！ 君に会えてうれしいよ！ どのくらいになるかな？

＊ if only ... は「ただ…でさえあればいいのに」という意味のフレーズ。

F: Hmmm ... when was the last time we met? I think it was that art show in SoHo.

うーん…最後に会ったのはいつだったかな？ あれはソーホーのアート・ショーだったよね。

＊ I think (that) ... は「私は…だと思う」という意味。

M: Really, that long? That was almost four years ago!

ホントに、そんなに前？ あれは、ほぼ4年前だよ！

STEP 3 日本語訳を見ながらスキットを演じてみよう。　CD 1-07

M :

ねえ、ちょっと、そこの人！ どこかでお会いしましたっけ？

F : Mark, hi! Long time, no see! You look great! You haven't changed a bit!

M :

ハハ、それがほんとうならいいね！ 君に会えてうれしいよ！ どのくらいになるかな？

F : Hmmm ... when was the last time we met? I think it was that art show in SoHo.

M :

ホントに、そんなに前？ あれは、ほぼ4年前だよ！

Unit 007 Introducing People 人を紹介するときの会話

STEP 1 各センテンスをシャドーイングしよう。　CD 1-08

STEP 2 テキストを見ながらスキットを演じてみよう。　CD 1-08

M : Jane, have you met my friend Frank before?

ジェーン、前に僕の友達のフランクに会ったことはある？

F : Not sure. Can you point him out to me?

さあ。彼を指さしてみてもらえる？

* point out A to B は「B に A を指さして選び出す；示す；教える」という意味。

M : He's the guy over there, waiting to buy a drink.

向こうの飲み物を買うのを待っている男性だよ。

* waiting to ... は「…している」という意味になる。

F : No, I've never met him. He's cute! Will you introduce me?

いいえ、彼には会ったことないわ。彼かわいいわね！　紹介してもらえる？

* Will you ...? は「…してくれませんか？」という依頼の文。

M : Of course! I think you two might like each other. Frank! This is someone I want you to meet.

もちろん！　君たちふたりはお互いを気に入るかもよ。フランク！　君に会ってほしい人がいるんだよ。

STEP 3 日本語訳を見ながらスキットを演じてみよう。　CD 1-08

M: Jane, have you met my friend Frank before?

F:

さあ。彼を指さしてみてもらえる？

M: He's the guy over there, waiting to buy a drink.

F:

いいえ、彼には会ったことないわ。彼かわいいわね！ 紹介してもらえる？

M: Of course! I think you two might like each other. Frank! This is someone I want you to meet.

Unit 008 天気の話題で話をする
Complaining About the Weather

STEP 1 各センテンスをシャドーイングしよう。　CD 1-09

STEP 2 テキストを見ながらスキットを演じてみよう。　CD 1-09

F: It has been so hot recently! I can't stand it!

最近かなり暑いわよね！ 耐えられないわ！

* has been は「ずっと…だ」という意味。

M: I know! I want to crawl inside my refrigerator!

そうだよね！ 冷蔵庫の中に入りたいよ！

* crawl は「(這って) 入る」という意味。

F: It has gone over 35 degrees for three days in a row! That's ridiculous!

3日間連続で35度を超えてるのよ！ バカげてるわ！

* go over ... で「…を超える」という意味。

M: And it's only the middle of July. We might have two more months of this.

それに、まだ7月の中旬だしね。これがあと2カ月も続くかもね。

* the middle of ... は「…の真ん中；半ば」、two more months of ... は、「さらに2カ月の…」。

F: Don't say that! I need to take a vacation someplace cool.

やめてよ！ どこか涼しいところで休暇を取りたいわ。

* someplace cool は「どこか涼しいところで」。

STEP 3 　日本語訳を見ながらスキットを演じてみよう。　CD 1-09

F :

最近かなり暑いわよね！ 耐えられないわ！

M : I know! I want to crawl inside my refrigerator!

F :

3日間連続で35度を超えてるのよ！ バカげてるわ！

M : And it's only the middle of July. We might have two more months of this.

F :

やめてよ！ どこか涼しいところで休暇を取りたいわ。

Unit 009 暇乞いするときの会話
Taking One's Leave

STEP 1 各センテンスをシャドーイングしよう。　CD 1-10

STEP 2 テキストを見ながらスキットを演じてみよう。　CD 1-10

F: Oh, it's ten already. I should be going.

ああ、もう10時だわ。行かないと。

* be going は「出かける状態になる」という意味。

M: Oh, that's too bad. Why do you have to leave so early?

ああ、それは残念だなあ。どうしてそんなに早く出なきゃならないの？

* bad は「悪い」ではなく「残念な」という意味で用いられている。

F: Well, tomorrow is a work day for me. I need to get up pretty early.

あのね、明日は私、仕事の日なのよ。けっこう早く起きないといけなくて。

* Well, ... は「あのね；うん；えーと」などの意味で、前置きに使われる。

M: Oh, I forgot. You work on weekends sometimes. Well, I hope to see you soon.

ああ、忘れてたよ。君はときどき週末も仕事をしているよね。じゃ、また近いうちにね。

* hope to ... は「…することを望む」という意味。

F: Yeah, I'll call you some time next week or so. Let's meet up for lunch!

ええ、来週あたりのどこかで電話するわ。ランチで待ち合わせましょうよ！

* ... or so は「…かそこいら」。

STEP 3 日本語訳を見ながらスキットを演じてみよう。　CD 1-10

F :

あぁ、もう 10 時だわ。行かないと。

M : Oh, that's too bad. Why do you have to leave so early?

F :

あのね、明日は私、仕事の日なのよ。けっこう早く起きないといけなくて。

M : Oh, I forgot. You work on weekends sometimes. Well, I hope to see you soon.

F :

ええ、来週あたりのどこかで電話するわ。ランチで待ち合わせましょうよ！

Unit 010 今夜は遅くなると連絡する
Calling to Say You'll Be Late

STEP 1 各センテンスをシャドーイングしよう。　CD 1-11

STEP 2 テキストを見ながらスキットを演じてみよう。　CD 1-11

F: Hi, I'm going to be late tonight. Sorry.

ハーイ、今夜は遅くなるわ。ごめんね。

M: Again? What time do you think you'll be back?

またなの？ 何時に戻れると思う？

F: I don't know. I think you should go ahead and eat without me.

わからないわ。私抜きで先に食べちゃったほうがいいと思うわ。

M: Oh, that's no fun. But you're going to eat here when you come back, right?

ああ、それはつまらないよ。でも、帰ってきたら、ここで食べるんでしょ？

* no fun は「ゼロの楽しみ」という意味。no は「ゼロの…；ひとつも…ない」。

F: Yeah, please make enough for me too. I'll try to be home before ten.

ええ、私にも十分な量を作ってね。10時前には戻るようにがんばるから。

* enough は「十分な量・数」という意味の名詞。

STEP 3 　日本語訳を見ながらスキットを演じてみよう。　CD 1-11

F : Hi, I'm going to be late tonight. Sorry.

M :

またなの？ 何時に戻れると思う？

F : I don't know. I think you should go ahead and eat without me.

M :

ああ、それはつまらないよ。でも、帰ってきたら、ここで食べるんでしょ？

F : Yeah, please make enough for me too. I'll try to be home before ten.

Unit 011 Talk After Arriving Home
帰宅したときの会話

STEP 1 各センテンスをシャドーイングしよう。　CD 1-12

STEP 2 テキストを見ながらスキットを演じてみよう。　CD 1-12

F : Hi! You're back already! That's unusual.

あら！ もう帰ったの！ めずらしいわね。

* unusual は「いつもと違った；めずらしい」という意味。

M : Yeah. I had a meeting with my client in the afternoon. So I came back when it finished.

うん。午後に顧客と打ち合わせがあってね。で、それが終わって戻ってきたんだ。

F : That's great. So you can have dinner with the kids tonight.

すばらしいわ。だったら、今夜は子どもたちと夕食が食べられるじゃない。

M : Yep. And we can watch a DVD or something before they go to bed.

うん。で、子どもが寝る前に DVD とかを観られるよ。

* ... or something は「…かなにか」という意味のフレーズ。

F : That sounds fun! They are playing in the back yard now. I'll call them.

それは楽しそうね！ いま子どもたちは裏庭で遊んでいるわ。呼ぶわね。

* sound fun は「楽しそうに聞こえる」→「楽しそうだ」と考える。

STEP 3 　日本語訳を見ながらスキットを演じてみよう。　CD 1-12

F :

あら！ もう帰ったの！ めずらしいわね。

M : Yeah. I had a meeting with my client in the afternoon. So I came back when it finished.

F :

すばらしいわ。だったら、今夜は子どもたちと夕食が食べられるじゃない。

M : Yep. And we can watch a DVD or something before they go to bed.

F :

それは楽しそうね！ いま子どもたちは裏庭で遊んでいるわ。呼ぶわね。

Unit 012 就寝前の会話
Talk Before Sleeping

STEP 1 各センテンスをシャドーイングしよう。　CD 1-13

STEP 2 テキストを見ながらスキットを演じてみよう。　CD 1-13

M: It seems like you are really enjoying that book.

その本をとても楽しんでるみたいだね。

* seem like ... で「…のように思える；…のようだ」という意味。

F: I can't put it down! Oh, sorry. Did you want to go to sleep?

本を読むのをやめられないのよ！ ああ、ごめん。眠りたかった？

M: That's okay. I'll listen to some music with my headphones.

大丈夫だよ。ヘッドホンでちょっと音楽を聴いてるからさ。

* I'll ... は「…するよ」と自分がいまから行うことを伝えている。

F: Just let me finish this chapter. I have about ten more pages to go.

この章だけ読み終わらせてね。あと 10 ページくらいよ。

* let me ... は「私に…させて」という意味。
* go はここでは「行く」ではなく、「読み進める」という意味。

M: Sure. And before we go to sleep, tell me why you like it so much!

もちろん。それで、眠る前に、なんでそんなに気に入っているのか教えてよ！

* tell me why ... は「どうして…なのか私に教えて；…の理由を私に教えて」という意味。

STEP 3 　日本語訳を見ながらスキットを演じてみよう。　CD 1-13

M: It seems like you are really enjoying that book.

F:

本を読むのをやめられないのよ！ ああ、ごめん。眠りたかった？

M: That's okay. I'll listen to some music with my headphones.

F:

この章だけ読み終わらせてね。あと 10 ページくらいよ。

M: Sure. And before we go to sleep, tell me why you like it so much!

Unit 013 いっしょに料理を作る
Preparing a Meal Together

STEP 1 各センテンスをシャドーイングしよう。　CD 1-14

STEP 2 テキストを見ながらスキットを演じてみよう。　CD 1-14

M: Okay, the water is boiling. Shall I put the pasta in?

よし、水が沸騰してるよ。パスタを入れようか？

* Shall I …? は「私が…しましょうか？」と提案する表現。

F: Put a pinch of salt in first, and then add the pasta. And stir it every once in a while.

まずは、塩をひとつまみ入れて、それからパスタを入れるの。で、ときどきかき混ぜるのよ。

* every once in a while は「ときどき」。once in a while でも同じ。

M: Okay. And for how long should I cook it?

わかった。で、どのくらいの時間、調理すればいいの？

* for how long は「どのくらい長く」と時間の長さをたずねている。

F: It should be al dente after about eight minutes. You need to be sure not to overcook it.

8分くらい経つとアルデンテになるはずよ。茹ですぎないようにしっかりやってね。

* not to overcook は「調理しすぎないことを；調理しすぎないように」という意味。

M: Got it. And let me just make sure about the amount; is this enough?

わかった。で、量について確認だけさせてよ。これで十分かな？

* Got it. は I got it. が省略されたもの。
* let me … は「僕に…させて」、make sure は「確認する」という意味。

STEP 3 日本語訳を見ながらスキットを演じてみよう。　CD 1-14

M :

よし、水が沸騰してるよ。パスタを入れようか？

F : Put a pinch of salt in first, and then add the pasta. And stir it every once in a while.

M :

わかった。で、どのくらいの時間、調理すればいいの？

F : It should be al dente after about eight minutes. You need to be sure not to overcook it.

M :

わかった。で、量について確認だけさせてよ。これで十分かな？

Unit 014 洋服を試着する
Trying On Clothes

STEP 1 各センテンスをシャドーイングしよう。　CD 1-15

STEP 2 テキストを見ながらスキットを演じてみよう。　CD 1-15

M: I like the design of this shirt. But, are these the only colors you have?

このシャツのデザイン、いいですね。でも、色はこれだけしかないんですか？

* the only ... は「ただそれだけの…」という意味。

F: I think so. What color did you want?

そうだと思います。何色が欲しかったんですか？

* so は「そのように」という意味の副詞。

M: I was hoping for the same style in purple. Of these, my favorite is the blue.

同じ形で紫のものが希望だったんです。この中なら、ブルーがいいかな。

* hope for ... は「…を望む」という意味のフレーズ。

F: Sorry, we don't have purple. Would you like to try on the blue one?

すみません、紫はないんです。ブルーのを試着なさいますか？

* Would you like to ...? は「…なさるのはどうですか？」というていねいな提案表現。

M: Yeah, I guess I will. I really like the style.

うん、そうしようかな。形はすごく気に入ってるんですよ。

* I guess that ... は「なんとなく…だと思う」という意味。「…かなあ」という日本語のニュアンスに近い表現。
* この I will は、I will try on the blue one が省略されたもの。

STEP 3 日本語訳を見ながらスキットを演じてみよう。 CD 1-15

M :

このシャツのデザイン、いいですね。でも、色はこれだけしかないんですか？

F : I think so. What color did you want?

M :

同じ形で紫のものが希望だったんです。この中なら、ブルーがいいかな。

F : Sorry, we don't have purple. Would you like to try on the blue one?

M :

うん、そうしようかな。形はすごく気に入ってるんですよ。

Unit 015 値引きしてもらう
Asking for a Discount

STEP 1 　各センテンスをシャドーイングしよう。　CD 1-16

STEP 2 　テキストを見ながらスキットを演じてみよう。　CD 1-16

F : I like this frame. But do you see here? It has a scratch.
このフレームがいいですね。でも、これが見えますか？ ひっかき傷があるんですよ。

M : Oh, yes, you're right. And that's the last one. I'm sorry.
ああ、はい、そうですね。それで、それが最後の品物なんです。すみません。

F : That's okay. I want to buy it. But I don't want to pay full price.
大丈夫ですよ。それを買いたいと思ってます。でも、満額は払いたくないですね。

M : Sure, I can give you a discount. How about if I take 30% off?
もちろん、値引きはできますよ。30％値引きしたらどうですか？

F : Let's see. That would be about seventeen dollars, right? Can you make it fifteen?
うーん。そうするとだいたい 17 ドルですよね？ それを 15 ドルにできますか？

＊ would be ... は「(なにかの場合には) …になる」という意味。

STEP 3　日本語訳を見ながらスキットを演じてみよう。　CD 1-16

F :

このフレームがいいですね。でも、これが見えますか？　ひっかき傷があるんですよ。

M : Oh, yes, you're right. And that's the last one. I'm sorry.

F :

大丈夫ですよ。それを買いたいと思ってます。でも、満額は払いたくないですね。

M : Sure, I can give you a discount. How about if I take 30% off?

F :

うーん。そうするとだいたい17ドルですよね？　それを15ドルにできますか？

Unit 016 カードで会計してもらう
Paying with a Credit Card

STEP 1 各センテンスをシャドーイングしよう。　CD 1-17

STEP 2 テキストを見ながらスキットを演じてみよう。　CD 1-17

M: I'd like to use my Diners Card to pay for everybody.

全員分の支払いに、私のダイナース・カードを使いたいんです。

F: Okay, that's fine. The total comes to two hundred and forty-seven dollars.

はい、大丈夫です。合計額は 247 ドルになります。

* come to ... は「合計で…になる」という意味。

M: Here's my card. Would you also write me a receipt?

こちらが私のカードです。領収書も書いてもらえますか？

F: Certainly, sir. To whom shall I make it out?

もちろんです、お客さま。どなた宛てにお書きしましょうか？

* to whom は「だれに対して」という意味。
* make out a receipt で「領収書を書く」という意味。

M: To Tom Hayes, please. H-A-Y-E-S.

トム・ヘイズ宛てでお願いします。H-A-Y-E-S です。

STEP 3 日本語訳を見ながらスキットを演じてみよう。　　CD 1-17

M :
[　　　　　　　　　　　　　　　　　　　　　　　]

全員分の支払いに、私のダイナース・カードを使いたいんです。

F : Okay, that's fine. The total comes to two hundred and forty-seven dollars.

M :
[　　　　　　　　　　　　　　　　　　　　　　　]

こちらが私のカードです。領収書も書いてもらえますか？

F : Certainly, sir. To whom shall I make it out?

M :
[　　　　　　　　　　　　　　　　　　　　　　　]

トム・ヘイズ宛てでお願いします。H-A-Y-E-S です。

Unit 017 Getting Free Delivery 無料で配送してもらう

STEP 1 各センテンスをシャドーイングしよう。　CD 1-18

STEP 2 テキストを見ながらスキットを演じてみよう。　CD 1-18

F : I'm not sure all of this will fit in my car. Do you charge for delivery?

これ全部が車に入るかどうかわからないわ。配送料はかかるんですか？

* I'm not sure (that) ... は「…ということはよくわからない」という意味。

M : Not for purchases over three hundred dollars. Your purchase comes to about two eighty.

300ドル以上の購入にはかかりません。お客さまの購入額はだいたい280ドルになりますね。

* Not for ... は We don't charge for ... が省略されたもの。
* come to ... は「合計額で…になる」という意味。

F : Oh, really? Maybe I'll pick up something else, so I can get free delivery.

あら、そうなんですね？ 無料配送をしてもらえるように、ほかのものを買おうかしら。

* Maybe I'll ... は「ひょっとすると…するかも；…しようかなあ」という意味になる。

M : Okay. Let's move your cart over here behind the counter while you shop.

わかりました。お買い物をしている間、こちらのカウンターの後ろにカートを移動しましょう。

F : Thanks. I think I know what I want, so I'll be back in a few minutes.

ありがとう。買いたいものはわかっていると思いますから、すぐに戻りますよ。

* I think I know は I think that I know の略。
* what I want は「私が欲しいもの」。

STEP 3　日本語訳を見ながらスキットを演じてみよう。　CD 1-18

F :

これ全部が車に入るかどうかわからないわ。配送料はかかるんですか？

M : Not for purchases over three hundred dollars. Your purchase comes to about two eighty.

F :

あら、そうなんですね？ 無料配送をしてもらえるように、ほかのものを買おうかしら。

M : Okay. Let's move your cart over here behind the counter while you shop.

F :

ありがとう。買いたいものはわかっていると思いますから、すぐに戻りますよ。

Unit 018 Birthday Present 誕生日のプレゼント

STEP 1 各センテンスをシャドーイングしよう。　CD 1-19

STEP 2 テキストを見ながらスキットを演じてみよう。　CD 1-19

M: Happy birthday, Mary.
誕生日おめでとう、メアリー。

F: Thank you, sweetie.
ありがとう、ダーリン。

M: I got something for you.
君にプレゼントを買ったんだ。

F: Did you?
そうなの？

M: Yeah. I thought of you when I saw it.
うん、見つけたときに、君のことが浮かんでさ。

F: What is it?
なんなの？

M: Open it!
開けてみて！

F: Oh, Richard! What a beautiful bracelet!
ああ、リチャード！ なんてきれいなブレスレットなの！

M: Do you like it?
気に入ったかい？

F: Yes, I do! It's perfect. Thank you. You always know how to make me feel special.
ええ！ 完璧よ。ありがとう。私を特別な気持ちにさせる方法を、いつだってあなたは知ってるわ。

STEP 3 日本語訳を見ながらスキットを演じてみよう。　CD 1-19

M :

誕生日おめでとう、メアリー。

F : Thank you, sweetie.

M :

君にプレゼントを買ったんだ。

F : Did you?

M :

うん、見つけたときに、君のことが浮かんでさ。

F : What is it?

M :

開けてみて！

F : Oh, Richard! What a beautiful bracelet!

M :

気に入ったかい？

F : Yes, I do! It's perfect. Thank you. You always know how to make me feel special.

Unit 019 ゴミ出し
Chores

STEP 1 各センテンスをシャドーイングしよう。　CD 1-20

STEP 2 テキストを見ながらスキットを演じてみよう。　CD 1-20

F: Did you remember to take the garbage out?
忘れないでゴミを出してくれた？

M: Ah, no. I forgot. Which trash goes out today?
ああ、ダメだ。忘れてたよ。今日はどのゴミを出すの？

F: Wait, and I'll check.
待ってね、チェックするわ。

M: I think it's flammables.
燃えるゴミだと思うよ。

F: Yeah, it's flammables.
ええ、燃えるゴミね。

M: Okay, there are two big bags in the garage.
わかった。ガレージに2つ大きな袋があるよね。

F: That's right. I think the truck will come soon.
そのとおり。トラックがもうすぐ来ると思うわ。

M: No problem. I'll take them out right now.
大丈夫。いますぐに出すからさ。

F: Thanks, hon.
ありがとう、あなた。

M: Sure thing.
任せておいて。

* Sure thing. は相手のお礼に対して「問題ないよ；どういたしまして；任せておいて」などと返事をするときのひとこと。

STEP 3 　日本語訳を見ながらスキットを演じてみよう。　CD 1-20

F :

忘れないでゴミを出してくれた？

M : Ah, no. I forgot. Which trash goes out today?

F :

待ってね、チェックするわ。

M : I think it's flammables.

F :

ええ、燃えるゴミね。

M : Okay, there are two big bags in the garage.

F :

そのとおり。トラックがもうすぐ来ると思うわ。

M : No problem. I'll take them out right now.

F :

ありがとう、あなた。

M : Sure thing.

Unit 020 Getting Dressed 着替え

STEP 1 各センテンスをシャドーイングしよう。 CD 1-21

STEP 2 テキストを見ながらスキットを演じてみよう。 CD 1-21

M: Is that the dress you are planning to wear?
そのドレスを着る予定なの？

F: Yes, why?
うん、どうして？

M: I want to wear something that matches it.
その服に合うものを着たいからさ。

F: Good idea. How about your new shirt?
いいアイデアね。新しいシャツはどう？

M: That works. What about pants?
いいね。ズボンはどうしよう？

F: I always like those light gray slacks.
明るいグレーのスラックスなら、いつ着てもバッチリよ。

M: I wear those a lot, but okay.
よく履いているけど、いいかな。

F: I think they'll look great with the shirt.
シャツにぴったりだと思うわ。

M: Yeah, and with your dress.
うん、それに君のドレスともね。

F: Perfect!
完璧よ！

STEP 3 　日本語訳を見ながらスキットを演じてみよう。　CD 1-21

M: Is that the dress you are planning to wear?

F:

うん、どうして？

M: I want to wear something that matches it.

F:

いいアイデアね。新しいシャツはどう？

M: That works. What about pants?

F:

明るいグレーのスラックスなら、いつ着てもバッチリよ。

M: I wear those a lot, but okay.

F:

シャツにぴったりだと思うわ。

M: Yeah, and with your dress.

F:

完璧よ！

Unit 021 Laundry 洗濯

STEP 1 各センテンスをシャドーイングしよう。　CD 1-22

STEP 2 テキストを見ながらスキットを演じてみよう。　CD 1-22

M: Honey, do I need to separate the laundry?
ハニー、洗濯物は分類する必要があるのかい？

F: Yes, please. Darks and lights.
ええ、お願い。色の濃いものと薄いものにね。

M: Okay, so I should run two loads?
わかった。じゃあ、2回分洗濯機を回すんだね？
* load「1回分の洗濯物」

F: Let me see. How much is there?
そうねえ。どのくらいあるの？

M: It's a pretty big pile.
かなりの嵩だよ。

F: Oh, gosh, yeah. It is!
ああ、まいったわ、そうね。ホントだわ！

M: So, maybe three loads?
じゃあ、おそらく3回分だよね？

F: Yeah, that seems right. Two darks and one lights.
うん、それでよさそう。2回、色の濃いのをやって、薄いのを1回ね。

M: Got it!
わかった！

STEP 3　日本語訳を見ながらスキットを演じてみよう。　CD 1-22

M :
　　　　　　　　　　　　　　　　　　　　　　　　　　　　

ハニー、洗濯物は分類する必要があるのかい？

F : Yes, please. Darks and lights.

M :

わかった。じゃあ、2 回分洗濯機を回すんだね？

F : Let me see. How much is there?

M :

かなりの高だよ。

F : Oh, gosh, yeah. It is!

M :

じゃあ、おそらく 3 回分だよね？

F : Yeah, that seems right. Two darks and one lights.

M :

わかった！

Unit 022　Walking the Dog　犬の散歩

STEP 1 各センテンスをシャドーイングしよう。　CD 1-23

STEP 2 テキストを見ながらスキットを演じてみよう。　CD 1-23

F : It's time for Mitzi's walk.
ミッチの散歩の時間よ。

M : Can you do it? I'm watching a game.
君が行ってくれる？ 試合を観てるんだよね。

F : I took her this morning. It's your turn!
今朝は私が連れていったのよ。今度はあなたの番よ！

M : Okay, okay. But just a short one.
わかった、わかった。でも、短い散歩だけだよ。

F : It's just a dumb game!
ただのくだらない試合じゃないの！

M : It's the playoffs! I'm just going to let her do her business and come back.
プレーオフなんだよ！ 用だけ足させたら、戻ってくるからね。

* do one's business「用を足す；便をする」

F : Oh, poor little Mitzi. That's no fun. I'll take her for a decent walk.
ああ、かわいそうなミッチ。それじゃあ、楽しくないわ。私がちゃんとしたお散歩に連れていくわよ。

M : Thanks, honey! I'll take her on two walks tomorrow.
ありがとう、ハニー。明日は僕が2回散歩させるから。

F : You'd better!
当然よ！

* You'd better.「そうしたほうがいい（さもないと…）」

STEP 3 　日本語訳を見ながらスキットを演じてみよう。　CD 1-23

F :

ミッチの散歩の時間よ。

M : Can you do it? I'm watching a game.

F :

今朝は私が連れていったのよ。今度はあなたの番よ！

M : Okay, okay. But just a short one.

F :

ただのくだらない試合じゃないの！

M : It's the playoffs! I'm just going to let her do her business and come back.

F :

ああ、かわいそうなミッチ。それじゃあ、楽しくないわ。私がちゃんとしたお散歩に連れていくわよ。

M : Thanks, honey! I'll take her on two walks tomorrow.

F :

当然よ！

Unit 023 手伝いを頼む

Getting Some Help

STEP 1 各センテンスをシャドーイングしよう。　CD 1-24

STEP 2 テキストを見ながらスキットを演じてみよう。　CD 1-24

F : Can you give me a hand?
ちょっと手伝ってもらえない？

M : Sure, what do you need?
いいよ、なにをすればいい？

F : I need to bring stuff inside from the car.
荷物を、車から中に運び込みたいの。

M : Okay. What is it?
わかった。それってなんなの？

F : I bought some frames so we can hang some photographs.
写真を吊って飾れるように、フレームを買ってきたのよ。

M : So they need to go upstairs, right?
じゃあ、2階に持っていくべきだよね？

F : Yeah. They're not heavy, but they are pretty big and awkward.
うん。重くはないけど、かなり大きくて厄介なの。
* awkward「不便な；厄介な」

M : No problem. Are they in the trunk?
問題ないよ。トランクの中にあるの？

F : Yep. Be careful taking them up the stairs, okay?
うん。注意して上に運んでちょうだいね！

STEP 3 　日本語訳を見ながらスキットを演じてみよう。　CD 1-24

F : Can you give me a hand?

M :

いいよ、なにをすればいい？

F : I need to bring stuff inside from the car.

M :

わかった。それってなんなの？

F : I bought some frames so we can hang some photographs.

M :

じゃあ、2階に持っていくべきだよね？

F : Yeah. They're not heavy, but they are pretty big and awkward.

M :

問題ないよ。トランクの中にあるの？

F : Yep. Be careful taking them up the stairs, okay?

Unit 024 電球の調整
Adjusting a Light Bulb

STEP 1 各センテンスをシャドーイングしよう。　CD 1-25

STEP 2 テキストを見ながらスキットを演じてみよう。　CD 1-25

M: That light seems to be flickering.
あの電気点滅してるみたいだね。
* flicker「点滅する；明滅する」

F: Yes, it's been doing that all day.
そう、一日中あの調子なの。

M: Time to change the bulb, I guess.
電球を替える時期かもね。

F: I feel like we just changed it.
替えたばかりみたいに思うんだけど。

M: Hmmm. Maybe it just became loose.
うーーん…おそらく、緩んできただけかもね。

F: Would you check?
見てみてくれる？

M: Yeah, I'm on it. Where do we keep the ladder?
わかった、すぐにやってみる。ハシゴはどこに置いてあったっけ？
* I'm on it.「（依頼を承諾して）すぐにやりますよ」

F: The step ladder is in the kitchen closet.
ハシゴはキッチンの収納の中よ。

M: Got it. Okay, hold it steady for me, would you?
あったよ。じゃあ、しっかり握っててくれる？

F: Sure. Be careful not to electrocute yourself!
いいわ。感電死しないようにね！
* electrocute「感電死させる」

STEP 3 　日本語訳を見ながらスキットを演じてみよう。　CD 1-25

M : That light seems to be flickering.

F :

そう、一日中あの調子なの。

M : Time to change the bulb, I guess.

F :

替えたばかりみたいに思うんだけど。

M : Hmmm. Maybe it just became loose.

F :

見てみてくれる？

M : Yeah, I'm on it. Where do we keep the ladder?

F :

ハシゴはキッチンの収納の中よ。

M : Got it. Okay, hold it steady for me, would you?

F :

いいわ。感電死しないようにね！

Unit 025 Shopping List 買い物のリスト

STEP 1 各センテンスをシャドーイングしよう。　CD 1-26

STEP 2 テキストを見ながらスキットを演じてみよう。　CD 1-26

F: Let's make a shopping list so we don't forget anything.
買い忘れるものがないように、買い物のリストを作りましょう。

M: Okay. I think we're almost out of mustard.
うん。マスタードがほとんどなくなってると思うよ。

F: Okay, good. We need toilet paper. What else?
いいわ。トイレット・ペーパーがいるわね。ほかには？

M: I should get some disposable razors for my camping trip.
キャンプ旅行用に、使い捨てのカミソリを買わないと。

F: Yeah, and maybe some instant noodles.
ええ、それと、たぶんインスタントの麺類もね。

M: Oh, that's a good idea. Hmm ... I'm thinking ...
ああ、それはいいアイデアだね。うーん…あとは〜…

F: Oh, I know! I need to pick up some stationery things.
ああ、そうだ！ ちょっと文房具を買わないと。
＊ stationery things「文具類」

M: Do they sell that at the store?
お店に売ってるかな？

F: I think so. Even if they don't we can stop someplace else.
あると思うわ。ないとしても、ほかの場所に寄ればいいわよ。

M: I think that's it.
以上だと思うな。
＊ that's it「それで全部だ；それで終わりだ」

STEP 3 　日本語訳を見ながらスキットを演じてみよう。　CD 1-26

F:

買い忘れるものがないように、買い物のリストを作りましょう。

M: Okay. I think we're almost out of mustard.

F:

いいわ。トイレット・ペーパーがいるわね。ほかには？

M: I should get some disposable razors for my camping trip.

F:

ええ、それと、たぶんインスタントの麺類もね。

M: Oh, that's a good idea. Hmm ... I'm thinking ...

F:

ああ、そうだ！ ちょっと文房具を買わないと。

M: Do they sell that at the store?

F:

あると思うわ。ないとしても、ほかの場所に寄ればいいわよ。

M: I think that's it.

Unit 026 — Package Delivery / 荷物の配送

STEP 1 各センテンスをシャドーイングしよう。　CD 1-27

STEP 2 テキストを見ながらスキットを演じてみよう。　CD 1-27

M: I have two packages for Fran Clark.
フラン・クラークさん宛に荷物がふたつ届いています。

F: That's me.
私です。

M: They're a little heavy. Shall I bring them inside?
ちょっと重いですよ。中に運びましょうか？

F: Oh, that's okay. Just leave them there.
ああ、大丈夫です。そこに置いておいてください。

M: You sure?
ほんとうに？

F: Yep, I'll manage.
ええ、なんとかしますので。

M: Okay. And I need you to sign.
わかりました。サインをいただきたいんですが。

F: For each package separately?
それぞれの荷物に別々にですか？

M: Yes, that's right. So here ... and here.
はい、そうです。なので、こちらと…こちらですね。

F: There you go. Thanks!
はい、どうぞ。どうも、ありがとう！

STEP 3　　日本語訳を見ながらスキットを演じてみよう。　　CD 1-27

M: I have two packages for Fran Clark.

F:

私です。

M: They're a little heavy. Shall I bring them inside?

F:

ああ、大丈夫です。そこに置いておいてください。

M: You sure?

F:

ええ、なんとかしますので。

M: Okay. And I need you to sign.

F:

それぞれの荷物に別々にですか？

M: Yes, that's right. So here ... and here.

F:

はい、どうぞ。どうも、ありがとう！

Unit 027 子どもを叱る
Scolding a Child

STEP 1 各センテンスをシャドーイングしよう。　CD 1-28

STEP 2 テキストを見ながらスキットを演じてみよう。　CD 1-28

F: You are not leaving here until you clean your room!
自分の部屋を掃除するまでは、あなたは家を出られないのよ！

M: But my friends are waiting.
でも、友達が待ってるんだよ。

F: Let them wait. Just look at this mess!
待たせておきなさい。この散らかり方を見なさいよ！

M: I promise I'll clean it when I get back.
戻ったら掃除するって約束するから。

F: Oh, no you don't! You always say that!
ダメよ、あなたはしないから！ いつもそう言うじゃないの！

M: Okay, okay! I'll clean it and then go play.
わかったよ！ 掃除してから、遊びに行くよ。

F: And do a GOOD job! Don't just move things around.
そうよ、ちゃんとやるのよ！ 物を移動するだけじゃダメだからね。

M: I will. Why do you make such a big deal?
やるよ。どうしてそんなに大騒ぎするのさ？

F: Because bad habits form when you're young, mister!
それはね、悪い癖が小さい頃にできあがるからよ！

＊ form「形成される」

STEP 3　日本語訳を見ながらスキットを演じてみよう。　CD 1-28

F :

自分の部屋を掃除するまでは、あなたは家を出られないのよ！

M : But my friends are waiting.

F :

待たせておきなさい。この散らかり方を見なさいよ！

M : I promise I'll clean it when I get back.

F :

ダメよ、あなたはしないから！ いつもそう言うじゃないの！

M : Okay, okay! I'll clean it and then go play.

F :

そうよ、ちゃんとやるのよ！ 物を移動するだけじゃダメだからね。

M : I will. Why do you make such a big deal?

F :

それはね、悪い癖が小さい頃にできあがるからよ！

Unit 028 Praising a Child / 子どもをほめる

STEP 1 各センテンスをシャドーイングしよう。　CD 1-29

STEP 2 テキストを見ながらスキットを演じてみよう。　CD 1-29

M: Was that you playing piano just now?
いまピアノを弾いていたのは君？

F: Yeah, why?
うん、どうして？

M: That was beautiful! I was so impressed!
きれいだったね！ 感心したよ！

F: Thanks, Dad!
ありがとう、パパ！

M: I mean it! I didn't realize how good you're getting.
ホントだよ！ 君がそんなにうまくなってきてるなんて、気づかなかったよ。

F: I do feel like I'm finally making progress.
ついに上達してきてるって感じがしてるの。
* make progress「上達する」

M: You sure are! I think you've got real talent!
確かに上達してるよ！ 君にはすごい才能があると思うよ！

F: I don't know about THAT! I just practice a lot.
それはわからないけど！ 練習をたくさんしてるだけよ。

M: Well, keep it up! I think what you've done so far is amazing!
うん、その調子でね！ これまで君がやってきたことはすばらしいよ！

F: Thanks so much, Dad!
ホントにありがとう、パパ！

STEP 3 　日本語訳を見ながらスキットを演じてみよう。　CD 1-29

M :

いまピアノを弾いていたのは君？

F : Yeah, why?

M :

きれいだったね！ 感心したよ！

F : Thanks, Dad!

M :

ホントだよ！ 君がそんなにうまくなってきてるなんて、気づかなかったよ。

F : I do feel like I'm finally making progress.

M :

確かに上達してるよ！ 君にはすごい才能があると思うよ！

F : I don't know about THAT! I just practice a lot.

M :

うん、その調子でね！ これまで君がやってきたことはすばらしいよ！

F : Thanks so much, Dad!

Unit 029 Offering Coffee
コーヒーをすすめる

STEP 1 各センテンスをシャドーイングしよう。 CD 1-30

STEP 2 テキストを見ながらスキットを演じてみよう。 CD 1-30

F: Can I get you some coffee or something?
コーヒーかなにか持ってきましょうか？

M: Sure! Coffee sounds great!
うん！ コーヒー、おいしそうだね！

F: How do you take it?
飲み方は？

M: Just black is fine.
ブラックでかまわないよ。

F: Okay. I'll serve you the good stuff!
わかったわ。おいしいのをいれるわね！

M: Ha ha, thanks!
ハハ、ありがとう！

F: I've got this gourmet Hawaiian brew.
グルメ・ハワイアン・ブルーの粉があるの。

M: Oh, wonderful!
へえ、いいね！

F: I always take mine with sugar and lots of cream.
私はいつもお砂糖とクリームをたくさん入れるのよ。

M: Actually, I think I'll add a little cream, too.
そうだなー、僕もちょっとクリームを入れようかなあ。

STEP 3　日本語訳を見ながらスキットを演じてみよう。　CD 1-30

F :
　　コーヒーかなにか持ってきましょうか？

M : Sure! Coffee sounds great!

F :
　　飲み方は？

M : Just black is fine.

F :
　　わかったわ。おいしいのをいれるわね！

M : Ha ha, thanks!

F :
　　グルメ・ハワイアン・ブルーの粉があるの。

M : Oh, wonderful!

F :
　　私はいつもお砂糖とクリームをたくさん入れるのよ。

M : Actually, I think I'll add a little cream, too.

Unit 030 メールを書く
Writing an Email

STEP 1 各センテンスをシャドーイングしよう。　CD 1-31

STEP 2 テキストを見ながらスキットを演じてみよう。　CD 1-31

F: I got an email from my cousin Sue. She found a new job.
いとこのスーからメールが来たの。新しい仕事を見つけたって。

M: That's nice. Did you write back to congratulate her?
いいね。お祝いの返事を書いたの？
* congratulate「祝福する」

F: Not yet. I thought you might want to add something.
まだなの。あなたもなにかつけ足したいかなと思ってさ。

M: Sure. Is it a good job?
もちろん。いい仕事なの？

F: Yeah, it's what she wants. But she has to move.
うん、彼女がやりたかった仕事なの。でも、引っ越さなきゃならないのよ。

M: Okay. Tell her I hope we can meet her before she moves.
そうか。彼女の引っ越し前に会いたいねって伝えてよ。

F: That's what I was hoping.
私もそうしたかったの。

M: When will she move?
彼女はいつ引っ越すの？

F: Beginning of next month.
来月の初旬よ。

M: That's soon! We'd better suggest some dates.
それはすぐじゃない！ 日取りを提案したほうがいいね。

STEP 3 　日本語訳を見ながらスキットを演じてみよう。　CD 1-31

F: I got an email from my cousin Sue. She found a new job.

M:

いいね。お祝いの返事を書いたの？

F: Not yet. I thought you might want to add something.

M:

もちろん。いい仕事なの？

F: Yeah, it's what she wants. But she has to move.

M:

そうか。彼女の引っ越し前に会いたいねって伝えてよ。

F: That's what I was hoping.

M:

彼女はいつ引っ越すの？

F: Beginning of next month.

M:

それはすぐじゃない！ 日取りを提案したほうがいいね。

Unit 031 ネット・サーフィン
Surfing the Net

STEP 1 各センテンスをシャドーイングしよう。　CD 1-32

STEP 2 テキストを見ながらスキットを演じてみよう。　CD 1-32

M : Hey, check this out!
ねえ、これ見てよ！

F : What is it?
なに？

M : It's a site I just discovered. It has lots of trivia quizzes.
最近、見つけたサイトなんだけど。トリビアのクイズが山ほど載ってるんだ。

F : Oh, no! Sounds addicting!
あれ、まあ！ 癖になりそうね！

M : Yeah, I've been hooked the last few days.
うん、ここ数日ハマっちゃってるんだ。

F : That reminds me of a site I wanted to show you. Look at this.
あなたに見せたかったサイトを思い出したわ。これを見て。
* remind「思い出させる」

M : Hey, that's cool! Amazing graphics!
へえ、すごいね！ グラフィックスがすごいよ！

F : Right? It turns your photographs into 3D images.
そうでしょ？ 写真を 3D イメージに変えてくれるのよ。

M : Internet!! Please stop making it so easy for me to waste time! Ha ha!
インターネットよ、僕に超かんたんに時間の無駄遣いをさせるのを、やめてくれよ〜！ ハハ！
* waste「無駄にする」

STEP 3 　日本語訳を見ながらスキットを演じてみよう。　CD 1-32

M: Hey, check this out!

F:

なに？

M: It's a site I just discovered. It has lots of trivia quizzes.

F:

あれ、まあ！ 癖になりそうね！

M: Yeah, I've been hooked the last few days.

F:

あなたに見せたかったサイトを思い出したわ。これを見て。

M: Hey, that's cool! Amazing graphics!

F:

そうでしょ？ 写真を 3D イメージに変えてくれるのよ。

M: Internet!! Please stop making it so easy for me to waste time! Ha ha!

Unit 032 Online Shopping ネット・ショッピング

STEP 1 各センテンスをシャドーイングしよう。　CD 1-33

STEP 2 テキストを見ながらスキットを演じてみよう。　CD 1-33

M: I don't really like to buy clothes online.
ネットで洋服を買うのはあまり好きじゃないんだ。

F: Because the color might not be the same?
色が違ってるかもしれないから？

M: Yeah, or the size.
うん、あるいはサイズがね。

F: Gotcha. What kind of things DO you like to buy online?
わかるわ。どんなものなら、ネットで買うのが好き？

M: Books, CDs, DVDs, fishing gear. Just not clothes.
本とか、CD、DVD、釣りの道具。洋服はダメだね。

F: I love online shopping!
私はネットの買い物は大好きよ！

M: Really? Why?
そうなの？ どうして？

F: It saves me so much time!
時間がすごく節約できるもの！

M: You don't miss going to the mall?
モールに行かなくてさみしくないの？

F: And waste time looking for a parking space? No way!
で、駐車スペースを探して時間を無駄に使うの？ あり得ないわ！

STEP 3 　日本語訳を見ながらスキットを演じてみよう。　CD 1-33

M :

ネットで洋服を買うのはあまり好きじゃないんだ。

F : Because the color might not be the same?

M :

うん、あるいはサイズがね。

F : Gotcha. What kind of things DO you like to buy online?

M :

本とか、CD、DVD、釣りの道具。洋服はダメだね。

F : I love online shopping!

M :

そうなの？どうして？

F : It saves me so much time!

M :

モールに行かなくてさみしくないの？

F : And waste time looking for a parking space? No way!

Unit 033 チャンネル
Changing the Channel

STEP 1 各センテンスをシャドーイングしよう。　CD 1-34

STEP 2 テキストを見ながらスキットを演じてみよう。　CD 1-34

M: Let's watch something else.
なにかほかのものを観ようよ。

F: You don't like this?
これ、嫌いなの？

M: Don't you think it's pretty boring?
かなり退屈だと思わない？

F: I guess. It's okay.
そうねえ。いいわよ。

M: Let me just see what else is on.
ほかになにをやってるか見させてね。
* let me ...「私に…させて」

F: Okay, but no sports.
いいわ、でもスポーツはダメよ。

M: Well, it doesn't really look like there's anything good on.
うーん、いいものは、あまりなにもやってなさそうだよね？
* look like ...「…のようだ」

F: Let's just go back to what we were watching.
観ていたものに戻そうよ。

M: Why don't we watch a DVD instead?
代わりに DVD を観るのはどう？

F: I don't want to start watching a movie now. I'm going to go to bed soon.
いま映画を観始めたくはないわ。すぐにベッドに入るのよ。

STEP 3 　日本語訳を見ながらスキットを演じてみよう。　CD 1-34

M: Let's watch something else.

F:

これ、嫌いなの？

M: Don't you think it's pretty boring?

F:

そうねえ。いいわよ。

M: Let me just see what else is on.

F:

いいわ、でもスポーツはダメよ。

M: Well, it doesn't really look like there's anything good on.

F:

観ていたものに戻そうよ。

M: Why don't we watch a DVD instead?

F:

いま映画を観始めたくはないわ。すぐにベッドに入るのよ。

Unit 034 気分が悪い
Not Feeling Well

STEP 1 各センテンスをシャドーイングしよう。　CD 1-35

STEP 2 テキストを見ながらスキットを演じてみよう。　CD 1-35

M: Stay clear of me! I don't want you to catch what I've got.
僕に近づかないで！ 君に病気をにうつしたくないんだ。
* stay clear of ...「…から離れている；…に近づかない」

F: Oh, no! Is it the flu or something?
あらまあ！ インフルエンザかなにかなの？

M: Maybe the flu, maybe a sinus infection.
インフルエンザかもしれないし、副鼻腔感染症かもしれない。
* sinus infection「副鼻腔感染症」

F: Oh, dear! Do you have a fever?
ああ、かわいそうに！ 熱があるの？

M: Maybe a small one. I haven't taken my temperature.
おそらくちょっとね。熱は計ってないんだよ。

F: You really need to see a doctor.
医者にちゃんと診てもらう必要があるわよ。

M: Yeah, I'm going today.
うん、今日行くんだよ。

F: Good. And you definitely should get some rest.
いいわ。それに絶対にカラダをちょっと休めるべきよ。

M: Yeah, I need to spend a day in bed.
うん、1日ベッドで過ごす必要があるよね。

F: Maybe two days! You don't want it to get worse!
おそらく2日よ！ 悪化させたくはないでしょ！

STEP 3　日本語訳を見ながらスキットを演じてみよう。　CD 1-35

M: Stay clear of me! I don't want you to catch what I've got.

F:

あらまあ！ インフルエンザかなにかなの？

M: Maybe the flu, maybe a sinus infection.

F:

ああ、かわいそうに！ 熱があるの？

M: Maybe a small one. I haven't taken my temperature.

F:

医者にちゃんと診てもらう必要があるわよ。

M: Yeah, I'm going today.

F:

いいわ。それに絶対にカラダをちょっと休めるべきよ。

M: Yeah, I need to spend a day in bed.

F:

おそらく2日よ！ 悪化させたくはないでしょ！

Unit 035 Directions 道順

STEP 1 各センテンスをシャドーイングしよう。 CD 1-36

STEP 2 テキストを見ながらスキットを演じてみよう。 CD 1-36

F: So, do we know how to get there?
で、そこへ行く方法はわかってるの？

M: I think so. We should be looking for Conrad Avenue.
わかると思う。コンラッド通りを探すべきなんだよ。

F: Slow down; that looks like it might be it coming up.
スピードを落として。近づいてきてるのがそれっぽいけど。

M: No, that was something else that began with C.
いや、あれはCで始まってたけど別のものだったよ。

F: Are you sure?
ホントに？

M: Yeah, Conrad should be a big street.
うん、コンラッドは大きな通りのはずなんだ。

F: Okay. And then what do we do?
わかったわ。で、それからはどうするの？

M: We turn left on Conrad, and then go to the second traffic light.
コンラッドで左折して、2番目の信号まで行くんだよ。

F: Uh huh. And then?
うん、で、それから？

M: It gets a little confusing after that. Lots of zigs and zags.
そのあとはちょっとややこしいんだ。たくさんジグザグがあってね。

* confusing「ややこしい；混乱させる」

STEP 3 日本語訳を見ながらスキットを演じてみよう。 CD 1-36

F: So, do we know how to get there?

M:

わかると思う。コンラッド通りを探すべきなんだよ。

F: Slow down; that looks like it might be it coming up.

M:

いや、あれはCで始まってたけど別のものだったよ。

F: Are you sure?

M:

うん、コンラッドは大きな通りのはずなんだ。

F: Okay. And then what do we do?

M:

コンラッドで左折して、2番目の信号まで行くんだよ。

F: Uh huh. And then?

M:

そのあとはちょっとややこしいんだ。たくさんジグザグがあってね。

Unit 036 電車の乗り換え
Changing Trains

STEP 1 各センテンスをシャドーイングしよう。 CD 1-37

STEP 2 テキストを見ながらスキットを演じてみよう。 CD 1-37

M: The next stop is where we have to change, right?
次の駅で乗り換えが必要だよね？

F: Yeah. And then we switch to the Green Line.
ええ。それからグリーン・ラインに乗り換えるの。

M: Then it's just two or three more stops, right?
そのあとは、あとほんの2、3駅だよね？

F: Three. We should get to Daffodil Square Station by three thirty.
3駅よ。3時半までに水仙広場駅に到着しなきゃダメなの。

M: How far from the station to the theater?
劇場までは、駅からどのくらい遠いの？

F: Not far at all. They're connected.
まったく遠くはないわよ。劇場と駅はつながっているから。
* connected「接続された」

M: You mean there's an underground tunnel?
地下トンネルがあるってことなの？

F: Yes, it's very convenient.
ええ、すごく便利なのよ。

STEP 3   日本語訳を見ながらスキットを演じてみよう。　CD 1-37

M :

次の駅で乗り換えが必要だよね？

F : Yeah. And then we switch to the Green Line.

M :

そのあとは、あとほんの2、3駅よね？

F : Three. We should get to Daffodil Square Station by three thirty.

M :

劇場までは、駅からどのくらい遠いの？

F : Not far at all. They're connected.

M :

地下トンネルがあるってことなの？

F : Yes, it's very convenient.

Unit 037 ドライブスルーの窓口
Ordering through a Drive-through Window

STEP 1 各センテンスをシャドーイングしよう。 CD 1-38

STEP 2 テキストを見ながらスキットを演じてみよう。 CD 1-38

F : Can I take your order?
ご注文、よろしいですか？

M : Yes, I'd like a deluxe burger and fries.
はい、デラックス・バーガーとフライド・ポテトをお願いします。

F : Small, medium or large fries?
ポテトは、スモール、ミディアム、ラージのどれにしましょう？

M : Hmmm. Medium, please.
うーん、ミディアムでお願いします。

F : Something to drink with that?
ごいっしょになにかお飲み物は？

M : Do you have iced coffee?
アイス・コーヒーはありますか？

F : No, sir. Iced tea or hot coffee.
恐縮ですが、ございません。アイス・ティーかホット・コーヒーになります。

M : Okay. Hot coffee, then. That's it.
そうですか。じゃあ、ホット・コーヒーで。以上です。

F : Your total comes to 11.79.
お支払い合計額は 11 ドル 79 セントになります。
* come to ... 「合計で…になる」

M : Okay, thanks.
はい、どうも。

STEP 3 　日本語訳を見ながらスキットを演じてみよう。　CD 1-38

F : Can I take your order?

M :

はい、デラックス・バーガーとフライド・ポテトをお願いします。

F : Small, medium or large fries?

M :

うーん、ミディアムでお願いします。

F : Something to drink with that?

M :

アイス・コーヒーはありますか？

F : No, sir. Iced tea or hot coffee.

M :

そうですか。じゃあ、ホット・コーヒーで。以上です。

F : Your total comes to 11.79.

M :

はい、どうも。

Unit 038 At Breakfast 朝食についての会話

STEP 1 各センテンスをシャドーイングしよう。　CD 1-39

STEP 2 テキストを見ながらスキットを演じてみよう。　CD 1-39

F: Good morning, honey.
ハニー、おはよう。
* honey「あなた；お前；愛しい人」夫、妻、恋人、子どもへの呼びかけ。

M: Mornin' sweetie.
やあ、おはよう。
* sweetie「愛しい人；かわいい人」

F: How about if I make us some breakfast? Do you want some eggs?
朝食を作ろうと思うけど？ 卵は欲しい？

M: Coffee and toast will do. I have to get in to the office early today. I have to give a presentation to some customers this afternoon.
コーヒーとトーストでいいよ。今日は早めにオフィスに行くから。午後に顧客にプレゼンをしないといけないんだよ。
* do「間に合う；役に立つ；ちょうどよい」 customer「顧客」

F: Are you sure that's all you want?
ホントにそれだけでいいのね？

M: If I change my mind, I can always stop at a drive-thru on the way.
気が変わったら、いつでも途中のドライブ・スルーに寄れるから。

F: Don't forget, we're supposed to have dinner with Tom and Julie tonight at seven.
忘れないでね。今夜7時にトムとジュリーといっしょに夕食を取ることになってるんだからね。
* be supposed to ...「…することになっている」

M: Our meeting is from three to five, so I should be home by six or so.
ミーティングは3時から5時だから、6時頃には家に戻ってるはずだよ。

STEP 3 　日本語訳を見ながらスキットを演じてみよう。　CD 1-39

F :

ハニー、おはよう。

M : Mornin' sweetie.

F :

朝食を作ろうと思うけど？ 卵は欲しい？

M : Coffee and toast will do. I have to get in to the office early today. I have to give a presentation to some customers this afternoon.

F :

ホントにそれだけでいいのね？

M : If I change my mind, I can always stop at a drive-thru on the way.

F :

忘れないでね。今夜7時にトムとジュリーといっしょに夕食を取ることになってるんだからね。

M : Our meeting is from three to five, so I should be home by six or so.

Unit 039 Today's Schedule 今日の予定に関する会話

STEP 1 各センテンスをシャドーイングしよう。　CD 1-40

STEP 2 テキストを見ながらスキットを演じてみよう。　CD 1-40

M: What does your day look like? Busy?
今日はどんな感じ？ 忙しいの？

F: Yes. In fact I might have to stay at the office pretty late.
うん、実は、かなり遅くまで会社にいなきゃならないかも。

M: The boys have soccer practice tonight. Do you want me to pick them up?
男の子たちは今晩サッカーの練習だよね。僕のほうで迎えにいこうか？
* pick someone up「…を（車で）拾う」

F: That would be great. Are you sure you'll get off work in time to do that?
それは助かるわ。確実に迎えに間に合う時間に仕事を終えられるの？
* get off work「仕事を終える」 in time「間に合って」

M: No problem. I have a light day today. They finish around six, right?
問題ないよ。今日の仕事は軽めだから。子どもたちは6時頃終わるんだよね？
* light day「仕事量が少ない日」

F: Yes. Thanks dear you're a sweetheart. I've got to go or I'm going to miss my bus.
うん。ありがとう、やさしいあなた。もう行かないとバスに乗り遅れちゃうわ。

M: Have a great day. If I take the afternoon off will you have time for lunch?
よい一日をね。午後休みを取ったらランチする時間はある？
* take the afternoon off「午後を休みにする」

F: Sorry ... I'm probably not even going to have time to eat anything.
ごめんね…おそらくなにか食べる時間さえないかも。

STEP 3 　日本語訳を見ながらスキットを演じてみよう。　CD 1-40

M: What does your day look like? Busy?

F:

うん、実は、かなり遅くまで会社にいなきゃならないかも。

M: The boys have soccer practice tonight. Do you want me to pick them up?

F:

それは助かるわ。確実に迎えに間に合う時間に仕事を終えられるの？

M: No problem. I have a light day today. They finish around six, right?

F:

うん。ありがとう、やさしいあなた。もう行かないとバスに乗り遅れちゃうわ。

M: Have a great day. If I take the afternoon off will you have time for lunch?

F:

ごめんね…おそらくなにか食べる時間さえないかも。

Unit 040　The Weather　今日の天気に関する会話

STEP 1 　各センテンスをシャドーイングしよう。　　CD 1-41

STEP 2 　テキストを見ながらスキットを演じてみよう。　　CD 1-41

F: You're not taking your umbrella with you?
　傘を持っていかないつもり？

M: Why? Is it supposed to rain today?
　どうして？ 今日は雨になるの？

F: Didn't you hear the weather report? We're supposed to get some heavy thunderstorms this afternoon.
　天気予報は聞いてないの？ 今日の午後は強い嵐になるはずだよ。
　＊ weather report「天気予報」　thunderstorm「嵐；雷雨」

M: Wow. I totally missed that! How long is the rain supposed to last?
　へえ。完全に知らなかった！ 雨はどのくらい続くの？
　＊ totally「完全に」　miss「逃す」　last「継続する」

F: The forecast said there is a 100% chance of rain for the next two or three days.
　予報ではこれから2日か3日は100％雨の確率になってるわよ。
　＊ forecast「予報」　chance of rain「雨の確率」

M: That stinks. Our company golf outing this weekend will probably have to be canceled.
　ちぇっ。今週末の会社のゴルフ・コンペはおそらくキャンセルだな。
　＊ stink「鼻持ちならない；いやになる」　outing「小旅行」

F: At least it's finally warmer. I thought this winter was never going to end.
　少なくともやっと暖かくはなったわよ。この冬は終わらないんじゃないかと思ってたもの。

M: You can say that again. Well ... see you later.
　そのとおりだね。じゃあ、行ってくるね。

STEP 3 日本語訳を見ながらスキットを演じてみよう。   CD 1-41

F : You're not taking your umbrella with you?

M :

どうして？ 今日は雨になるの？

F : Didn't you hear the weather report? We're supposed to get some heavy thunderstorms this afternoon.

M :

へえ。完全に知らなかった！ 雨はどのくらい続くの？

F : The forecast said there is a 100% chance of rain for the next two or three days.

M :

ちぇっ。今週末の会社のゴルフ・コンペはおそらくキャンセルだな。

F : At least it's finally warmer. I thought this winter was never going to end.

M :

そのとおりだね。じゃあ、行ってくるね。

Unit 041 Arriving Home 帰宅したときの会話

STEP 1 各センテンスをシャドーイングしよう。　CD 1-42

STEP 2 テキストを見ながらスキットを演じてみよう。　CD 1-42

M : Mom! I'm home.
母さん、ただいま。
* mom「母さん；母ちゃん」momma, mommy の短縮。

F : Welcome home dear. How was your day at school?
お帰り。学校はどうだったの？
* welcome home「お帰り」　dear「かわいい人；いい人（恋人や家族への呼びかけ）」

M : It was good. We went on a field trip to the history museum.
よかったよ。歴史博物館に見学に行ったんだよ。
* field trip「校外の見学旅行」　museum「博物館；美術館」

F : Did you have a good time? What was your favorite exhibit?
楽しかった？ どの展示が気に入ったの？
* exhibit「展示」

M : It was really cool. I liked learning about native American Indians the best.
すごかったよ。ネイティヴ・アメリカンについて学べたのがいちばんよかった。

F : Do you have any homework?
宿題はないの？

M : Nope. Can I go over to Danny's house and play?
いや。ダニーの家に遊びにいってもいいかな？

F : Sure. Just be home before dark.
もちろん。暗くなる前には戻ってきてね。

STEP 3 日本語訳を見ながらスキットを演じてみよう。　CD 1-42

M : Mom! I'm home.

F :

お帰り。学校はどうだったの？

M : It was good. We went on a field trip to the history museum.

F :

楽しかった？ どの展示が気に入ったの？

M : It was really cool. I liked learning about native American Indians the best.

F :

宿題はないの？

M : Nope. Can I go over to Danny's house and play?

F :

もちろん。暗くなる前には戻ってきてね。

Unit 042 掃除についての会話

Cleaning/Housework

STEP 1 各センテンスをシャドーイングしよう。　CD 1-43

STEP 2 テキストを見ながらスキットを演じてみよう。　CD 1-43

F : Did you clean your room like I asked? It was a mess!
頼んでたけど、自分の部屋は掃除したの？ ぐちゃぐちゃだったでしょ！
* mess「滅茶苦茶な状態；散乱；乱雑」

M : Yes, Mom.
うん、やったよ。

F : Okay. Now I need you to vacuum the living room and dining room for me.
よかったわ。じゃあ、リビングとダイニングに掃除機をかけてね。
* vacuum「掃除機をかける」

M : But I was going to go to Jimmy's house to play baseball!
でも、ジミーの家に野球をしにいこうと思ってたんだよ！

F : You can go play when you're finished helping me with the housework.
家事の手伝いが終わったら、遊びに出かけてもいいわ。

M : Oh alright. I'll go get the vacuum cleaner.
わかったよ。掃除機を取ってくる。

F : I already got it out for you. It's in the living room. Just make sure you put it away when you're done.
もう取り出しておいたから。リビングにあるわよ。終わったら片付けを忘れないで。
* get something out「…を出す」　put away「片づける」　be done「終わる」

M : I'll be done before you know it!
すぐに終わるから！
* before you know it「あなたがそれに気づく前に；あっという間に」

STEP 3 》》 日本語訳を見ながらスキットを演じてみよう。　　CD 1-43

F: Did you clean your room like I asked? It was a mess!

M: ☐

うん、やったよ。

F: Okay. Now I need you to vacuum the living room and dining room for me.

M: ☐

でも、ジミーの家に野球をしにいこうと思ってたんだよ！

F: You can go play when you're finished helping me with the housework.

M: ☐

わかったよ。掃除機を取ってくる。

F: I already got it out for you. It's in the living room. Just make sure you put it away when you're done.

M: ☐

すぐに終わるから！

Unit 043 スーパーでの会話
At the Supermarket

STEP 1 各センテンスをシャドーイングしよう。　CD 1-44

STEP 2 テキストを見ながらスキットを演じてみよう。　CD 1-44

M: Hey, we haven't had fresh fruit in a while. How about if we get some mangos?

ねえ、しばらく新鮮な果物を食べてないよね。マンゴーを買うのはどうかな？

* How about if ...?「…するのはどうだろう？」

F: That's a good idea. Look at this, they're on sale too!

いいわね。これ見て、安売りにもなってるわよ！

M: How do you know which ones to pick?

どれを買うべきかどうやって判断するの？

F: Don't pay attention to the color. Squeeze them gently and ripe ones give slightly.

色は気にしないのよ。やさしく押すと、熟したやつはちょっとへこむのよ。

* pay attention to ...「…に注意を払う」　squeeze「押す；絞る」　give「へこむ；たわむ」

M: Sort of like peaches, huh? I never knew that.

桃みたいだね？　知らなかったよ。

F: That's right. Also perfect ones will smell sweet around the stem.

そうなの。それと、完璧なやつは茎のあたりから甘いにおいがするの。

* stem「茎」

M: What else should we get? Do you want some grapes?

ほかにはなにを買う？　ブドウはどう？

F: That's not a bad idea ... just make sure they're seedless. I don't like grapes with seeds.

悪くないわね…種がないのをしっかり確認してね。種のあるやつは嫌いなのよ。

* seedless「種のない」

STEP 3 日本語訳を見ながらスキットを演じてみよう。　　CD 1-44

M : [　　　　　　　　　　　　　　　　　　　　　　　]

ねえ、しばらく新鮮な果物を食べてないよね。マンゴーを買うのはどうかな？

F : That's a good idea. Look at this, they're on sale too!

M : [　　　　　　　　　　　　　　　　　　　　　　　]

どれを買うべきかどうやって判断するの？

F : Don't pay attention to the color. Squeeze them gently and ripe ones give slightly.

M : [　　　　　　　　　　　　　　　　　　　　　　　]

桃みたいだね？ 知らなかったよ。

F : That's right. Also perfect ones will smell sweet around the stem.

M : [　　　　　　　　　　　　　　　　　　　　　　　]

ほかにはなにを買う？ ブドウはどう？

F : That's not a bad idea ... just make sure they're seedless. I don't like grapes with seeds.

Unit 044 帰りの時間を知らせる電話
Calling to Say When You'll Be Home

STEP 1 各センテンスをシャドーイングしよう。　CD 1-45

STEP 2 テキストを見ながらスキットを演じてみよう。　CD 1-45

F: Hello?
もしもし。

M: Hey babe it's me. Listen, I'm going to be late coming home tonight.
やあ、僕だよ。あのね、今日は帰りが遅くなるんだ。
* babe「あなた；お前（妻や夫への呼びかけ）」　be late coming home「帰宅が遅くなる」

F: Again!? How come?
またなの？ どうしてよ？

M: We have clients in from out of town and the boss wants me to take them out for dinner and drinks tonight.
顧客が出張で来ていてね、今晩、彼らをディナーとお酒に連れていってくれって、上司が言うんだよ。
* have clients in「来客がある」　from out of town「よそ（の街）から」

F: What time do you think you'll be home?
何時に戻れると思う？

M: I really can't say for sure, so don't wait up for me.
はっきりはわからないから、僕を待っていないで先に寝ててよ。
* for sure「確実に」　wait up for ...「…を起きて待つ」

F: Alright. I'm making pasta for dinner, so there'll be leftovers in the fridge if you're hungry later.
わかった。夕食にパスタを作るの。あとでおなかが空いたら、冷蔵庫に残りがあるからね。
* leftovers「残り物」　fridge「冷蔵庫」

M: Thanks. I love you. Tell the kids I love them too.
ありがとう。愛してるよ。子どもたちにも愛してるって伝えてよ。

STEP 3　日本語訳を見ながらスキットを演じてみよう。　CD 1-45

F :

もしもし。

M : Hey babe it's me. Listen, I'm going to be late coming home tonight.

F :

またなの？ どうしてよ？

M : We have clients in from out of town and the boss wants me to take them out for dinner and drinks tonight.

F :

何時に戻れると思う？

M : I really can't say for sure, so don't wait up for me.

F :

わかった。夕食にパスタを作るの。あとでおなかが空いたら、冷蔵庫に残りがあるからね。

M : Thanks. I love you. Tell the kids I love them too.

Unit 045 What's for Dinner 夕食のメニューの相談

STEP 1 各センテンスをシャドーイングしよう。　CD 1-46

STEP 2 テキストを見ながらスキットを演じてみよう。　CD 1-46

M: What do you want to do for dinner tonight?
今夜の夕食はどうしたい？

* What do you want to do for dinner tonight?　この文への返事には、「外食する」「家で作る」「公園でバーベキューする」などの答えが可能。

F: I don't know. Do you want to go out to eat?
さあ。外食したいの？

M: I wouldn't mind trying that new Chinese restaurant that opened.
開店した新しい中華料理店を試してみたいな。

* wouldn't mind -ing「…したい」

F: Mary told me it was pretty expensive, but the food was good.
メアリーはすごく高かったって言ってたわ、でも食べ物はおいしかったって。

M: I wonder if we'll need a reservation on a weekday.
平日には予約は必要かなあ？

* reservation「予約」　weekday「平日」

F: I've seen people waiting in line outside. Maybe we should make one just to be safe.
外で並んでいる人を見たことあるわよ。念のため、予約したほうがいいかもね。

* in line「列に」　just to be safe「念のため」

M: Yeah. Better safe than sorry. I'll call and get us a table for 6:30. How does that sound?
うん。後悔するよりはやったほうが安全だね。電話して6時半に席を予約するよ。どうかな？

F: That works for me.
それでいいわ。

STEP 3　日本語訳を見ながらスキットを演じてみよう。　CD 1-46

M: What do you want to do for dinner tonight?

F:

さあ。外食したいの？

M: I wouldn't mind trying that new Chinese restaurant that opened.

F:

メアリーはすごく高かったって言ってたわ、でも食べ物はおいしかったって。

M: I wonder if we'll need a reservation on a weekday.

F:

外で並んでいる人を見たことあるわよ。念のため、予約したほうがいいかもね。

M: Yeah. Better safe than sorry. I'll call and get us a table for 6:30. How does that sound?

F:

それでいいわ。

Unit 046 Cooking 料理中の会話

STEP 1 各センテンスをシャドーイングしよう。　CD 1-47

STEP 2 テキストを見ながらスキットを演じてみよう。　CD 1-47

M: Dinner will be ready in five minutes. Can you set the table for me?
5分で夕食ができるよ。テーブルを準備してもらえる？

F: Sure. Hey, that smells great. What are you cooking?
うん。ああ、いいにおいだね。なにを作ってるの？

M: I made your favorite dinner tonight. Bacon-wrapped filet mignon and baked potatoes.
今夜の夕食は君の好物を作ったよ。ヒレ肉のベーコン巻とベークド・ポテトだよ。
* filet mignon「高級ヒレ肉」 bake「(直火に当てずに) 焼く」

F: Is that asparagus you're grilling?! I'm not really a fan of asparagus.
焼いているのはアスパラガス？　アスパラはあまり好きじゃないんだよね。
* grill「網焼きにする」

M: You're going to like this. Trust me. I marinated it in olive oil and garlic.
好きになるよ。信じて。オリーブ・オイルとニンニクでマリネにしたから。
* marinate「マリネにする」

F: Oh, that does sound pretty good. I've never had it like that before.
うひょ〜、それはすごくおいしそうね。そんなふうにして食べたことはないわ。
* like that「そんなふうに」

M: You want your steak medium-rare like always, right?
いつものようにステーキはミディアム・レアでいいんだよね？

F: Of course. That's the way steak should be eaten. I like them pink in the middle.
もちろん。それこそステーキが食べられるべき姿よ。真ん中がピンクなのが好きなのよね。

STEP 3 　日本語訳を見ながらスキットを演じてみよう。　CD 1-47

M: Dinner will be ready in five minutes. Can you set the table for me?

F:

うん。ああ、いいにおいだね。なにを作ってるの？

M: I made your favorite dinner tonight. Bacon-wrapped filet mignon and baked potatoes.

F:

焼いているのはアスパラガス？ アスパラはあまり好きじゃないんだよね。

M: You're going to like this. Trust me. I marinated it in olive oil and garlic.

F:

うひょ〜、それはすごくおいしそうね。そんなふうにして食べたことはないわ。

M: You want your steak medium-rare like always, right?

F:

もちろん。それこそステーキが食べられるべき姿よ。真ん中がピンクなのが好きなのよね。

Unit 047 What to Watch 観たい番組についての会話

STEP 1 各センテンスをシャドーイングしよう。　CD 1-48

STEP 2 テキストを見ながらスキットを演じてみよう。　CD 1-48

F: Can we watch something other than football tonight?
今夜はアメフト以外になにか観るものはないの？
* other than ...「…のほかに」　football「アメフト」英国では「サッカー」の意で用いられる。

M: But it's the playoffs and the Patriots are playing! I've got to watch that!
でも、プレーオフでペイトリオッツがやってるんだよ！ 観なきゃダメなんだよ！

F: There's a really good movie on tonight. I've been looking forward to watching.
今夜は、すごくいい映画があるのよ。観るのを楽しみにしていたの。

M: I'll tell you what ... we'll DVR the movie and let's watch it tomorrow night.
こうしようよ…映画は録画して、明日の夜に観よう。
* DVR「デジタル・ビデオ録画（する）」

F: You always say that, and I end up watching them alone.
いつもそう言うわよね。で、結局、私ひとりで観ることになるのよね。
* end up -ing「結局…することになる」

M: How about if we put a TV in the bedroom? Then you can watch whatever you want to!
ベッドルームにテレビを１台置くのはどう？ そうすれば君の観たいものがなんでも観られるよ！

F: But then we'll never be spending time together! I want to watch TV with you, just not sports!
でも、それじゃあ、全然いっしょに時間が過ごせないわ！ あなたといっしょにテレビを観たいのよ。スポーツだけじゃなくてね！
* just not ...「…に限らず；…だけではなく」

M: Okay ... We'll record the football game. But as soon as the movie is over I'm watching it!
わかったよ…アメフトを録画しよう。でも、映画が終わったら、僕はすぐにアメフトを観るからね！

STEP 3 　日本語訳を見ながらスキットを演じてみよう。　CD 1-48

F :

今夜はアメフト以外になにか観るものはないの？

M : But it's the playoffs and the Patriots are playing! I've got to watch that!

F :

今夜は、すごくいい映画があるのよ。観るのを楽しみにしていたの。

M : I'll tell you what ... we'll DVR the movie and let's watch it tomorrow night.

F :

いつもそう言うわよね。で、結局、私ひとりで観ることになるのよね。

M : How about if we put a TV in the bedroom? Then you can watch whatever you want to!

F :

でも、それじゃあ、全然いっしょに時間が過ごせないわ！ あなたといっしょにテレビを観たいのよ。スポーツだけじゃなくてね！

M : Okay ... We'll record the football game. But as soon as the movie is over I'm watching it!

Unit 048 Before Bedtime 就寝前のちょっとした会話

STEP 1 各センテンスをシャドーイングしよう。 CD 1-49

STEP 2 テキストを見ながらスキットを演じてみよう。 CD 1-49

M: Well ... I can hardly keep my eyes open so I am going to hit the hay.
うーん、目を開けてられないから寝るよ。
* keep one's eyes open「目を開けている」 hit the hay「床に就く；寝る」

F: I won't be too far behind you. I just want to finish reading this article.
私もそんなに遅くならないから。この記事だけ読み終わりたいの。
* not be too far behind you「あなたにそれほど遅れない」

M: I need to go in to work a little early tomorrow, so I am going to set the alarm clock for 5:30.
明日はちょっと早く仕事に行くから、目覚まし時計を5時半にセットするよ。

F: That's fine. It's my turn to drive the kids' school carpool, so I should get up early too.
いいわよ。子どもを学校まで相乗りで送るのが私の順番なの。だから私も早起きしなくちゃ。
* carpool「相乗り」

M: Why don't you finish reading that magazine in bed?
その雑誌ベッドで読み終えたらどうなの？

F: That's okay. I don't want to keep you up.
大丈夫。あなたを起こしたくないし。

M: Okay. Good night my love.
わかった。じゃあ、おやすみ。
* love「愛する君；あなた（親しみのこもった呼びかけ）」

F: Good night to you too, dear. See you in the morning.
おやすみ、あなた。また朝にね。

STEP 3 　日本語訳を見ながらスキットを演じてみよう。　CD 1-49

M: Well ... I can hardly keep my eyes open so I am going to hit the hay.

F:

私もそんなに遅くならないから。この記事だけ読み終わりたいの。

M: I need to go in to work a little early tomorrow, so I am going to set the alarm clock for 5:30.

F:

いいわよ。子どもを学校まで相乗りで送るのが私の順番なの。だから私も早起きしなくちゃ。

M: Why don't you finish reading that magazine in bed?

F:

大丈夫。あなたを起こしたくないし。

M: Okay. Good night my love.

F:

おやすみ、あなた。また朝にね。

Unit 049 Planning a Trip
旅行の計画に関する会話

STEP 1 　各センテンスをシャドーイングしよう。　CD 1-50

STEP 2 　テキストを見ながらスキットを演じてみよう。　CD 1-50

M: You have this coming Friday off, right?
今度の金曜日は休暇を取るんだよね？
* coming「次の；来たるべき」

F: Yes. I haven't taken any time off yet this year, so I wanted to have a three-day weekend.
うん。今年はまだ休んでないから、3連休にしたかったのよ。
* take time off「休暇を取る」　three-day weekend「3連休の週末」

M: I was thinking about taking the day off too. We haven't had much time together lately. What do you say we take a little trip?
僕も休もうかと思ってるんだ。最近はあまりいっしょに時間が過ごせてないよね。小旅行に行くのはどうかな？

F: That sounds great! What do you have in mind?
それはいいわね！ なにか考えていることがあるの？
* have ... in mind「…が頭の中にある」

M: I was thinking maybe the beach ... someplace warm. We could fly down to Florida Friday night and come back on Sunday.
ビーチとか…暖かいところを考えてたんだ。金曜の夜にフロリダに飛んで日曜に戻ってくることだってできるよ。

F: We haven't been there in ages!
フロリダは長いこと行ってないわね！
* in ages「長い間」

M: Not since we got married, in fact.
実際、結婚したとき以来、行ってないよ。

F: This can be our second honeymoon!
2回目のハネムーンになるかもね！

STEP 3 　日本語訳を見ながらスキットを演じてみよう。　CD 1-50

M: You have this coming Friday off, right?

F:

うん。今年はまだ休んでないから、3連休にしたかったのよ。

M: I was thinking about taking the day off too. We haven't had much time together lately. What do you say we take a little trip?

F:

それはいいわね！ なにか考えていることがあるの？

M: I was thinking maybe the beach ... someplace warm. We could fly down to Florida Friday night and come back on Sunday.

F:

フロリダは長いこと行ってないわね！

M: Not since we got married, in fact.

F:

2回目のハネムーンになるかもね！

Unit 050 休暇の不満を漏らす会話

Having to Work on One's Day Off

> **STEP 1** 各センテンスをシャドーイングしよう。　CD 1-51

> **STEP 2** テキストを見ながらスキットを演じてみよう。　CD 1-51

M: I know I promised we'd go to the mountains this weekend, but I have to work Saturday.

今週末に山に行くって約束したのはわかってるんだけど、土曜は仕事になっちゃって。

F: What!? You've been working overtime the last three weekends!

えっ！ この3週間はずっと週末に残業してたじゃない！

M: I know. We're just so short-handed at work, there's no way I can say no.

そうなんだ。職場がすごい人手不足で、断ることはできないんだよ。

* short-handed「人手不足で」

F: Are they at least paying you overtime? You should be getting double for working weekends.

少なくとも残業手当は出るのよね？ 週末の仕事は2倍もらわなきゃね。

* pay someone overtime「…に残業手当を払う」　double「2倍」

M: They're only giving me time and a half. My yearly review is next week, and I am going to demand a raise.

1.5倍しか払ってくれないんだよね。来週、僕の1年ごとの査定があるから、昇給を要求しようと思ってる。

* time and a half「1.5倍」　review「査定」　demand a raise「昇給を要求する」

F: You definitely should. I think you ought to tell them they need to hire more people too.

絶対に、そうすべきよ。それにもっと人を雇うように話をするべきよ。

M: You're right. Listen, I know you're disappointed about the trip. I promise I'll make it up to you next weekend.

そのとおりだよ。あのね、旅行のこと、残念に思ってるよね。次の週末はなんとかするって約束するからさ。

* disappointed「がっかりした」　make it up to ...「…に償いをする」

F: You better.

それは当然よ。

STEP 3 　日本語訳を見ながらスキットを演じてみよう。　CD 1-51

M: I know I promised we'd go to the mountains this weekend, but I have to work Saturday.

F:

えっ！ この 3 週間はずっと週末に残業してたじゃない！

M: I know. We're just so short-handed at work, there's no way I can say no.

F:

少なくとも残業手当は出るのよね？ 週末の仕事は 2 倍もらわなきゃね。

M: They're only giving me time and a half. My yearly review is next week, and I am going to demand a raise.

F:

絶対に、そうすべきよ。それにもっと人を雇うように話をするべきよ。

M: You're right. Listen, I know you're disappointed about the trip. I promise I'll make it up to you next weekend.

F:

それは当然よ。

Unit 051 Family Finances 家計についての議論

STEP 1 各センテンスをシャドーイングしよう。 CD 1-52

STEP 2 テキストを見ながらスキットを演じてみよう。 CD 1-52

M : I was thinking about looking for a new car this weekend.
今週末、新しい車を探そうと思っていたんだ。

F : Honey! We can't afford that! Plus, there's nothing wrong with the car we have!
あなた！ そんなお金はないわよ！ それに、いまの車もどこも悪くなってないし！
* afford ...「…を買う余裕がある」 there's nothing wrong with ...「…に悪いところはない」

M : But it's so old I'm embarrassed to drive it!
でも、すごく古くて運転するのが恥ずかしいんだよ！
* be embarrassed to ...「…するのが恥ずかしい」

F : We are barely making it from paycheck to paycheck as it is.
いまうちはギリギリの生活をしているのよ。
* make it from paycheck to paycheck「給料日の間を食いつなぐ」 as it is「現状では」

M : I guess you're right. Maybe we can save up for one though.
そうだと思うよ。でも、たぶん車1台分は貯金できると思うんだけど。

F : Remember we are going to have to start saving for the kids' college tuition too.
子どもたちの大学の学費のための貯金も始めないといけないことを忘れないでよ。
* tuition「学費」

M : They're only three years old! We have plenty of time for that.
子どもたちはまだ3歳じゃないか！ まだ時間はたっぷりあるよ。

F : Have you seen how much tuition is rising every year?! We need to start saving now.
毎年どれだけ学費が値上げされているかわかってるの？ いま貯金を始めないとダメなのよ。

111

STEP 3 日本語訳を見ながらスキットを演じてみよう。　CD 1-52

M :

今週末、新しい車を探そうと思っていたんだ。

F : Honey! We can't afford that! Plus, there's nothing wrong with the car we have!

M :

でも、すごく古くて運転するのが恥ずかしいんだよ！

F : We are barely making it from paycheck to paycheck as it is.

M :

そうだと思うよ。でも、たぶん車 1 台分は貯金できると思うんだけど。

F : Remember we are going to have to start saving for the kids' college tuition too.

M :

子どもたちはまだ 3 歳じゃないか！ まだ時間はたっぷりあるよ。

F : Have you seen how much tuition is rising every year?! We need to start saving now.

Unit 052 Gardening ガーデニングに関する会話

STEP 1 各センテンスをシャドーイングしよう。　CD 1-53

STEP 2 テキストを見ながらスキットを演じてみよう。　CD 1-53

M: I was thinking about hiring someone to landscape our yard.
庭の手入れのために人を雇おうと思ってたんだけど。
* landscape「(庭を美しく) 手入れする」

F: I don't know about that. That can cost a lot of money.
それはどうかなあ。お金がかなりかかるかもね。

M: That's true, but it looks good and adds to the value of the house.
そのとおりなんだけど、外観がよくなるし、家の価値も上がるよね。
* add to ...「…(の価値など) が増える」　value「価値」

F: What are you thinking about planting?
なにを植えようと考えているの？

M: I want to put some flower beds in along the side of the house.
家の横に花壇をいくつか置きたいんだ。

F: I wouldn't mind putting some hedges up too. They would provide shade and privacy.
生け垣を作るのもいいわよね。日陰もできるしプライバシーも保てるから。
* wouldn't mind -ing「…したい」　hedge「生け垣」　shade「日陰」

M: Why don't we go to the nursery and see what would look good. Maybe we can do it ourselves.
園芸店に行って、なにがいいのか見てみようよ。自分たちでできるかも。
* nursery「園芸店」　do it oneself「自分自身でそれをやる」

F: That's a lot of work. But if you really want to do it, I'll help.
大変な労力だよ。でも、あなたがホントにそうしたいのなら手伝うけど。

STEP 3 　日本語訳を見ながらスキットを演じてみよう。　CD 1-53

M: I was thinking about hiring someone to landscape our yard.

F:

それはどうかなあ。お金がかなりかかるかもね。

M: That's true, but it looks good and adds to the value of the house.

F:

なにを植えようと考えているの？

M: I want to put some flower beds in along the side of the house.

F:

生け垣を作るのもいいわよね。日陰もできるしプライバシーも保てるから。

M: Why don't we go to the nursery and see what would look good. Maybe we can do it ourselves.

F:

大変な労力だよ。でも、あなたがホントにそうしたいのなら手伝うけど。

Unit 053 Inviting Someone to Dinner
食事に招待する会話

STEP 1 各センテンスをシャドーイングしよう。　CD 1-54

STEP 2 テキストを見ながらスキットを演じてみよう。　CD 1-54

M: Hey Linda. Do you have plans for this Saturday?
やあ、リンダ。今度の土曜は計画とかあるの？

F: I'm not doing anything in particular. What's up?
特になにもする予定はないわ。どうしたの？

* in particular「特に」　What's up?「どうしたの？」相手の状況をたずねる表現。

M: My wife and I are planning on having some people over and cooking out. I was hoping you and John could come.
奥さんと僕で、何人か人を呼んで外で料理しようかと思っててね。君とジョンが来られればいいなと思って。

* have ... over「…を（自宅などに）呼ぶ」　cook out「外で料理する」

F: That sounds like fun. I'll run it past him tonight. What time are you thinking?
楽しそうね。今夜、彼の意見を聞いてみる。何時を考えてるの？

* sound like fun「楽しそうだ」　run it past someone「それについて…の意見を聞く」

M: Most people are probably going to show up around three o'clock. We'll probably eat around four-thirty.
おそらく、ほとんどの人は3時頃やってくると思うよ。たぶん4時半くらいに食べると思うな。

F: Can I bring something? A side dish maybe?
なにか持ってこようか？　サイド・ディッシュとか？

M: That would be great! In fact, I'd love it if you could bring that famous potato salad of yours.
それはいいね！　実は、君のあの有名なポテト・サラダを持ってきてくれると、すごくうれしいよ。

F: You got it. I'm almost positive we'll be there, but let me check with John and I'll call you to confirm.
わかった。ほぼ行けると思うけど、ジョンに確認させてね。それから確認の電話をするわ。

* almost「ほとんど」　positive「肯定的な」

STEP 3　日本語訳を見ながらスキットを演じてみよう。　CD 1-54

M: Hey Linda. Do you have plans for this Saturday?

F:

特になにもする予定はないわ。どうしたの？

M: My wife and I are planning on having some people over and cooking out. I was hoping you and John could come.

F:

楽しそうね。今夜、彼の意見を聞いてみる。何時を考えてるの？

M: Most people are probably going to show up around three o'clock. We'll probably eat around four-thirty.

F:

なにか持ってこようか？ サイド・ディッシュとか？

M: That would be great! In fact, I'd love it if you could bring that famous potato salad of yours.

F:

わかった。ほぼ行けると思うけど、ジョンに確認させてね。それから確認の電話をするわ。

Unit 054 Meeting for the First Time 初対面の人との会話

STEP 1 各センテンスをシャドーイングしよう。　CD 1-55

STEP 2 テキストを見ながらスキットを演じてみよう。　CD 1-55

M: Hi, I don't think we've met before. My name's William, but you can call me Bill.
こんにちは、前に会ってはいませんよね。ウィリアムといいますが、ビルって呼んでくださいね。

F: Nice to meet you Bill. My name is Sarah. I am Susan's sister.
はじめましてビル。私はサラといいます。スーザンの姉なんですよ。

M: Oh yes. Susan talks about you all the time. I work with her husband Jim.
ああ、そうですか。スーザンはあなたのことをいつも話してますよ。僕は、彼女の夫のジムといっしょに働いているんです。

F: So you're in real estate too, huh?
ということは、あなたも不動産業界ですか？
* real estate「不動産（業界）」

M: Well, sort of. I'm actually the company accountant. Here's my business card. What do you do for a living?
ええ、そんな感じです。実は会社の会計士なんですよ。これが僕の名刺です。あなたはどんなお仕事なんですか？
* sort of「ある意味；ある種」　accountant「会計士」　for a living「生活のために」

F: I am a freelance graphic designer. I work out of my home.
私はフリーのグラフィック・デザイナーです。家で仕事をしてるんです。
* work out of one's home「自分の家で仕事をしている」

M: Well it has been a pleasure talking with you. I'm sure I'll see you around.
お話できて楽しかったです。必ずまた会いましょう。
* pleasure「よろこび」　I'm sure (that) I'll ...「きっと…しましょう」

F: The pleasure was all mine.
私のほうこそ。

STEP 3　日本語訳を見ながらスキットを演じてみよう。　CD 1-55

M: Hi, I don't think we've met before. My name's William, but you can call me Bill.

F:

はじめましてビル。私はサラといいます。スーザンの姉なんですよ。

M: Oh yes. Susan talks about you all the time. I work with her husband Jim.

F:

ということは、あなたも不動産業界ですか？

M: Well, sort of. I'm actually the company accountant. Here's my business card. What do you do for a living?

F:

私はフリーのグラフィック・デザイナーです。家で仕事をしてるんです。

M: Well it has been a pleasure talking with you. I'm sure I'll see you around.

F:

私のほうこそ。

Unit 055 Arranging to Meet 待ち合わせの約束

STEP 1 各センテンスをシャドーイングしよう。 CD 1-56

STEP 2 テキストを見ながらスキットを演じてみよう。 CD 1-56

M: We're still on for dinner tonight, right? Where do you want to meet?
今夜の夕食の約束まだ生きているよね？ どこで会う？
* be on「(約束などが) 有効だ」

F: How about Shibuya Station? I'll meet you at the South Entrance.
渋谷駅はどう？ 南口で会いましょう。

M: That's fine. What time works best for you?
いいよ。君は何時が都合がいいの？

F: I might be a little late leaving the office. How does seven o'clock sound?
オフィスを出るのがちょっと遅くなるかもしれないの。7時はどうかな？

M: Actually, if it's okay, can we make it seven thirty? I need to stop by the bank.
うーん、もし大丈夫なら7時半でもいいかな？ 銀行に寄る用があるんだ。
* make A B「A を B にする」 stop by「立ち寄る」

F: That's fine with me. That way I don't have to rush.
私はいいわよ。それなら急ぐ必要もないしね。
* that way「それなら」 rush「急ぐ；慌てる」

M: Great. I guess I'll see you there at seven thirty then.
OK。じゃあ、そこで7時半にね。

F: Sounds like a plan. I'll see you then. If something comes up just call me.
OK。じゃあ、そのときに。なにかあったら電話してくれればいいからね。
* come up「起こる」

STEP 3   日本語訳を見ながらスキットを演じてみよう。   CD 1-56

M: We're still on for dinner tonight, right? Where do you want to meet?

F:

渋谷駅はどう？ 南口で会いましょう。

M: That's fine. What time works best for you?

F:

オフィスを出るのがちょっと遅くなるかもしれないの。7時はどうかな？

M: Actually, if it's okay, can we make it seven thirty? I need to stop by the bank.

F:

私はいいわよ。それなら急ぐ必要もないしね。

M: Great. I guess I'll see you there at seven thirty then.

F:

OK。じゃあ、そのときに。なにかあったら電話してくれればいいからね。

Unit 056 外出準備中の会話
Getting Ready to Leave

STEP 1 各センテンスをシャドーイングしよう。　CD 1-57

STEP 2 テキストを見ながらスキットを演じてみよう。　CD 1-57

M: The play starts at 8 o'clock. We need to leave in half an hour. Are you ready?

芝居は8時に始まるよ。30分で出かけないといけないけど、準備はできてる？

* half an hour「30分」

F: Not quite. I can't decide on which dress to wear. Which of these do you like better?

まだなの。どっちのドレスを着ていくか決まらないのよ。あなたはどっちが好き？

* not quite「完全に…ではない」

M: They both look great, but I think the black dress is the one.

どっちもすごくいいけど、僕は黒がいいと思うな。

F: Do you have the tickets?

チケットは持ったの？

M: Yes. They're in my wallet.

うん、財布に入ってるよ。

F: Did you call to confirm our dinner reservations?

ディナーの予約確認の電話をしてくれた？

* confirm「確認する」　reservation「予約」

M: That's what I forgot! I'll do that right now while you finish getting ready.

それ忘れてたね！いますぐにやるよ。君の準備が終わるまでにね。

* forget「忘れる」　right now「すぐに」

F: I'll be just a few more minutes.

もうちょっとでできるから。

STEP 3 　日本語訳を見ながらスキットを演じてみよう。　CD 1-57

M : The play starts at 8 o'clock. We need to leave in half an hour. Are you ready?

F :

まだなの。どっちのドレスを着ていくか決まらないのよ。あなたはどっちが好き？

M : They both look great, but I think the black dress is the one.

F :

チケットは持ったの？

M : Yes. They're in my wallet.

F :

ディナーの予約確認の電話をしてくれた？

M : That's what I forgot! I'll do that right now while you finish getting ready.

F :

もうちょっとでできるから。

Unit 057 At the Department Store デパートでの会話

STEP 1 各センテンスをシャドーイングしよう。　CD 1-58

STEP 2 テキストを見ながらスキットを演じてみよう。　CD 1-58

F: Good afternoon. Are you finding everything okay?
こんにちは。お探しものは全部見つかりましたか？

M: Actually, I am looking for a new wallet.
実は、財布を探しているんですよ。
* wallet「財布；札入れ」

F: Those are located in the Menswear section, next to the belts and neckties.
お財布はメンズウェアのセクションにございます。ベルトとネクタイの隣です。

M: I looked there, but I couldn't seem to find them.
そこは見たんですけど、見つけられないみたいだったんです。

F: Here let me show you. They should be right over here.
ではご案内いたします。ちょうどこちらのほうにあるはずですが。
* show「案内する」　right over here「ちょうどこっちに」

M: They sure are. I don't know how I missed them! Thank you.
ホントだ。どうして見逃したのかわからないなあ！ありがとう。

F: You're welcome. Also, I think there are some up by the checkout aisles that are on sale too.
どういたしまして。それから、レジの通路のそばにもセール品が少しあると思いますよ。
* checkout「レジ；チェックアウト」　aisle「通路」

M: I'll be sure to check those out. Thank you again.
そっちもチェックしてみますよ。ありがとう。
* check out「見てみる」

STEP 3 日本語訳を見ながらスキットを演じてみよう。 CD 1-58

F: Good afternoon. Are you finding everything okay?

M:

実は、財布を探しているんですよ。

F: Those are located in the Menswear section, next to the belts and neckties.

M:

そこは見たんですけど、見つけられないみたいだったんです。

F: Here let me show you. They should be right over here.

M:

ホントだ。どうして見逃したのかわからないなあ！ ありがとう。

F: You're welcome. Also, I think there are some up by the checkout aisles that are on sale too.

M:

そっちもチェックしてみますよ。ありがとう。

Unit 058 試着室での会話
In the Fitting Room

STEP 1 各センテンスをシャドーイングしよう。　CD 1-59

STEP 2 テキストを見ながらスキットを演じてみよう。　CD 1-59

M: Excuse me. Where are your fitting rooms located?
すみません。試着室はどこにあるでしょうか？

F: They're right through this door. How many items do you have?
ちょうどこのドアを抜けたところです。いくつ商品をお持ちですか？

M: I want to try on these three pairs of slacks.
この3本のスラックスを試着したいんです。
* three pairs of ...「3本の…；3組の…」

F: Let me take them off the hangers for you.
ハンガーからお外ししましょう。
* take off「取り外す」

M: Also, I was wondering if you had this size and style in navy blue.
それと、このサイズとスタイルでネイビー・ブルーはないですかね？

F: Let me check the computer ... I'm sorry, we're out of stock in that color.
コンピューターでお調べしますね…すみません、その色は品切れになっております。
* out of stock「在庫が切れて」

M: I see. They're on sale now. Can I get the sale price when you get them in stock again?
そうですか。いまが安売りなんですよね。また入荷したときにセール価格で購入できますかね？
* in stock「在庫に」

F: Unfortunately not. That sale is only for while products last.
残念ながらできません。セールは商品がある期間限定ですので。
* unfortunately「残念ながら」　last「続く；持続する」

STEP 3 日本語訳を見ながらスキットを演じてみよう。　CD 1-59

M :

すみません。試着室はどこにあるでしょうか？

F : They're right through this door. How many items do you have?

M :

この 3 本のスラックスを試着したいんです。

F : Let me take them off the hangers for you.

M :

それと、このサイズとスタイルでネイビー・ブルーはないですかね？

F : Let me check the computer ... I'm sorry, we're out of stock in that color.

M :

そうですか。いまが安売りなんですよね。また入荷したときにセール価格で購入できますかね？

F : Unfortunately not. That sale is only for while products last.

Unit 059 At the Register レジでの支払い時の会話

STEP 1 各センテンスをシャドーイングしよう。　CD 1-60

STEP 2 テキストを見ながらスキットを演じてみよう。　CD 1-60

F : Were you able to find everything you needed today?

お探しのものはすべて見つかりましたでしょうか？

M : Yes. Thank you. Actually, I don't need it today but I am curious, do you guys sell charcoal?

ええ、ありがとう。実は今日は必要ないんですが、興味があって。こちらでは木炭は売っていますか？

* curious「興味のある」　charcoal「木炭」

F : We sure do. It's in aisle 10. Do you have your MEGAMART member's card?

もちろんございます。10番通路にございますよ。メガマートのメンバーズ・カードはお持ちですか？

* aisle「通路；廊下」

M : I know I have it here somewhere in my wallet. Ah, here you go.

この財布のどこかに入っていると思うんですけど。はい、ありました。

* somewhere「どこかに」　here you go「はいどうぞ」

F : Your total with your savings from your MEGAMART card comes to $44.50. Do you have any coupons today?

貯まっているメガマート・ポイント［のお預かり額］を使ったお買い物の合計金額は、44ドル50セントになります。本日はなにかクーポンはお持ちですか？

* savings「貯まっていたもの（ここでは換金可能ポイントを指す）」　come to ...「合計で…になる」

M : Nope. I sure don't. I'll just pay cash.

いいえ。ありません。現金だけで支払います。

F : Okay. Out of fifty ... $5.50 is your change, and here is your receipt. Have a wonderful day.

わかりました。50ドルからですから…5ドル50セントのお釣りになります。それとこちらがレシートです。すばらしい一日をお過ごしください。

* out of ...「…から」　change「釣り銭」

M : Thank you. You do the same.

ありがとう。あなたのほうもね。

STEP 3 　日本語訳を見ながらスキットを演じてみよう。　CD 1-60

F : Were you able to find everything you needed today?

M :

ええ、ありがとう。実は今日は必要ないんですが、興味があって。こちらでは木炭は売っていますか？

F : We sure do. It's in aisle 10. Do you have your MEGAMART member's card?

M :

この財布のどこかに入っていると思うんですけど。はい、ありました。

F : Your total with your savings from your MEGAMART card comes to $44.50. Do you have any coupons today?

M :

いいえ。ありません。現金だけで支払います。

F : Okay. Out of fifty ... $5.50 is your change, and here is your receipt. Have a wonderful day.

M :

ありがとう。あなたのほうもね。

Unit 060 Returning an Item 返品する場面での会話

STEP 1 各センテンスをシャドーイングしよう。　CD 1-61

STEP 2 テキストを見ながらスキットを演じてみよう。　CD 1-61

F: I need to return this shirt. I didn't notice it when I bought it, but it's missing some buttons.

このシャツを返品したいんです。買ったとき気づかなかったのですが、ボタンがいくつか取れているんですよ。

* return「返品する」　notice「気づく」　missing「あるべきところにない」

M: I can certainly help you with that. Do you have your receipt?

もちろん大丈夫です。レシートをお持ちですか？

F: Yes. Here it is. I bought it last weekend.

はい、こちらです。先週末に購入しました。

M: Would you like cash back, or would you like to exchange it?

キャッシュ・バックがよろしいですか？ 交換いたしますか？

* cash back「返金」　exchange「交換する」

F: I'd like to exchange it for this one. This one is a little cheaper. Can I get the difference back in cash?

こちらに交換したいんです。こっちのほうがちょっと安いですよね。差額分は現金で返金いただけますか？

M: We can't give you cash for an exchange, but we can give you the difference in in-store credit. That's our store policy.

交換では現金は差し上げられないのですが、差額分は店内で使えるクレジットを差し上げることができます。それが当店の方針でして。

* in-store credit「店内で使えるクレジット」　policy「方針」

F: I guess that will be okay.

まあ、それでいいですよ。

M: Okay. Here is your new receipt, and here is your credit voucher for $7.50. Have a wonderful day.

わかりました。こちらが新しいレシートで、こちらが7ドル50セントのクレジット・クーポンです。ありがとうございました。

* voucher「クーポン」

STEP 3 日本語訳を見ながらスキットを演じてみよう。 CD 1-61

F :

このシャツを返品したいんです。買ったとき気づかなかったのですが、ボタンがいくつか取れているんですよ。

M : I can certainly help you with that. Do you have your receipt?

F :

はい、こちらです。先週末に購入しました。

M : Would you like cash back, or would you like to exchange it?

F :

こちらに交換したいんです。こっちのほうがちょっと安いですよね。差額分は現金で返金いただけますか？

M : We can't give you cash for an exchange, but we can give you the difference in in-store credit. That's our store policy.

F :

まあ、それでいいですよ。

M : Okay. Here is your new receipt, and here is your credit voucher for $7.50. Have a wonderful day.

Unit 061 Talking Over Drinks お酒を飲みながらの会話

STEP 1 各センテンスをシャドーイングしよう。　CD 2-01

STEP 2 テキストを見ながらスキットを演じてみよう。　CD 2-01

F : We haven't been out for drinks in a while. It's good to see you.
しばらく外に飲みにきてなかったね。久しぶり。

M : Yeah. I've just been so busy at work lately. What are you having? First round's on me.
うん、最近仕事がすごく忙しくてね。君はなにを飲む？ 最初の1杯は僕がおごるよ。
* first round「1巡目；1杯目」 on me「私のおごりで」

F : I think I'll have a glass of Merlot.
メルローのグラスをいただこうかな。

M : Wine, huh? That's a change. You always used to be a beer drinker.
ワインかい？ いつもと違うじゃない。ずっとビールばかり飲んでたのに。

F : I've been on a diet so I'm trying to cut down on my calorie intake. How about you ... still drinking Scotch?
ダイエット中なの。だからカロリー摂取を抑えてるのよ。あなたは…まだスコッチを飲んでるの？
* on a diet「ダイエット中で」 cut down on ...「…を控える」

M : Usually yes, but I went out with some co-workers last night and we got hammered. Just beer today.
たいていはそうだけど、昨日同僚と飲みにいってひどく酔っちゃったんだ。今日はビールだけ。
* co-worker「同僚」 get hammered「ひどく酔う」

F : I forgot what a hangover feels like it's been so long. But I don't miss it!
長い間、二日酔いになってないから、どんな感じだか忘れちゃった。でも、いいことだよね！
* I don't miss it. は「私はそれ [二日酔い] がなくてさみしく思うことはない」が直訳。

STEP 3　日本語訳を見ながらスキットを演じてみよう。　CD 2-01

F :

しばらく外に飲みにきてなかったね。久しぶり。

M : Yeah. I've just been so busy at work lately. What are you having? First round's on me.

F :

メルローのグラスをいただこうかな。

M : Wine, huh? That's a change. You always used to be a beer drinker.

F :

ダイエット中なの。だからカロリー摂取を抑えてるのよ。あなたは…まだスコッチを飲んでるの？

M : Usually yes, but I went out with some co-workers last night and we got hammered. Just beer today.

F :

長い間、二日酔いになってないから、どんな感じだか忘れちゃった。でも、いいことだよね！

Unit 062 At the Bank 銀行での会話

STEP 1 各センテンスをシャドーイングしよう。　CD 2-02

STEP 2 テキストを見ながらスキットを演じてみよう。　CD 2-02

F : Good afternoon. Welcome to AMERICA BANK. What can I do for you today?
こんにちは。アメリカ・バンクへようこそ。本日はどのようなご用件でしょうか？

M : I'd like to deposit this check, but I don't know my account number.
この小切手を預けたいんですが、口座番号がわからなくて。
* deposit「預け入れる」　check「小切手」　account「口座」

F : That's quite alright. Do you have your ATM card with you?
それはまったく問題ありません。キャッシュ・カードはお持ちですか？

M : Yes. Here you go. I'd like the money to go into my savings account please.
はい、こちらです。私の普通預金口座にお金を入れたいんです。
* Here you go.「はいどうぞ（手渡すときの決まり文句）」　savings account「普通預金口座」

F : Please endorse the check for me by signing the back.
裏面に署名して、小切手を裏書きしてください。
* endorse「裏書きする」　sign「署名する」

M : Oh, by the way. Is it possible for me to get $100 cash back?
ああ、ところで、100 ドルをキャッシュで受け取ることはできますか？

F : Sure. Would you like that in small bills or will five twenty-dollar bills do?
もちろんです。小額紙幣がいいでしょうか、それとも 20 ドル札 5 枚でいいですか？
* small bills「小額紙幣」一般的に、20 ドル札以上は big bills という印象。それより小さい額の紙幣が small bills と呼ばれる。

M : If it's okay I'd like six tens and two twenties, please.
もし大丈夫なら、10 ドル札を 6 枚と、20 ドル札を 2 枚でお願いします。

STEP 3 日本語訳を見ながらスキットを演じてみよう。 2-02

F: Good afternoon. Welcome to AMERICA BANK. What can I do for you today?

M:

この小切手を預けたいんですが、口座番号がわからなくて。

F: That's quite alright. Do you have your ATM card with you?

M:

はい、こちらです。私の普通預金口座にお金を入れたいんです。

F: Please endorse the check for me by signing the back.

M:

ああ、ところで、100ドルをキャッシュで受け取ることはできますか？

F: Sure. Would you like that in small bills or will five twenty-dollar bills do?

M:

もし大丈夫なら、10ドル札を6枚と、20ドル札を2枚でお願いします。

Unit 063 At the Post Office
郵便局の窓口でのやりとり

STEP 1 各センテンスをシャドーイングしよう。　CD 2-03

STEP 2 テキストを見ながらスキットを演じてみよう。　CD 2-03

F: Next in line please. What can we do for you today?
次にお並びの方どうぞ。今日はどのようなご用件でしょう？

M: I'd like to mail this package via express mail. How much would that cost?
速達でこの荷物を送りたいのですが。料金はいくらになりますか？
＊ mail「郵送する」　via express mail「速達で」

F: Let's put it on the scale here. Okay, it weighs about four pounds. The postage would be $10.50.
こちらの秤に載せてみますね。はい、約4ポンドですね。郵便料金は10ドル50セントになります。
＊ scale「台秤」　weigh ...「…の重さだ」　pound「ポンド（重さの単位）」　postage「郵便料金」

M: That's fine. If it goes out today, when will it arrive at the destination?
そうですか。今日発送したら、宛先にいつ到着しますか？
＊ go out「出荷される」　destination「宛先；行き先」

F: Well, it's going to California, so transit would be two business days.
えー、カリフォルニア宛ですね。でしたら、配送に2営業日かかります。
＊ transit「輸送；配送」　business day「営業日」

M: That means it would be there by Wednesday afternoon, right?
ということは、水曜の午後までには到着するということですね？

F: That's right. If you need it to get there sooner we can send it Priority Overnight, but that would cost more.
そのとおりです。もっと早く届けたければ翌日配達便で送れますが、料金が高くなります。
＊ need A to B「AがBすることを必要とする」　priority overnight「翌日配達の優先便」

M: No thank you. As long as it arrives by Wednesday that will be fine.
いいえ、けっこうです。水曜までに到着するのであれば、それでかまいませんので。

STEP 3 　日本語訳を見ながらスキットを演じてみよう。　CD 2-03

F : Next in line please. What can we do for you today?

M :

速達でこの荷物を送りたいのですが。料金はいくらになりますか？

F : Let's put it on the scale here. Okay, it weighs about four pounds. The postage would be $10.50.

M :

そうですか。今日発送したら、宛先にいつ到着しますか？

F : Well, it's going to California, so transit would be two business days.

M :

ということは、水曜の午後までには到着するということですね？

F : That's right. If you need it to get there sooner we can send it Priority Overnight, but that would cost more.

M :

いいえ、けっこうです。水曜までに到着するのであれば、それでかまいませんので。

Unit 064 At the Hospital 病院での医者との会話

STEP 1 各センテンスをシャドーイングしよう。　CD 2-04

STEP 2 テキストを見ながらスキットを演じてみよう。　CD 2-04

F: So Mr. Jameson, what seems to be bothering you today?
で、ジェイムソンさん、今日はどこの具合が悪いようでしょうか？

M: I feel dizzy and light-headed. My heart is racing too.
めまいがしてふらふらするんです。胸もどきどきするんですよ。
* dizzy「めまいがする」　light-headed「ふらふらした」　race「どきどきする；早く脈打つ」

F: How long have you been experiencing these symptoms?
これらの徴候はいつからでしょう？
* symptom「徴候」

M: It started the day before yesterday, but it's been getting worse each day.
一昨日から始まりましたが、日増しに悪くなっているんです。

F: Okay. Let's take your blood pressure and I want to do some blood tests too.
そうですか。血圧を測りましょう。それと、血液検査もしておきたいですね。
* blood pressure「血圧」　blood test「血液検査」

M: If you must.
必要ならどうぞ。

F: Well, your blood pressure is rather high. Do you have a history of high blood pressure?
血圧がかなり高いですね。高血圧になったことはありますか？
* history「病歴；履歴」　high blood pressure「高血圧」

M: It runs in the family, but I have personally never had any problems before.
血統なんですよ。でも僕は個人的には、これまで一度も問題なかったんですが。
* run in the family「家族に流れる；血統だ」　personally「個人的には」

F: Well ... I think we should keep you overnight while we wait for the test results.
ああ…テストの結果が出るまで、ひと晩こちらでお過ごしいただければと思います。

STEP 3　日本語訳を見ながらスキットを演じてみよう。　CD 2-04

F : So Mr. Jameson, what seems to be bothering you today?

M :

めまいがしてふらふらするんです。胸もどきどきするんですよ。

F : How long have you been experiencing these symptoms?

M :

一昨日から始まりましたが、日増しに悪くなっているんです。

F : Okay. Let's take your blood pressure and I want to do some blood tests too.

M :

必要ならどうぞ。

F : Well, your blood pressure is rather high. Do you have a history of high blood pressure?

M :

血統なんですよ。でも僕は個人的には、これまで一度も問題なかったんですが。

F : Well ... I think we should keep you overnight while we wait for the test results.

Unit 065 緊急通報の会話
Calling 911

STEP 1 各センテンスをシャドーイングしよう。　CD 2-05

STEP 2 テキストを見ながらスキットを演じてみよう。　CD 2-05

F : 911. What is your emergency?

911番です。緊急ですか？

* 911「【米国】緊急通報用の電話番号」　emergency「緊急事態」

M : I can see smoke coming from my neighbor's house! Send the fire department!

隣の家から煙が出ているのが見えるんです！ 消防隊を派遣してください！

* fire department「消防隊；消防署」

F : It looks like you're calling me from 2415 River Road, is that correct?

リバー・ロードの2415からお電話いただいているようですが、正しいでしょうか？

M : Yes. My neighbor's address is 2417. Please hurry!

はい。隣の家の住所は2417です。急いでください！

F : Fire crews are on their way. Stay calm. Do you know if anyone is inside the house?

消防団員がそちらへ向かっています。落ち着いてください。家の中に人がいるかどうかわかりますか？

* fire crews「消防団員」　on one's way「(向かっている) 途中で」

M : I'm not sure. I don't think so because their car is not there.

わかりません。自動車がないので、いないのだと思います。

F : Can you see any fire or just smoke?

火が見えますか？ それとも煙だけですか？

M : Right now just smoke ... it's coming out of the second floor windows.

いまは煙だけです…2階の窓から出ています。

F : Okay. Maintain a safe distance. Help is on the way.

わかりました。距離を置いて安全な場所にいてください。救助スタッフがそちらに向かっていますので。

* maintain「持続する；維持する」

STEP 3 　日本語訳を見ながらスキットを演じてみよう。　　●CD 2-05

F : 911. What is your emergency?

M :

隣の家から煙が出ているのが見えるんです！ 消防隊を派遣してください！

F : It looks like you're calling me from 2415 River Road, is that correct?

M :

はい。隣の家の住所は 2417 です。急いでください！

F : Fire crews are on their way. Stay calm. Do you know if anyone is inside the house?

M :

わかりません。自動車がないので、いないのだと思います。

F : Can you see any fire or just smoke?

M :

いまは煙だけです…2階の窓から出ています。

F : Okay. Maintain a safe distance. Help is on the way.

Unit 066 Talking About Fashion
ファッションについての会話

STEP 1 各センテンスをシャドーイングしよう。　CD 2-06

STEP 2 テキストを見ながらスキットを演じてみよう。　CD 2-06

M: Hi Mary. You look fantastic today! I really like that dress.

やあ、メアリー。今日はすてきだね！ そのドレスすごくいいね。

F: Thanks John. You're the third person who's complimented me on it today.

ありがとう、ジョン。あなたは今日服をほめてくれた3人目の人よ。

* compliment A on B「BについてAをほめる」

M: Those earrings match it perfectly too. Did you buy them together?

イヤリングも完璧にマッチしてるよ。いっしょに買ったの？

F: You're not going to believe it, but I got this dress at a discount store at half price!

信じないと思うけど、このドレスはディスカウント・ショップで半額で買ったのよ！

* discount store「安売り店」　half price「半値」

M: And the earrings? Did you get them there too?

で、イヤリングも？ そこで買ったの？

F: Actually, my friend gave me these as a birthday present and they happened to match the dress perfectly!

実はね、友達が誕生日のプレゼントにくれたのよ。で、偶然ドレスに完璧に合ったの。

* actually「実は」　as ...「…として」

M: You're lucky! I have at least ten ties in the closet I got as gifts but never wear!

ラッキーだね！ プレゼントでもらったネクタイで全然着けないやつが、少なくとも10本はクローゼットに入ってるよ。

F: Well, the ones you do wear always look great on you.

ふーん、あなたがしてるネクタイはいつもすてきだよ。

* look great on ...「…にすごく似合う」

STEP 3　日本語訳を見ながらスキットを演じてみよう。　CD 2-06

M :
　　　やあ、メアリー。今日はすてきだね！ そのドレスすごくいいね。

F : Thanks John. You're the third person who's complimented me on it today.

M :
　　　イヤリングも完璧にマッチしてるよ。いっしょに買ったの？

F : You're not going to believe it, but I got this dress at a discount store at half price!

M :
　　　で、イヤリングも？ そこで買ったの？

F : Actually, my friend gave me these as a birthday present and they happened to match the dress perfectly!

M :
　　　ラッキーだね！ プレゼントでもらったネクタイで全然着けないやつが、少なくとも10本はクローゼットに入ってるよ。

F : Well, the ones you do wear always look great on you.

Unit 067 旅の感想についての会話
Impressions of a Trip

STEP 1 各センテンスをシャドーイングしよう。　CD 2-07

STEP 2 テキストを見ながらスキットを演じてみよう。　CD 2-07

M: You were just on a business trip to Japan, right? How was it?
君、日本に出張していたんだよね？ どうだった？
* business trip「出張旅行」

F: It was fantastic. We were in Tokyo for three nights and four days.
すばらしかったわよ。東京に3泊4日したの。

M: I hear the view of the skyline at night is spectacular.
夜空に浮かぶ街並みが壮観だって聞いたけど。
* skyline「空に浮かぶ街並みのライン」 spectacular「壮観な」

F: It sure is. Another impressive thing was the mixture of old and modern architecture.
そのとおりよ。古い建築と新しい建築の融合も印象的な点ね。
* impressive「印象的な」 mixture「混合；混じり合い」 architecture「建築」

M: Did you get to do any sightseeing when you were there?
東京では、観光する機会はあったの？

F: We went to Ginza and Akihabara, two of the main shopping districts, and to an ancient temple.
銀座と秋葉原に行ったの。どちらも大規模なショッピング・エリアよ。それと、古いお寺にもね。
* district「地域；区域」 ancient「大昔の；古代の」

M: I've always wanted to go there someday.
日本へはいつか行きたいってずっと思ってるんだよね。

F: I definitely recommend it. I can't wait to go back.
絶対におすすめよ。次の機会が待ちきれないわ。

STEP 3　日本語訳を見ながらスキットを演じてみよう。　CD 2-07

M: You were just on a business trip to Japan, right? How was it?

F:

すばらしかったわよ。東京に3泊4日したの。

M: I hear the view of the skyline at night is spectacular.

F:

そのとおりよ。古い建築と新しい建築の融合も印象的な点ね。

M: Did you get to do any sightseeing when you were there?

F:

銀座と秋葉原に行ったの。どちらも大規模なショッピング・エリアよ。それと、古いお寺にもね。

M: I've always wanted to go there someday.

F:

絶対におすすめよ。次の機会が待ちきれないわ。

Unit 068 スポーツについての会話
Talking About Sports

STEP 1 各センテンスをシャドーイングしよう。　CD 2-08

STEP 2 テキストを見ながらスキットを演じてみよう。　CD 2-08

M: You like baseball, right? Did you see the Braves game last night?
野球が好きなんだよね？ 昨夜のブレーブスの試合は観た？

F: I only watched the first half, then I fell asleep.
前半しか観なかったの。で、眠っちゃった。
* first half「前半」「後半」は second half と表現できる。

M: Wow. You missed a great game. They won in extra innings.
へえ、君はすばらしい試合を見逃したね。ブレーブスが延長戦で勝利したんだよ。

F: They've won six games in a row now, right? What's their record?
じゃあ、もう6連勝よね？ ブレーブスの記録はどうなの？
* in a row「連続して」 record「記録」

M: They are six and one. The only game they lost was the season opener.
6勝1敗だよ。シーズン最初の試合だけ落としたんだ。

F: Do you think they have a chance to go all the way this year?
今年、ブレーブスが優勝するチャンスはあると思う？
* go all the way「優勝する」

M: It's too early to tell, but they are certainly playing well.
まだ判断するには早すぎるよ。でも、かなりいいプレーをしているよね。

F: Last year I was really disappointed when they lost in the playoffs.
去年、プレーオフで負けたときには、すごくがっかりしたのよ。

M: Tell me about it. I was sure that was our year to win it all.
そのとおりだよね。去年こそ確実に優勝できると思ってたんだよ。
* Tell me about it.「そのとおり」 win it all「優勝する」

STEP 3 日本語訳を見ながらスキットを演じてみよう。　CD 2-08

M: You like baseball, right? Did you see the Braves game last night?

F:

前半しか観なかったの。で、眠っちゃった。

M: Wow. You missed a great game. They won in extra innings.

F:

じゃあ、もう6連勝よね？ ブレーブスの記録はどうなの？

M: They are six and one. The only game they lost was the season opener.

F:

今年、ブレーブスが優勝するチャンスはあると思う？

M: It's too early to tell, but they are certainly playing well.

F:

去年、プレーオフで負けたときには、すごくがっかりしたのよ。

M: Tell me about it. I was sure that was our year to win it all.

Unit 069 趣味についての会話

Talking About Hobbies/Interests

STEP 1 各センテンスをシャドーイングしよう。 CD 2-09

STEP 2 テキストを見ながらスキットを演じてみよう。 CD 2-09

M : What do you like to do in your free time?
暇なときにはなにをするのが好きなの？
* free time「自由な時間；暇なとき」

F : I love the outdoors. Camping, fishing, hiking. Anything having to do with nature.
アウトドアが好きなの。キャンプや釣り、ハイキングとか。自然と関係のあることならなんでも。
* outdoors「アウトドア活動」

M : Me too! I love to go hiking. How often do you usually go?
僕もだよ！ ハイキングに行くのが好きなんだ。君はどのくらいの頻度で行くの？

F : In the summertime I try to go every weekend, but it depends on the weather, of course.
夏には毎週末行くようにしてるけど、もちろんお天気にもよるわね。
* depend on ...「…による」 weather「天候」

M : Have you ever done any mountain climbing?
山登りはしたことあるの？

F : No I haven't. I've always wanted to try it though.
ないわ。でも、ずっとやってみたいと思ってたの。

M : I'm a member of a club that meets monthly. Would you like to come next month?
僕は月に一度集まるクラブのメンバーなんだよ。来月、来てみたいかい？

F : I'd love to! Just let me know where and when and I'll be there!
ぜひ行きたいわ！ 場所と日取りを教えてくれたら、絶対に行くから！
* let someone know「…に知らせる」

STEP 3 日本語訳を見ながらスキットを演じてみよう。　CD 2-09

M : [　　　　　　　　　　　　　　　　　　　　　　　]

暇なときにはなにをするのが好きなの？

F : I love the outdoors. Camping, fishing, hiking. Anything having to do with nature.

M : [　　　　　　　　　　　　　　　　　　　　　　　]

僕もだよ！ ハイキングに行くのが好きなんだ。君はどのくらいの頻度で行くの？

F : In the summertime I try to go every weekend, but it depends on the weather, of course.

M : [　　　　　　　　　　　　　　　　　　　　　　　]

山登りはしたことあるの？

F : No I haven't. I've always wanted to try it though.

M : [　　　　　　　　　　　　　　　　　　　　　　　]

僕は月に一度集まるクラブのメンバーなんだよ。来月、来てみたいかい？

F : I'd love to! Just let me know where and when and I'll be there!

Unit 070 書籍についての会話

Book Review

STEP 1 各センテンスをシャドーイングしよう。　CD 2-10

STEP 2 テキストを見ながらスキットを演じてみよう。　CD 2-10

F: What are you reading? It looks interesting.
なにを読んでるの？ おもしろそうね。

M: It's the new publication of the Lord of the Rings, by J. R. R. Tolkien.
J. R. R. トールキンの『ロード・オブ・ザ・リング』の新刊だよ。
* new publication「新刊」

F: Is it good? I've seen the movies but never read the books.
おもしろいの？ 映画は観たけど、本は読んだことないわ。

M: The movies are good, but the books are way better!
映画はいいね。でも、本のほうがはるかにいいよ！
* way「はるかに」

F: How many books are there in the series?
シリーズには何巻あるの？

M: There are five total, but most people haven't read the fifth one called the Silmarillion.
全部で5巻だけど、ほとんどの人は第5巻の『シルマリルの物語』は読んでないよ。
* total「【口語】合計で」

F: Would you mind if I borrow them from you? I would love to read them.
本を貸してもらってもいいかな？ 読んでみたいわ。
* mind「いやだと思う；気にする」　borrow「借りる」

M: Sure. Just promise me you'll return them to me when you're finished.
もちろん。読み終わったら返すって約束してくれればね。

STEP 3 　日本語訳を見ながらスキットを演じてみよう。　CD 2-10

F :

なにを読んでるの？ おもしろそうね。

M : It's the new publication of the Lord of the Rings, by J. R. R. Tolkien.

F :

おもしろいの？ 映画は観たけど、本は読んだことないわ。

M : The movies are good, but the books are way better!

F :

シリーズには何巻あるの？

M : There are five total, but most people haven't read the fifth one called the Silmarillion.

F :

本を貸してもらってもいいかな？ 読んでみたいわ。

M : Sure. Just promise me you'll return them to me when you're finished.

Unit 071 Movie Review 映画についての会話

STEP 1 各センテンスをシャドーイングしよう。　CD 2-11

STEP 2 テキストを見ながらスキットを演じてみよう。　CD 2-11

M: I was thinking about going to see the movie "Iron Man 3" this weekend. Want to come?

今週末、映画の『アイアンマン3』を観にいこうと思ってたんだ。君も行きたい？

F: Actually, I already saw it. I went to the opening night premiere.

実は、もう観ちゃったの。初日の夜の封切りを観たのよ。

* premiere「初演；初日；封切り」

M: Really? Did you like it? I hear it's getting rave reviews.

そうなの？ どうだった？ すごくいい評価だって聞いたよ。

* rave review「激賞」

F: It's by far the best one yet. The special effects were incredible!

これまででは、断トツで最高よ。特殊効果は信じられないすばらしさだったわ！

* by far「はるかに；断然」　incredible「信じられない；すばらしい」

M: My ten-year-old son wants to go see it. Do you think it's suitable for kids?

うちの10歳の息子が観たがってるんだよ。子どもに向いていると思う？

F: Well, there is some violence and adult language of course, but I think it's okay.

うーん、もちろん多少の暴力シーンや大人の会話もあるけど、大丈夫だと思うな。

M: I'd like to watch it myself first to be sure. Would you be interested in watching it again?

確認したいから自分で観ておきたいな。もう一度観る気はある？

* to be sure「確認のため；念のため」　be interested in ...「…に興味がある」

F: Sure! I've been a Marvel comic fan ever since I was young.

もちろん！ 小さい頃からマーベル・コミックのファンなのよ。

STEP 3 日本語訳を見ながらスキットを演じてみよう。　CD 2-11

M: I was thinking about going to see the movie "Iron Man 3" this weekend. Want to come?

F:

実は、もう観ちゃったの。初日の夜の封切りを観たのよ。

M: Really? Did you like it? I hear it's getting rave reviews.

F:

これまででは、断トツで最高よ。特殊効果は信じられないすばらしさだったわ！

M: My ten-year-old son wants to go see it. Do you think it's suitable for kids?

F:

うーん、もちろん多少の暴力シーンや大人の会話もあるけど、大丈夫だと思うな。

M: I'd like to watch it myself first to be sure. Would you be interested in watching it again?

F:

もちろん！ 小さい頃からマーベル・コミックのファンなのよ。

Unit 072 Talking About Smart Phones 携帯電話についての会話

STEP 1 各センテンスをシャドーイングしよう。　CD 2-12

STEP 2 テキストを見ながらスキットを演じてみよう。　CD 2-12

M: Wow! Is that the new smartphone from Pine!?
へえ！ それってパイン社の新しいスマートフォン？

F: It sure is. I just bought it yesterday. I had to stand in line for hours!
そのとおり。昨日、買ったばかりなの。何時間も列に並ばなきゃならなかったの！

M: I heard the high definition screen was unbelievable!
高精細のスクリーンがすごいって聞いたよ！
* definition「解像度；精細度」　unbelievable「信じられない（ほどすばらしい）」

F: It is. And with 4G network speed I can watch live TV and everything.
そうなの。それに 4G ネットワークのスピードだから、ライブのテレビとかなんでも観られるの。
* ... and everything「…やほかのものすべて」

M: How much did you have to pay for it? I'll bet it wasn't cheap.
いくら支払ったの？ 安かったはずはないよね。

F: I got a discount through my current wireless provider. It only cost me $299.
いま使っている無線のプロバイダーからディスカウントをもらったの。たったの 299 ドルだったわよ。
* discount「値引き」　wireless「無線の」　cost someone「…にお金がかかる」

M: That's a great deal. Maybe I'll get one too.
いい買い物をしたね。僕も買おうかなあ。

F: You had better hurry. They are selling out fast.
急いだほうがいいよ。すぐに売り切れちゃうからね。
* sell out「売り切れる」

STEP 3 　日本語訳を見ながらスキットを演じてみよう。　CD 2-12

M :
　　へえ！ それってパイン社の新しいスマートフォン？

F : It sure is. I just bought it yesterday. I had to stand in line for hours!

M :
　　高精細のスクリーンがすごいって聞いたよ！

F : It is. And with 4G network speed I can watch live TV and everything.

M :
　　いくら支払ったの？ 安かったはずはないよね。

F : I got a discount through my current wireless provider. It only cost me $299.

M :
　　いい買い物をしたね。僕も買おうかなあ。

F : You had better hurry. They are selling out fast.

Unit 073 Talking About the Seasons
季節についての会話

STEP 1 各センテンスをシャドーイングしよう。　CD 2-13

STEP 2 テキストを見ながらスキットを演じてみよう。　CD 2-13

F: The autumn leaves are beautiful, aren't they?
紅葉が美しいわよね。

M: They sure are. It seems that fall is here early this year.
そうだねえ。ここには今年は秋が早くやってきたようだね。

F: It was a brutally hot summer. I'm glad it's cooling down finally.
ものすごい酷暑だったよね。やっと涼しくなってきてうれしいわ。
* brutally「容赦なく」　cool down「涼しくなる」

M: I'm not looking forward to winter though. I can't stand the cold.
でも、僕は冬はあまり楽しみじゃないんだよね。寒さには耐えられないよ。

F: I'm with you there. I'd rather have sweltering heat than bitter cold.
その点は私も同じ。ものすごい寒さよりは、うだるような暑さのほうがいいわ。
* there「そこは；それに関しては」　I'd rather ...「…するほうがいい」　sweltering「うだるような」
  bitter「つらい；厳しい」

M: They say when the leaves change color early it's going to be a harsh winter.
葉が早く色づくと厳しい冬になるそうだよ。
* They say ...「…だそうだ；…と言われている」　harsh「厳しい」

F: Well ... I guess all we can do is enjoy this nice weather while we have it.
そっか、私たちにできることは、いいお天気の間にそれを楽しむことだけだね。

M: Yep. Before you know it we'll be right back to complaining about spring showers!
うん。あっという間に、僕たちはまた春の雨に文句を言っていると思うよ！
* before you know it「あっという間に」　be back to ...「…に戻る」　complain「不平・文句を言う」

155

STEP 3 　日本語訳を見ながらスキットを演じてみよう。　CD 2-13

F :

紅葉が美しいわよね。

M : They sure are. It seems that fall is here early this year.

F :

ものすごい酷暑だったよね。やっと涼しくなってきてうれしいわ。

M : I'm not looking forward to winter though. I can't stand the cold.

F :

その点は私も同じ。ものすごい寒さよりは、うだるような暑さのほうがいいわ。

M : They say when the leaves change color early it's going to be a harsh winter.

F :

そっか、私たちにできることは、いいお天気の間にそれを楽しむことだけだね。

M : Yep. Before you know it we'll be right back to complaining about spring showers!

Unit 074 Talking About Volunteer Work
ボランティアについての会話

STEP 1 各センテンスをシャドーイングしよう。　CD 2-14

STEP 2 テキストを見ながらスキットを演じてみよう。　CD 2-14

M: Hey, Mary. I heard you do volunteer work at the hospital on weekends.
やあ、メアリー。週末に病院でボランティアをやってるって聞いたけど。
* volunteer work「ボランティアの仕事」　on weekends「週末に」

F: Yes I do. I've been doing it for about two years now and I love it.
そうなの。もう2年くらいになるの。気に入ってるのよ。

M: What do you do there?
病院でなにをやってるの？

F: Lots of things. Most of the time we visit patients who don't get many visitors.
いろいろなことね。ほとんどは訪問者が少ない患者さんのところに顔を出してるの。

M: I'll bet they enjoy having someone to talk to. What else do you do?
話し相手ができて、きっとうれしいだろうね。ほかにはなにをするの？

F: Sometimes we help the hospital with fundraisers and charity events to raise money.
ときどき、病院の募金集めのパーティーやチャリティー・イベントを手伝うわ。
* fundraiser「募金のためのパーティー」　raise money「資金・基金などを集める」

M: That sounds like really rewarding work. I'd like to volunteer some of my time too.
とてもやりがいのある仕事みたいだね。僕も自分の時間をちょっとボランティアで使いたいな。
* rewarding「やりがいのある；有益な」　some of ...「…のうちのいくらか」

F: Anyone can do it. If you want, just come with me this Saturday!
だれにでもできるのよ。やりたければ、今度の土曜にいっしょにおいでよ！

STEP 3 　日本語訳を見ながらスキットを演じてみよう。　CD 2-14

M: Hey, Mary. I heard you do volunteer work at the hospital on weekends.

F:

そうなの。もう2年くらいになるの。気に入ってるのよ。

M: What do you do there?

F:

いろいろなことね。ほとんどは訪問者が少ない患者さんのところに顔を出してるの。

M: I'll bet they enjoy having someone to talk to. What else do you do?

F:

ときどき、病院の募金集めのパーティーやチャリティー・イベントを手伝うわ。

M: That sounds like really rewarding work. I'd like to volunteer some of my time too.

F:

だれにでもできるのよ。やりたければ、今度の土曜にいっしょにおいでよ！

Unit 075　Hometown Talk　故郷についての会話

STEP 1 　各センテンスをシャドーイングしよう。　CD 2-15

STEP 2 　テキストを見ながらスキットを演じてみよう。　CD 2-15

F: So where are you from? Were you born here in New York City?

で、あなたはどちらのご出身なの？ このニューヨーク市で生まれたの？

M: No. I just moved here last year. I'm from Destin, Florida. Have you ever heard of it?

いや、去年引っ越してきたばかりなんですよ。フロリダのデスティン出身です。聞いたことはありますか？

* move「引っ越す」　hear of ...「…について聞く」

F: No. Is it anywhere near Miami?

いいえ、どこかマイアミに近いところですか？

M: No. It's on the Gulf of Mexico in the Florida panhandle. It's a popular tourist location because of the beautiful beaches and sport fishing.

いや、フロリダ半島のメキシコ湾沿いなんですよ。美しいビーチがあって、スポーツ・フィッシングもできるので、有名な観光地になっているんです。

* gulf「湾」　panhandle「細長い地域」　tourist location「観光地」

F: It must be quite a shock moving to a big city like this.

こういう大都市に引っ越してくるのはすごくショックでしょ。

* quite a shock「かなりのショック」

M: I'm still getting used to all the people and congestion here. The cost of living is also much higher here.

こちらの人の多さと混み具合に、まだ慣れているところですよ。こっちは生活費もかなり高いですね。

* get used to ...「…に慣れる」　congestion「混雑；密集」　cost of living「生活コスト」

F: What do you like about being here?

こちらで気に入っていることはなんですか？

M: I really enjoy having four seasons. In Florida it is pretty much summer all year round.

四季があるところがすごくいいですね。フロリダでは年中ほぼ夏ですからね。

STEP 3 　日本語訳を見ながらスキットを演じてみよう。　CD 2-15

F :

で、あなたはどちらのご出身なの？ このニューヨーク市で生まれたの？

M : No. I just moved here last year. I'm from Destin, Florida. Have you ever heard of it?

F :

いいえ、どこかマイアミに近いところですか？

M : No. It's on the Gulf of Mexico in the Florida panhandle. It's a popular tourist location because of the beautiful beaches and sport fishing.

F :

こういう大都市に引っ越してくるのはすごくショックでしょ。

M : I'm still getting used to all the people and congestion here. The cost of living is also much higher here.

F :

こちらで気に入っていることはなんですか？

M : I really enjoy having four seasons. In Florida it is pretty much summer all year round.

Unit 076 People 人物についての会話

STEP 1 各センテンスをシャドーイングしよう。　CD 2-16

STEP 2 テキストを見ながらスキットを演じてみよう。　CD 2-16

M: So what do you think of the new CEO?
で、君は新しい CEO についてどう思ってるの？
* CEO「最高経営責任者」

F: He's only been here a few days so it's hard to say. He seems to be very principled and organized.
彼がここに来てまだ数日だから難しいけどね。とても信念があって有能そうね。
* principled「信念のある」 organized「物事の整理ができしっかりした；有能な」

M: I hear he's well qualified for the position, but rumor has it he's really hard on his subordinates.
彼は役職に就くのに十分な資格があるそうだけど、部下にはとても厳しいそうだよ。
* qualified「資格のある」 position「地位」 hard on ...「…に厳しい」

F: Where did you hear that?
どこで聞いたのよ？

M: I have a friend that used to work under him at UNITEL Corporation. They said all the department managers couldn't stand him.
ユニテル社で彼の部下だった友人がいるんだ。部長連中みんな彼が嫌いだったって。
* work under ...「…のもとで働く」 department manager「部長」 stand「我慢する」

F: He seems like a nice-enough guy. I didn't get that impression at all.
十分いい人に見えるけど。そんな印象はちっとも受けなかったわ。

M: I guess we'll find out what he's really like soon enough.
彼が実際どんな人かは、すぐにわかるだろうけどね。

F: He must be talented as a manager to be hired so young. I was shocked when I heard his age.
あれほど若くして雇われてるんだから経営者として有能なんでしょうね。彼の年齢を聞いたときショックを受けたわ。

M: No kidding. He's already saved two global companies from bankruptcy ... so he must be good.
まったくだね。もう 2 社も国際的な大企業を倒産から救ってるんだから、有能に違いないね。
* No kidding.「まったくだ」「冗談ではない」が直訳。

161

STEP 3 日本語訳を見ながらスキットを演じてみよう。　CD 2-16

M : So what do you think of the new CEO?

F :

彼がここに来てまだ数日だから難しいけどね。とても信念があって有能そうね。

M : I hear he's well qualified for the position, but rumor has it he's really hard on his subordinates.

F :

どこで聞いたのよ？

M : I have a friend that used to work under him at UNITEL Corporation. They said all the department managers couldn't stand him.

F :

十分いい人に見えるけど。そんな印象はちっとも受けなかったわ。

M : I guess we'll find out what he's really like soon enough.

F :

あれほど若くして雇われてるんだから経営者として有能なんでしょうね。彼の年齢を聞いたときショックを受けたわ。

M : No kidding. He's already saved two global companies from bankruptcy ... so he must be good.

Unit 077 消息についての会話
Long Time No See

STEP 1 各センテンスをシャドーイングしよう。　CD 2-17

STEP 2 テキストを見ながらスキットを演じてみよう。　CD 2-17

M: You know John Smith, right? I haven't seen him at the bar in a long time.
ジョン・スミスを知ってるよね？ 長いこと彼をバーで見かけないんだよね。

F: Of course. You didn't hear? He moved to New York three months ago.
当然よ。聞いてないの？ 彼は3カ月前にニューヨークに引っ越したのよ。

M: Really?! Was he transferred for work or something?
そうなの？！ 仕事で異動かなにかになったの？
* transfer「異動させる；転任させる」

F: No! He met a girl from New York City and they got engaged.
全然！ ニューヨーク市の女の子と出会って婚約したのよ。
* get engaged「婚約する」

M: No kidding? I had no idea. I was wondering why he disappeared.
うっそー！ 知らなかったよ。どうしていなくなったのかなあって思ってたんだ。
* wonder「あれこれ思い巡らす；不思議に思う」

F: I heard she comes from a family with money.
彼女の家がお金持ちだって聞いたわよ。

M: Do you have a way to get in touch with him?
彼と連絡を取る方法はあるかな？
* get in touch with ...「…と連絡を取る」

F: I have his contact information at home. I can e-mail it to you if you like.
家に帰れば連絡先の情報はわかるわよ。よかったらEメールで送るけど。

M: Please do. I'd like to stay in touch. I always liked him.
そうして。連絡を取りたいんだ。ずっと彼のこと気に入ってたからさ。

STEP 3 　日本語訳を見ながらスキットを演じてみよう。　CD 2-17

M: You know John Smith, right? I haven't seen him at the bar in a long time.

F:

当然よ。聞いてないの？ 彼は3カ月前にニューヨークに引っ越したのよ。

M: Really?! Was he transferred for work or something?

F:

全然！ ニューヨーク市の女の子と出会って婚約したのよ。

M: No kidding? I had no idea. I was wondering why he disappeared.

F:

彼女の家がお金持ちだって聞いたわよ。

M: Do you have a way to get in touch with him?

F:

家に帰れば連絡先の情報はわかるわよ。よかったらEメールで送るけど。

M: Please do. I'd like to stay in touch. I always liked him.

Unit 078 Talking About the Kids 子供についての会話

STEP 1 各センテンスをシャドーイングしよう。　CD 2-18

STEP 2 テキストを見ながらスキットを演じてみよう。　CD 2-18

F : Hi Jim! Long time no see! How've you been?
ジム、こんにちは！久しぶりね！どうしてた？
* Long time no see!「久しぶり」 直訳は「長い時間、会っていない」。

M : I'm doing great, Cindy. How about you?
元気にやってるよ、シンディー。そっちはどう？

F : I'm good, thanks. How are the kids?
いいわよ。お子さんたちはどう？

M : They're great. Jack's about to graduate from high school and Jill is a sophomore in college.
元気だよ。ジャックは高校を卒業するところで、ジルは大学の2年生なんだ。
* be about to ...「ちょうど…するところだ」　graduate from ...「…を卒業する」
  sophomore「大学2年生」

F : Wow! They were just little the last time I saw them.
へえ！最後に会ったときは、ほんの小さな子どもだったのに。

M : Yeah, they grow up fast! Jill actually just got engaged!
うん、成長するのが早いよね！実は、ジルは婚約したばかりなんだよ！
* get engaged「婚約する」

F : That's great! Did they set a wedding date yet?
すばらしいわ！もう結婚式の日取りは決まってるの？
* yet「もう」

M : No. They're going to wait until they both finish school.
いや。ふたりが学校を卒業するまで待つつもりなんだよ。

STEP 3 　日本語訳を見ながらスキットを演じてみよう。　CD 2-18

F :

ジム、こんにちは！ 久しぶりね！ どうしてた？

M : I'm doing great, Cindy. How about you?

F :

いいわよ。お子さんたちはどう？

M : They're great. Jack's about to graduate from high school and Jill is a sophomore in college.

F :

へえ！ 最後に会ったときは、ほんの小さな子どもだったのに。

M : Yeah, they grow up fast! Jill actually just got engaged!

F :

すばらしいわ！ もう結婚式の日取りは決まってるの？

M : No. They're going to wait until they both finish school.

Unit 079 婚約した人との会話

Significant Others

STEP 1 各センテンスをシャドーイングしよう。　CD 2-19

STEP 2 テキストを見ながらスキットを演じてみよう。　CD 2-19

M: I hear you got engaged ... congratulations! When is the wedding?
婚約したんだってね…おめでとう！ 式はいつなの？
* get engaged「婚約する」　congratulations「おめでとう」

F: We are getting married next October, but we haven't set a date yet.
来年の10月に結婚する予定だけど、まだ日取りは決めてないの。
* set a date「日取りを決める」

M: What kind of ceremony are you going to have?
どんな結婚式にする予定？

F: I've always wanted an outdoor wedding. We're thinking about a small wedding on the beach.
ずっとアウトドアの結婚式がしたいと思ってたの。ビーチで小さな式をしようと考えてるの。

M: What are your plans for the honeymoon?
ハネムーンの計画は？

F: We haven't decided yet, but we definitely want to go overseas ... maybe to France.
まだ決めてはいないけど、海外へは絶対に行きたいの…たぶんフランスね。

M: That's where my wife and I went! You'll love it! If you need any recommendations, just let me know.
フランスは僕とワイフが行った場所だよ！ 気に入ると思うよ。おすすめが聞きたかったら、言ってね。
* recommendation「推薦；おすすめ」

F: It's just so expensive! Even though we have a year it's pretty overwhelming.
すごく高いのよね！ 1年あるとはいえ、かなり大変だわ。
* overwhelming「(圧倒的に) 大変な」

STEP 3   日本語訳を見ながらスキットを演じてみよう。   CD 2-19

M: I hear you got engaged ... congratulations! When is the wedding?

F:

来年の10月に結婚する予定だけど、まだ日取りは決めてないの。

M: What kind of ceremony are you going to have?

F:

ずっとアウトドアの結婚式がしたいと思ってたの。ビーチで小さな式をしようと考えてるの。

M: What are your plans for the honeymoon?

F:

まだ決めてはいないけど、海外へは絶対に行きたいの…たぶんフランスね。

M: That's where my wife and I went! You'll love it! If you need any recommendations, just let me know.

F:

すごく高いのよね！1年あるとはいえ、かなり大変だわ。

Unit 080 Making Up 仲直りするときの会話

STEP 1 各センテンスをシャドーイングしよう。　CD 2-20

STEP 2 テキストを見ながらスキットを演じてみよう。　CD 2-20

M : Kelly. I want to apologize for some of the things I said last night.
ケリー、昨日の夜、僕が言ったこと謝りたいんだ。

F : I still can't believe you said that. You really hurt my feelings!
あなたがあんなこと言うなんて、まだ信じられないわ。私、ホントに傷ついたのよ！

M : I know. I was stressed out because of problems at work and I took it out on you.
わかってる。仕事のトラブルでイライラが溜まってたんだよ。それで、君に八つ当たりしちゃったんだ。
* take it out on someone「そのことで…に八つ当たりする」

F : You made me so upset! I cried all night!
滅茶苦茶な気持ちになって、ひと晩中泣いてたのよ！
* upset「動揺して；動転して；怒って」

M : I know. And I don't want to leave things like that. I'm really sorry.
そうだね。だから、そのままにはしておきたくないんだ。ほんとうにごめんね。

F : Do you promise never to say anything like that again?!
あんなこと二度と言わないって約束する？

M : I swear on my life. You're my best friend. Can you forgive me?
誓うよ。君は僕の親友だから。許してくれるかい？
* swear「誓う」　on one's life「命にかけて」　forgive「許す」

F : I'll think about it. If you buy me dinner it will help me think better.
考えさせて。夕食をごちそうしてくれたら、うまく考えられるかも。

M : You got it! You just name the time and place!
わかったよ！時間と場所を指定して！
* name「指定する」

STEP 3 　日本語訳を見ながらスキットを演じてみよう。　CD 2-20

M: Kelly. I want to apologize for some of the things I said last night.

F:

あなたがあんなこと言うなんて、まだ信じられないわ。私、ホントに傷ついたのよ！

M: I know. I was stressed out because of problems at work and I took it out on you.

F:

滅茶苦茶な気持ちになって、ひと晩中泣いてたのよ！

M: I know. And I don't want to leave things like that. I'm really sorry.

F:

あんなこと二度と言わないって約束する？

M: I swear on my life. You're my best friend. Can you forgive me?

F:

考えさせて。夕食をごちそうしてくれたら、うまく考えられるかも。

M: You got it! You just name the time and place!

Chapter 2
旅行会話

レベル 1 ★★★ ……… p. 173
レベル 2 ★★★ ……… p. 231

Unit 081 レストランを予約する

Making a Restaurant Reservation

STEP 1 各センテンスをシャドーイングしよう。　　CD 2-21

STEP 2 テキストを見ながらスキットを演じてみよう。　　CD 2-21

M: Good evening. Terry's Oyster Bar. How can I help you?

こんばんは。テリーのオイスター・バーです。どんなご用件でしょうか？

F: Hi. I'd like to make reservations for five people for tomorrow evening.

こんにちは。明日の夕方、5名で予約がしたいのですが。

＊ make reservations「予約する」

M: For Wednesday, the 18th? All right. And what about the time?

18日の水曜日ですね？　承知しました。で、時間はいかがでしょう？

F: I guess eight o'clock is best. Is that too late to get a table by the window?

おそらく8時がベストだと思います。窓辺の席を取るのには遅すぎますか？

M: No, you're fine. We're usually not that crowded on Wednesday. I just need a name.

いいえ、大丈夫です。水曜日はいつもそれほど混み合いませんから。あと、お名前をいただけますか。

＊ that crowded の that は「そんなに；それほど」という意味。

STEP 3 　日本語訳を見ながらスキットを演じてみよう。　CD 2-21

M : Good evening. Terry's Oyster Bar. How can I help you?

F :

こんにちは。明日の夕方、5名で予約がしたいのですが。

M : For Wednesday, the 18th? All right. And what about the time?

F :

おそらく8時がベストだと思います。窓辺の席を取るのには遅すぎますか?

M : No, you're fine. We're usually not that crowded on Wednesday. I just need a name.

Unit 082 レストランに入店する
Entering a Restaurant

STEP 1 各センテンスをシャドーイングしよう。 CD 2-22

STEP 2 テキストを見ながらスキットを演じてみよう。 CD 2-22

M: Hi. We don't have a reservation. Can we get a table?

こんにちは。予約がないのですが。テーブルはありますか？

F: Well, as you can see we're very busy tonight. I'll have to put you on a waiting list.

えー、ご覧のとおり、今夜はとても忙しいんです。お客様さまを順番待ちのリストに載せなければなりません。

* waiting list は「(お店での) 順番待ちのリスト」。

M: How far down the list will we be?

リストのどのくらい下になりますか？

* how far は「どのくらい遠く」、down the list は「リストを下って」。

F: You're just two, right? You'll be fourth. It will probably be an hour before I can seat you.

おふたりだけですね？ 4番目になります。おそらく着席いただくまでに1時間かかります。

M: That long? Okay, thanks. Please put us down. My name is Mike Stevens.

そんなにですか？ わかりました、ありがとう。私たちを登録してください。名前はマイク・スティーヴンスです。

* put ... down で「…を登録する；書き留める」という意味になる。

STEP 3 　日本語訳を見ながらスキットを演じてみよう。　CD 2-22

M :

こんにちは。予約がないのですが。テーブルはありますか？

F : Well, as you can see we're very busy tonight. I'll have to put you on a waiting list.

M :

リストのどのくらい下になりますか？

F : You're just two, right? You'll be fourth. It will probably be an hour before I can seat you.

M :

そんなにですか？ わかりました、ありがとう。私たちを登録してください。名前はマイク・スティーヴンスです。

Unit 083 おすすめ料理をたずねる
Asking for Meal Recommendations

STEP 1 各センテンスをシャドーイングしよう。 CD 2-23

STEP 2 テキストを見ながらスキットを演じてみよう。 CD 2-23

F: Which dishes do you recommend?

どの料理がおすすめですか？

M: Well, I think tonight's risotto is pretty special. It has brussel sprouts and anchovies.

えー、今晩のリゾットはかなり特別だと思います。芽キャベツとアンチョビが入っています。

* I think (that) … は「私は…ということを思う」という意味。

F: Wow, that does sound really good! What else?

うわあ、ほんとうにおいしそうね！ ほかには？

* sound … は「…に聞こえる；響く；思える」という意味。

M: Our pasta Genovese is always good. We use cashews instead of pine nuts in our pesto.

当店のパスタ・ジェノベーゼはいつもおいしゅうございます。グリーン・ソースには、松の実の代わりにカシュー・ナッツを使用しております。

* in stead of … は「…の代わりに」という意味。

F: Oh, that sounds delightful! I think I'll go with that!

へえ、それはすばらしいわ！ それをいただきます！

* go with … は「…で行く」。ここでは「…をいただく；選ぶ」という意味。

STEP 3 　日本語訳を見ながらスキットを演じてみよう。　CD 2-23

F :

どの料理がおすすめですか？

M : Well, I think tonight's risotto is pretty special. It has brussel sprouts and anchovies.

F :

うわあ、ほんとうにおいしそうね！ ほかには？

M : Our pasta Genovese is always good. We use cashews instead of pine nuts in our pesto.

F :

へえ、それはすばらしいわ！ それをいただきます！

Unit 084 食事を注文する
Ordering at a Restaurant

STEP 1 各センテンスをシャドーイングしよう。　CD 2-24

STEP 2 テキストを見ながらスキットを演じてみよう。　CD 2-24

M : The lamb curry sounds really good. But is it very spicy?

ラム・カレーがとてもおいしそうですね。でも、かなり辛いですか？

F : I'd say it's medium spicy. It's more like a North African dish than an Indian one.

中程度の辛さだと思います。インド料理というより、北アフリカの料理に似ていますよ。

* more like A than B は「B というより、もっと A に似ている」という意味。

M : Oh, I see. So is it served on couscous?

ああ、そうですか。じゃあ、クスクスの上にかけて出されるんですか？

F : We can do that, or you can have it with saffron rice.

それはできますよ。あるいは、サフラン・ライスといっしょに食べることもできます。

* ... or ... は「…あるいは…」と選択を表す。

M : I'll have it with couscous. And I'd like a baked potato, too.

クスクスといっしょにいただきます。それと、ベークド・ポテトもください。

* I'll have ... は「…をいただきます」という意味で注文の場面でよく使う。I'd like ... も同様。

旅行会話 ★★★

179

STEP 3　日本語訳を見ながらスキットを演じてみよう。　CD 2-24

M:

ラム・カレーがとてもおいしそうですね。でも、かなり辛いですか？

F: I'd say it's medium spicy. It's more like a North African dish than an Indian one.

M:

ああ、そうですか。じゃあ、クスクスの上にかけて出されるんですか？

F: We can do that, or you can have it with saffron rice.

M:

クスクスといっしょにいただきます。それと、ベークド・ポテトもください。

Unit 085 お酒を注文する

Ordering Drinks with a Meal

STEP 1 各センテンスをシャドーイングしよう。　CD 2-25

STEP 2 テキストを見ながらスキットを演じてみよう。　CD 2-25

M: And what can I get you to drink?

それから、お酒はなにをお持ちしましょう？

* get は「準備して持ってくる；買ってくる；取ってくる」という意味。

F: We'd like to order a bottle of wine. What do you recommend?

ワインをボトルで注文したいんです。おすすめはなんですか？

* would like to ... は「…したいのです」とていねいに希望を表す。

M: This month we are featuring wines from the Russian River, in California.

今月はカリフォルニアのロシアン・リヴァーのワインを呼び物にしています。

* feature は「呼び物にする；特集する」という意味の動詞。

F: Oh, that sounds nice! Is that in Napa Valley?

へえ、それはおいしそうですね！ ナパ・ヴァレーにあるんですか？

M: The Russian River is in Sonoma Valley, just next to Napa. Some of the best wine in America is produced there.

ロシアン・リヴァーは、ナパに隣接するソノマ・ヴァレーにあます。アメリカでも指折りのワインがそこで作られています。

旅行会話 ★

STEP 3 日本語訳を見ながらスキットを演じてみよう。　CD 2-25

M: And what can I get you to drink?

F:

ワインをボトルで注文したいんです。おすすめはなんですか？

M: This month we are featuring wines from The Russian River, in California.

F:

へえ、それはおいしそうですね！ ナパ・ヴァレーにあるんですか？

M: The Russian River is in Sonoma Valley, just next to Napa. Some of the best wine in America is produced there.

Unit 086 デザートを注文する

Ordering Dessert

STEP 1 》 各センテンスをシャドーイングしよう。　CD 2-26

STEP 2 》 テキストを見ながらスキットを演じてみよう。　CD 2-26

M: I hope that you saved some room for dessert!

デザートを食べる分のおなかを空けておいていただけましたか？

F: You bet I did! You're famous for your pies, right?

もちろん！ おたくのパイは有名ですよね？

* You bet ... は「もちろん…」という意味のフレーズ。

M: Indeed! They get written up in magazines a lot. Especially our cream pies.

そうなんです！ 雑誌にもたくさん取り上げられて書かれています。クリーム・パイは特にそうです。

* write up は「(新聞・雑誌などの記事として) 書き上げる」という意味。

F: That's what I want. What kind do you have?

それが食べたいですね。どんな種類がありますか？

* what I want は「私が望んでいるもの」。

M: We have several varieties. Regular, tropical, chocolate and peanut butter. Which would you like?

いくつか種類があります。レギュラー、トロピカル、チョコレート、それにピーナツ・バター。どちらがよろしいですか？

STEP 3 　日本語訳を見ながらスキットを演じてみよう。　CD 2-26

M: I hope that you saved some room for dessert!

F:

もちろん！ おたくのパイは有名ですよね？

M: Indeed! They get written up in magazines a lot. Especially our cream pies.

F:

それが食べたいですね。どんな種類がありますか？

M: We have several varieties. Regular, tropical, chocolate and peanut butter. Which would you like?

Unit 087 At the Cashier 支払い時の会話

STEP 1 各センテンスをシャドーイングしよう。　CD 2-27

STEP 2 テキストを見ながらスキットを演じてみよう。　CD 2-27

M: Do you accept personal checks as payment?

個人小切手を支払いに使えますか？

F: Yes, but only local banks'. We don't accept checks from out of state.

はい、しかし地元の銀行だけになります。州外の小切手は承れません。

* from out of ... 「…の外から来た」

M: I was afraid of that. I'm from out of town. You do accept traveler's checks, right?

それを恐れていたんです。私はよそから来たんですよ。トラベラーズ・チェックなら受け取れますよね？

* be afraid of ... は「…を恐れている；心配している」という意味。

F: Yes, we do, sir. Is that how you would like to pay?

ええ、もちろんです、お客さま。そのようにお支払いになりたいのですか？

* sir は男性の顧客などへの呼びかけ。女性の場合は ma'am を用いる。
* how は the way how の省略。how は後ろのセンテンスとつながって「どのように…するか；…の方法；…の仕方」という意味になる。

M: Yeah, let me just make sure I have enough to pay for all of this.

ええ、これ全部を支払うのに十分なのか、ちょっと確認させてください。

* let me ... は「私に…させて」の意。

STEP 3　日本語訳を見ながらスキットを演じてみよう。　CD 2-27

M:

個人小切手を支払いに使えますか？

F: Yes, but only local banks'. We don't accept checks from out of state.

M:

それを恐れていたんです。私はよそから来たんですよ。トラベラーズ・チェックなら受け取れますよね？

F: Yes, we do, sir. Is that how you would like to pay?

M:

ええ、これ全部を支払うのに十分なのか、ちょっと確認させてください。

Unit 088 アテンダントとの会話①
Talking with a Flight Attendant 1

STEP 1 各センテンスをシャドーイングしよう。　CD 2-28

STEP 2 テキストを見ながらスキットを演じてみよう。　CD 2-28

F : Would you like the fish or chicken entree?
メインは魚料理がよろしいですか、それとも鶏肉料理でしょうか？

M : I think I ordered vegetarian.
私はヴェジタリアン料理を注文したと思います。

F : Oh, I'm sorry! 36H ... that's right. I'm sorry. I'll bring that to you when I have finished serving these.
あっ、失礼しました！ 36のH…そのとおりです。すみません。これらを出し終えたらそちらをお持ちいたします。

* serve は「(食事を) 出す」という意味。

M : Thanks. And can you bring me some white wine too?
どうも。それと、白ワインも持ってきてくれますか？

F : I sure will. It will just be a few more minutes.
お持ちします。あとほんの数分お待ちください。

STEP 3 　日本語訳を見ながらスキットを演じてみよう。　　CD 2-28

F : Would you like the fish or chicken entree?

M : ［　　　　　　　　　　　　　　　　　　　　　］

私はヴェジタリアン料理を注文したと思います。

F : Oh, I'm sorry! 36H ... that's right. I'm sorry. I'll bring that to you when I have finished serving these.

M : ［　　　　　　　　　　　　　　　　　　　　　］

どうも。それと、白ワインも持ってきてくれますか？

F : I sure will. It will just be a few more minutes.

Unit 089 アテンダントとの会話②
Talking with a Flight Attendant 2

STEP 1 　各センテンスをシャドーイングしよう。　　CD 2-29

STEP 2 　テキストを見ながらスキットを演じてみよう。　　CD 2-29

M : Could you give me a little help?

ちょっと手伝っていただけますか？

F : Sure, what can I do for you?

もちろんです、どういたしましょう？

＊ Sure. は「もちろんです」となにかをポジティヴに引き受ける言葉。

M : I can't figure out the entertainment channels. I want to watch this Chinese movie with English subtitles.

エンターテインメント・チャンネルがわからないんです。この中国の映画を英語の字幕で観たいんです。

＊ figure out は「理解する；わかる」という意味のフレーズ。
＊ with English subtitles は「英語の字幕で」。

F : Oh, I see. That can be a little confusing. Let me set that up for you.

ああ、そうですか。ちょっと難しいかもしれません。私に設定させてください。

＊ can はこの場合、「時に…する場合もある」という意味になる。

M : Thanks, I really appreciate that! Oh, great! Now I can hear what they are talking about!

どうも、助かります！ すばらしい！ これで、彼らの話していることが聞こえますね！

＊ now は「いまや；こうなると」という意味。

STEP 3　日本語訳を見ながらスキットを演じてみよう。　CD 2-29

M :

ちょっと手伝っていただけますか？

F : Sure, what can I do for you?

M :

エンターテインメント・チャンネルがわからないんです。この中国の映画を英語の字幕で観たいんです。

F : Oh, I see. That can be a little confusing. Let me set that up for you.

M :

どうも、助かります！　すばらしい！　これで、彼らの話していることが聞こえますね！

Unit 090 入国審査 At the Immigration Counter

STEP 1 各センテンスをシャドーイングしよう。　CD 2-30

STEP 2 テキストを見ながらスキットを演じてみよう。　CD 2-30

M: Next in line, please. Good afternoon. Can I see your documents?

次にお並びの方、どうぞ。こんにちは。書類を拝見できますか？

F: Here is my passport and my airline ticket.

こちらが、私のパスポートと航空券です。

* Here is ... は「こちらが…です；ここに…があります」という意味になる。

M: Thank you. Will you be traveling to any other countries?

どうも。どこかほかの国へも旅行なさいますか？

F: No, I'll be in the United States the whole time.

いいえ、ずっとアメリカにいます。

* I'll be の be はここでは「いる」と存在を表す。

M: Okay, and I see that your return flight is on the 14th, from this airport. Have a nice stay.

わかりました。それと、帰国のフライトはこの空港から 14 日になりますね。すてきな滞在を。

* I see that ... は「私は…をわかっている」という意味になる。

旅行会話 ★

STEP 3 　日本語訳を見ながらスキットを演じてみよう。　CD 2-30

M : Next in line, please. Good afternoon. Can I see your documents?

F :

こちらが、私のパスポートと航空券です。

M : Thank you. Will you be traveling to any other countries?

F :

いいえ、ずっとアメリカにいます。

M : Okay, and I see that your return flight is on the 14th, from this airport. Have a nice stay.

Unit 091 荷物の預け入れ
Checking In Luggage on a Flight

STEP 1 各センテンスをシャドーイングしよう。　CD 2-31

STEP 2 テキストを見ながらスキットを演じてみよう。　CD 2-31

F: Sir, this bag is too heavy. I'll have to charge you extra.

お客さま、このバッグは重すぎます。余分にお支払いいただかねばなりません。

* extra は「余分に」。

M: Oh, I was afraid of that. How much extra?

ああ、それを恐れていたんですよ。どのくらい余分にですか？

F: Seventy-five dollars. It's quite a bit over our weight limit.

75 ドルです。重量制限をかなり超えています。

* quite a bit は「かなり」。

M: Wow, that's a lot. But I don't really have any choice. Okay.

うわあ、それは多いですね。でも、選択肢はありませんね。わかりました。

* not any ... で「ひとつも…ない」という意味になる。

F: The other bags are okay. So altogether you are checking in three bags, right?

ほかのバッグは大丈夫です。結局、全部でお荷物 3 つをお預けになるんですね？

* check in は「(空港で荷物を) 預ける」という意味。

旅行会話 ★

STEP 3　日本語訳を見ながらスキットを演じてみよう。　CD 2-31

F : Sir, this bag is too heavy. I'll have to charge you extra.

M :

ああ、それを恐れていたんですよ。どのくらい余分にですか？

F : Seventy-five dollars. It's quite a bit over our weight limit.

M :

うわあ、それは多いですね。でも、選択肢はありませんね。わかりました。

F : The other bags are okay. So altogether you are checking in three bags, right?

Unit 092 Converting Currency
お金を両替する

STEP 1 各センテンスをシャドーイングしよう。　CD 2-32

STEP 2 テキストを見ながらスキットを演じてみよう。　CD 2-32

M : I'd like to convert some Japanese yen into dollars, please.

日本円をドルに交換したいんですが。

* please はていねいな依頼を表す。

F : Japanese yen into U.S. dollars? What's the amount?

日本円を米ドルにですか？ 総額はいくらでしょう？

M : Let's see. I guess I'll do twenty-five thousand yen.

えーと。2万5千円かなあ。

* I guess ... は「…かなあ」という意味。

F : 25,000? At today's exchange that comes to two hundred seventy dollars and eighty-three cents. How would you like it?

2万5千円ですね？ 本日の交換レートでは、270ドルと83セントになります。どのように両替しますか？

* come to ... は「(合計で) …になる」という意味。

M : I want it in four fifties and seven tens.

50ドル札4枚と、10ドル札7枚でお願いします。

* in ... は「…の状態で」という意味。

旅行会話 ★★★

STEP 3 　日本語訳を見ながらスキットを演じてみよう。　　CD 2-32

M :

日本円をドルに交換したいんですが。

F : Japanese yen into U.S. dollars? What's the amount?

M :

えーと。2万5千円かなあ。

F : 25,000? At today's exchange that comes to two hundred seventy dollars and eighty-three cents. How would you like it?

M :

50ドル札4枚と、10ドル札7枚でお願いします。

Unit 093 Making Hotel Reservations ホテルを予約する

STEP 1 各センテンスをシャドーイングしよう。　CD 2-33

STEP 2 テキストを見ながらスキットを演じてみよう。　CD 2-33

M: Hi. Do you have vacancies?

こんにちは。部屋の空きはありますか？

* vacancy は「空室；空席；空き」などの意味。

F: Yes, we do, sir. How many nights do you plan to stay?

はい、ございます、お客さま。何泊ご滞在の予定ですか？

* plan to stay は「滞在する予定だ」という意味。

M: Tonight and the next two nights. For one. And I'd like an ocean view.

ええ、今晩とそのあと2泊です。1名で。海の見える部屋がいいんですが。

F: All our rooms face the ocean, sir. Is a single room okay?

当ホテルは全室海に面しております、お客さま。シングルでよろしいんですね？

M: Yes, please. Oh, and I need a room with internet access.

はい、お願いします。ああ、それと、インターネット接続のある部屋でお願いします。

STEP 3 　日本語訳を見ながらスキットを演じてみよう。　CD 2-33

M :

こんにちは。部屋の空きはありますか?

F : Yes, we do, sir. How many nights do you plan to stay?

M :

ええ、今晩とそのあと2泊です。1名で。海の見える部屋がいいんですが。

F : All our rooms face the ocean, sir. Is a single room okay?

M :

はい、お願いします。ああ、それと、インターネット接続のある部屋でお願いします。

Unit 094 チェックイン時の会話
Checking In (to a Hotel)

STEP 1 各センテンスをシャドーイングしよう。　CD 2-34

STEP 2 テキストを見ながらスキットを演じてみよう。　CD 2-34

M: Hi, I'm checking in. My name is Tom O'Brien.

こんにちは、チェックインをお願いします。名前はトム・オブライエンです。

* check in は、ここでは「(ホテルに) チェックインする」という意味。

F: Yes, Mr. O'Brien. Two adults and two children, right?

はい、オブライエンさま。大人2名と子ども2名でよろしいでしょうか？

* ..., right? は「…でしょうか？；正しいでしょうか？」という確認。

M: That's right. And we booked a suite.

そのとおりです。それと、スイートを予約しています。

* suite は「スイート・ルーム」。寝室、浴室のほか、居間などのある広めの部屋。

F: Yes, you did. We have a lovely room for you. You're here for four nights, right?

はい、そのとおりです。すてきなお部屋をご用意いたしました。4泊でございますね？

M: That's right.

そうです。

F: Okay, I just need to see all your passports. And I'll get your keys ready. Will three be enough?

では、みなさまのパスポートだけ拝見させてください。それから、お客さまのキーをご用意いたします。3本で大丈夫でしょうか？

* get ... ready は「…を準備の整った状態にする」=「…の準備をする」という意味。

STEP 3 日本語訳を見ながらスキットを演じてみよう。　CD 2-34

M :
>
> こんにちは、チェックインをお願いします。名前はトム・オブライエンです。

F : Yes, Mr. O'Brien. Two adults and two children, right?

M :
>
> そのとおりです。それと、スイートを予約しています。

F : Yes, you did. We have a lovely room for you. You're here for four nights, right?

M :
>
> そうです。

F : Okay, I just need to see all your passports. And I'll get your keys ready. Will three be enough?

Unit 095 Making a Complaint (at a Hotel) ホテルで苦情を伝える

STEP 1 各センテンスをシャドーイングしよう。　CD 2-35

STEP 2 テキストを見ながらスキットを演じてみよう。　CD 2-35

F: I'm afraid I have to complain about the person staying in the room above me.

すみませんが、上の部屋に泊まっている人について苦情があるんです。

* I'm afraid (that) ... は「…(ということ)を残念に思う」という意味。

M: Oh, I'm very sorry. How is that guest bothering you?

ああ、申し訳ありません。そのお客さまは、どのようにご迷惑をおかけしていますか？

* bother は「悩ませる；迷惑をかける」という意味。

F: Well, it sounds as if people are dancing up there.

ええ、まるで上でみんながダンスしているように聞こえるんです。

* sound as if ... は「まるで…のように聞こえる」という意味。

M: I'll have someone go up there right away and tell them to stop. I'm terribly sorry for the inconvenience.

すぐに上階に人を向かわせて、やめるように伝えます。ご迷惑をおかけしてほんとうに申し訳ありません。

* have someone go up there は「だれかを上に行かせる」という意味。

旅行会話 ★

STEP 3 日本語訳を見ながらスキットを演じてみよう。　CD 2-35

F :

すみませんが、上の部屋に泊まっている人について苦情があるんです。

M : Oh, I'm very sorry. How is that guest bothering you?

F :

ええ、まるで上でみんながダンスしているように聞こえるんです。

M : I'll have someone go up there right away and tell them to stop. I'm terribly sorry for the inconvenience.

Unit 096 Asking to Change Rooms
部屋を変更してもらう

STEP 1 各センテンスをシャドーイングしよう。　CD 2-36

STEP 2 テキストを見ながらスキットを演じてみよう。　CD 2-36

F : Hi. We were wondering if we could change to a suite for the rest of our stay.

こんにちは。滞在の残りの期間、スイートに変更してもらえるか知りたくて。

* wonder は「…を知りたいと思う；…だろうかと思いを巡らす」という意味。

M : Let me check. How many more days will you be here?

確認させてください。あと何日こちらにご滞在ですか？

* how many more ... は「あとどのくらい多くの…」という意味。

F : We'll stay four more nights, and check out on Thursday.

あと4泊で、木曜にチェック・アウトします。

M : And that's from tonight, correct? Yes, we can do that for you.

で、それは今夜からですね？ はい、お客さまのために、そうすることはできますよ。

F : Great! My kids will be so happy!

すばらしい！ うちの子どもたちがすごくよろこびます！

旅行会話 ★☆☆

STEP 3 　日本語訳を見ながらスキットを演じてみよう。　CD 2-36

F :

こんにちは。滞在の残りの期間、スイートに変更してもらえるか知りたくて。

M : Let me check. How many more days will you be here?

F :

あと4泊で、木曜にチェック・アウトします。

M : And that's from tonight, correct? Yes, we can do that for you.

F :

すばらしい！ うちの子どもたちがすごくよろこびます！

Unit 097 Calling Room Service
ルーム・サービスを頼む

STEP 1 各センテンスをシャドーイングしよう。　CD 2-37

STEP 2 テキストを見ながらスキットを演じてみよう。　CD 2-37

M: Hi, you've reached the kitchen. How can I help you?

こんにちは、こちらはキッチンでございます。ご用件はなんでしょう？

* reach は、ここでは「(かけた電話が) …につながる」という意味。

F: I don't see pizza on the room service menu. Don't you serve it?

ルーム・サービス・メニューにピザが見当たらないんです。出していないんですか？

* serve は「提供する；料理を出す」という意味。

M: We don't make it here. But I can order for you from the place across the street.

こちらでは作っておりません。しかし、お客さまのために、通りの向かいの店に注文することはできます。

F: Oh! I'm just looking at it out my window now! Is it good?

ああ！ いま窓の外にちょうどそれが見えています！ おいしいですか？

* be just looking at ... は「ちょうど…を見ているところだ」という意味。

M: It's wonderful! They have won several awards.

すばらしいですよ！ あそこは、いくつか賞を受賞しているんです。

STEP 3 　日本語訳を見ながらスキットを演じてみよう。　CD 2-37

M: Hi, you've reached the kitchen. How can I help you?

F:

ルーム・サービス・メニューにピザが見当たらないんです。出していないんですか？

M: We don't make it here. But I can order for you from the place across the street.

F:

ああ！ いま窓の外にちょうどそれが見えています！ おいしいですか？

M: It's wonderful! They have won several awards.

Unit 098 コンシェルジェにたずねる
Getting Tips from a Hotel Concierge

STEP 1 各センテンスをシャドーイングしよう。　CD 2-38

STEP 2 テキストを見ながらスキットを演じてみよう。　CD 2-38

M: I want to pick up a lot of souvenirs while I'm here. Where do you suggest?

ここにいる間にたくさんお土産を買いたいんです。どこがおすすめですか？

* ここでは pick up は「買う；購入する」という意味。

F: Well, Fisherman's Wharf is probably the best place for that. They have tons of shops.

えーと、おそらく、それにはフィッシャーマンズ・ワーフが最高だと思います。すごくたくさんお店がありますよ。

* They have の they は、ここでは「フィッシャーマンズ・ワーフ（という地域）」を指す。

M: Oh, that's good to know. Thanks. And how do I get there?

それはいいことを聞きました。ありがとう。で、どうやって行けばいいんですか？

* That's good to know. は「それがわかってよかったです；ありがたいです」という意味。

F: You can just take the cable car that stops in front of the hotel. It runs straight down to the Wharf.

ただホテルの前に停まるケーブルカーに乗るだけでいいんです。埠頭までまっすぐに行きますから。

* down は「（話し手のいる場所から）離れて・遠ざかって」という意味になる。

M: Great, thanks. I'm glad it's so easy.

すばらしいですね。ありがとう。かんたんでうれしいです。

STEP 3 日本語訳を見ながらスキットを演じてみよう。　CD 2-38

M :

ここにいる間にたくさんお土産を買いたいんです。どこがおすすめですか？

F : Well, Fisherman's Wharf is probably the best place for that. They have tons of shops.

M :

それはいいことを聞きました。ありがとう。で、どうやって行けばいいんですか？

F : You can just take the cable car that stops in front of the hotel. It runs straight down to the Wharf.

M :

すばらしいですね。ありがとう。かんたんでうれしいです。

Unit 099 Checking Out (of a Hotel) チェックアウト時の会話

STEP 1 各センテンスをシャドーイングしよう。　CD 2-39

STEP 2 テキストを見ながらスキットを演じてみよう。　CD 2-39

F : Hi. I'd like to check out now.

どうも。チェックアウトをお願いします。

* would like to ... は「…したいのです」とていねいに希望を述べる言い方。

M : Okay. I just need you to agree to these extra charges.

わかりました。こちらの追加料金にご同意いただくだけでかまいません。

* need A to B で「A（人）に B してもらう必要がある」という意味になる。

F : The spa and the massage. Sure. So, do I need to sign here?

スパとマッサージですね。もちろん。で、私はここにサインするんですね？

* need to sign は「署名する必要がある」という意味。

M : Yes, and the charges will be added to your card. Shall I arrange a cab for you?

はい、それで料金はお客さまのカードに追加されます。タクシーを手配いたしましょうか？

* Shall I ...? は「私が…しましょうか？」と申し出る表現。

F : Yes, thanks. I'm planning to go directly to the airport from here.

ええ、お願いします。ここから直接、空港に行く予定にしていますので。

* plan to ... は「する予定だ」という意味。

STEP 3 　日本語訳を見ながらスキットを演じてみよう。　CD 2-39

F :

どうも。チェックアウトをお願いします。

M : Okay. I just need you to agree to these extra charges.

F :

スパとマッサージですね。もちろん。で、私はここにサインするんですね？

M : Yes, and the charges will be added to your card. Shall I arrange a cab for you?

F :

ええ、お願いします。ここから直接、空港に行く予定にしていますので。

Unit 100 乗り換えについて聞く
Train Transfer

STEP 1 　各センテンスをシャドーイングしよう。　CD 2-40

STEP 2 　テキストを見ながらスキットを演じてみよう。　CD 2-40

F : Does Amtrak stop at Gatlinburg?

アムトラックはガトリンバーグに停まりますか？

* Amtrak はアメリカを走る鉄道・バス路線網。

M : No, I'm afraid it doesn't. The nearest we go is Knoxville.

いいえ、すみませんが停まりません。いちばん近いのはノックスビルになります。

F : Oh, I see. So how can I get from there to Gatlinburg?

ああ、そうですか。で、そこからガトリンバーグへはどう行けばいいんでしょう？

M : Most people rent a car. But there are also tour buses that go there from Knoxville.

ほとんどの人は車を借ります。でも、ノックスビルからそこへ行くツアー・バスもありますよ。

* there are ... は「…がある」という意味で存在を表す。

F : Well, I don't have a driver's license. Do you have information about the tour bus?

うーん、私は免許証をもってないんです。ツアー・バスに関する情報はわかりますか？

STEP 3 日本語訳を見ながらスキットを演じてみよう。   CD 2-40

F :

アムトラックはガトリンバーグに停まりますか？

M : No, I'm afraid it doesn't. The nearest we go is Knoxville.

F :

ああ、そうですか。で、そこからガトリンバーグへはどう行けばいいんでしょう？

M : Most people rent a car. But there are also tour buses that go there from Knoxville.

F :

うーん、私は免許証をもってないんです。ツアー・バスに関する情報はわかりますか？

Unit 101 Asking for Directions 道順をたずねる

STEP 1 各センテンスをシャドーイングしよう。　CD 2-41

STEP 2 テキストを見ながらスキットを演じてみよう。　CD 2-41

F : Can you help me? I'm lost, and I'm trying to find the Historical District.

助けてもらえますか？ 道に迷っていて、歴史地区を探そうとしているんですけど。

* try to find は「探そうとする；探そうと努力する」。

M : Oh, you're pretty close. You need to turn left at the next stoplight. That's Greene Street.

ああ、けっこう近いですよ。次の信号で左折しないといけません。そこがグリーン通りです。

* turn left/right で「左／右に曲がる」という意味。

F : Okay, thanks. And then what?

わかります、どうも。で、それからどうすれば？

* what は「なにを；どんな」の意。

M : After walking for about five minutes, you will start to see signs for the Historical District. It's about a quarter of a mile from here.

約5分歩くと、歴史地区の標識が見え始めますよ。ここから4分の1マイルほどです。

* after walking は「歩くことのあと」＝「歩いたあと」。

F : Got it! Thank you so much!

わかりました！ ほんとうにありがとうございます！

旅行会話 ★

STEP 3　　日本語訳を見ながらスキットを演じてみよう。　　CD 2-41

F :

助けてもらえますか？ 道に迷っていて、歴史地区を探そうとしているんですけど。

M : Oh, you're pretty close. You need to turn left at the next stoplight. That's Greene Street.

F :

わかります、どうも。で、それからどうすれば？

M : After walking for about five minutes, you will start to see signs for the Historical District. It's about a quarter of a mile from here.

F :

わかりました！ ほんとうにありがとうございます！

Unit 102 タクシーでの会話
Talking to a Taxi Driver

STEP 1 各センテンスをシャドーイングしよう。 CD 2-42

STEP 2 テキストを見ながらスキットを演じてみよう。 CD 2-42

F: I'm meeting a friend in front of The Ansonia Hotel. Do you know where that is?

アンソニア・ホテルの前で友人に会う予定なんです。それがどこにあるかわかりますか？

＊ I'm meeting は「私は会う予定だ」という意味。

M: I know that it's on the Upper West Side. Do you have the address?

アッパー・ウェスト・サイドにあることは知っています。住所はわかりますか？

＊ I know that ... は「…ということを知っている」という意味。

F: My friend says it's at Broadway and 72nd Street.

友人が言うには、それはブロードウェーと72番街の交差点にあるそうです。

＊ be at A and B は「AとBの交差点にある」という意味。

M: Oh, yeah, I know it. It's right in front of the subway entrance. It's a beautiful building.

ああ、はい、それ、わかりますよ。地下鉄の入り口のちょうど目の前にありますね。美しい建物ですよ。

F: Yeah, she showed me a picture. It looks really old.

ええ、彼女が写真を見せてくれたんですよ。とても古く見えますよね。

STEP 3 日本語訳を見ながらスキットを演じてみよう。　CD 2-42

F :

アンソニア・ホテルの前で友人に会う予定なんです。それがどこにあるかわかりますか？

M : I know that it's on the Upper West Side. Do you have the address?

F :

友人が言うには、それはブロードウェーと 72 番街の交差点にあるそうです。

M : Oh, yeah, I know it. It's right in front of the subway entrance. It's a beautiful building.

F :

ええ、彼女が写真を見せてくれたんですよ。とても古く見えますよね。

Unit 103 レンタカーを返却する
Returning a Rented Car

STEP 1 各センテンスをシャドーイングしよう。　CD 2-43

STEP 2 テキストを見ながらスキットを演じてみよう。　CD 2-43

M: Hi, I'm returning the car I rented. I'm a few hours late.

こんにちは。借りた車の返却なんですが。数時間遅くなりました。

F: That's fine, sir. Did you read the part of the agreement about late returns?

かまいませんよ。契約書の返却の遅延に関する部分を読みましたか？

M: Yeah, I did. It's going to be about thirty extra dollars, right?

ええ、読みました。約 30 ドルの割り増しになりますよね？

* thirty extra dollars の extra は「余分の；追加の；割り増しの」。

F: Yes, it's pretty close to that. And did you fill up the gas tank?

はい、それにかなり近い額です。それから、ガソリン・タンクは満タンにしましたか？

* fill up は「満たす」という意味になるフレーズ。

M: Yep, just a couple blocks from here. It's a full tank now.

ええ、ここからほんの数ブロックのところで。いまは満タンですよ。

* a full tank は「満タン（のガソリン・タンク）」。

STEP 3 日本語訳を見ながらスキットを演じてみよう。　CD 2-43

M:

こんにちは。借りた車の返却なんですが。数時間遅くなりました。

F: That's fine, sir. Did you read the part of the agreement about late returns?

M:

ええ、読みました。約30ドルの割り増しになりますよね？

F: Yes, it's pretty close to that. And did you fill up the gas tank?

M:

ええ、ここからほんの数ブロックのところで。いまは満タンですよ。

Unit 104 チケットを買う
Buying Tickets to a Performance

STEP 1 各センテンスをシャドーイングしよう。　　CD 2-44

STEP 2 テキストを見ながらスキットを演じてみよう。　　CD 2-44

F : Unfortunately, all our B seats are sold out for this performance. We just have A and C.

残念ながら、この上演のB席はすべて売り切れています。AとCだけしかございません。

＊ sold out は「売り切れている」という意味。

M : Oh, shoot! The price is probably very different, right?

ああ、しまった！ おそらく値段はだいぶ違うんでしょ？

＊ Shoot! は「しまった；くそー」という意味。Shit! をやんわりと表現したもの。

F : Yes, that's right. A seats are eighty-five dollars, and C seats are forty dollars.

はい、そのとおりです。A席は85ドルで、C席は40ドルになります。

M : More than double, huh? Are the views that much better?

2倍以上ですって？ 眺めはそんなにいいんですか？

＊ more than ... は「…よりも多い」という意味。double は「2倍」。
＊ huh? は「…ですって？」と驚きを表す。

F : Yes, they are, sir. If you can afford it, it's worth the extra money.

はい、そうです、お客さま。余裕がおありでしたら、追加料金の価値はございます。

＊ worth ... は「…に値する；…の価値がある」という意味。

旅行会話 ★

STEP 3 　日本語訳を見ながらスキットを演じてみよう。　CD 2-44

F : Unfortunately, all our B seats are sold out for this performance. We just have A and C.

M :

ああ、しまった！ おそらく値段はだいぶ違うんでしょ？

F : Yes, that's right. A seats are eighty-five dollars, and C seats are forty dollars.

M :

2倍以上ですって？ 眺めはそんなにいいんですか？

F : Yes, they are, sir. If you can afford it, it's worth the extra money.

Unit 105 モールで店をたずねる
At a Mall Information Booth

STEP 1 各センテンスをシャドーイングしよう。　CD 2-45

STEP 2 テキストを見ながらスキットを演じてみよう。　CD 2-45

F: Hi! How can I help you today?

こんにちは！ いらっしゃいませ。

＊ How can I help you? は店員が客に声をかけるときの決まり文句。

M: This is my first time in this mall, and it's so huge! I want to buy cowboy boots.

このモールははじめてなんです、それにとても巨大ですよね！ カウボーイ・ブーツを買いたいんです。

＊ huge は「巨大な；莫大な」という意味。

F: Well, the main department store might have them on the sixth floor. That's right behind you.

えー、それはメインのデパートの6階にあるかもしれませんね。ちょうどお客さまの後ろです。

＊ might have は「持っているかもしれない；在庫しているかもしれない」という意味。

M: I just came from there. Their shoe department doesn't carry cowboy boots.

僕はちょうどそこから来たんです。あそこの靴売り場にはカウボーイ・ブーツはありませんでした。

＊ carry は、ここでは「在庫として置いている」という意味。

F: Oh, I see. Well, we have two specialty shops for shoes. Let me get you a map.

ああ、そうですか。えー、モールにはふたつの靴専門店があります。地図をお持ちいたしますね。

＊ Let me ... は「私に…させて」という意味。

STEP 3　日本語訳を見ながらスキットを演じてみよう。　CD 2-45

F : Hi! How can I help you today?

M :

このモールははじめてなんです、それにとても巨大ですよね！ カウボーイ・ブーツを買いたいんです。

F : Well, the main department store might have them on the sixth floor. That's right behind you.

M :

僕はちょうどそこから来たんです。あそこの靴売り場にはカウボーイ・ブーツはありませんでした。

F : Oh, I see. Well, we have two specialty shops for shoes. Let me get you a map.

Unit 106 品揃えをたずねる
Finding the Item You Wish to Purchase

STEP 1 各センテンスをシャドーイングしよう。　CD 2-46

STEP 2 テキストを見ながらスキットを演じてみよう。　CD 2-46

F : I've been trying to find a place that sells Persian rugs. Do you carry them?

ペルシャ絨毯を売っているところを探しているんです。そちらには置いていますか？

M : We do have a few, but I'm afraid our selection isn't very large.

少しはございますが、残念ながら品揃えはそれほど多くありません。

* I'm afraid (that) ... は「残念ながら…です；申し訳ないが…です」という意味の表現。

F : Oh, that's too bad. Do you have long ones, like for a hallway?

ああ、それは残念です。廊下用のような長いのはありますか？

* That's too bad. は残念な気持ちを表すときの決まり文句。

M : Well, if we do, it would just be one or two. But we have some other really nice varieties of rugs.

ええ、あるとすれば、ひとつかふたつでしょう。しかし、ほかにとてもいい絨毯を揃えております。

* nice varieties of ... は「すばらしいバラエティーの…」という意味。

F : I'm sure you do. But I think I'll do a little more searching. Thanks!

そうでしょうね。でも、もうちょっと探してみようと思います。ありがとうございます！

* I'm sure (that) ... は「きっと…だと思う」という意味。

STEP 3　日本語訳を見ながらスキットを演じてみよう。　CD 2-46

F :

ペルシャ絨毯を売っているところを探しているんです。そちらには置いていますか？

M : We do have a few, but I'm afraid our selection isn't very large.

F :

ああ、それは残念です。廊下用のような長いのはありますか？

M : Well, if we do, it would just be one or two. But we have some other really nice varieties of rugs.

F :

そうでしょうね。でも、もうちょっと探してみようと思います。ありがとうございます！

Unit 107 お土産を買う
Choosing Souvenirs

STEP 1 各センテンスをシャドーイングしよう。　CD 2-47

STEP 2 テキストを見ながらスキットを演じてみよう。　CD 2-47

F : What are the most popular souvenirs from your town?

こちらの町でいちばん人気のあるお土産はなんですか？

* the most popular は「もっとも人気のある」という意味。

M : Well, we are known for our miniature wood carvings. They are really popular as gifts.

えー、ここはミニチュアの木彫りで有名なんです。贈り物としてとても人気がありますよ。

* be known for ... は「…で知られている；有名だ」という意味のフレーズ。

F : Oh, I see. You mean like that row of little houses over there?

へえ、そうなんですね。つまり向こうに並んでいる小さな家みたいなもののことですよね？

* mean like ... は「…のように意味する」という意味。

M : Exactly. Each one of those is a model of an actual Victorian house here in town.

そのとおりです。そのそれぞれが、この町にある、本物のビクトリア様式家屋の模型なんです。

* Exactly. は「まさに；まさしく」。

F : They are adorable! Perfect! My souvenir problem is solved!

とてもかわいいですよね！ 完璧！ 私のお土産問題は解決しましたよ！

* solve は「解決する」。

旅行会話 ★☆☆

STEP 3 日本語訳を見ながらスキットを演じてみよう。 CD 2-47

F :

こちらの町でいちばん人気のあるお土産はなんですか？

M : Well, we are known for our miniature wood carvings. They are really popular as gifts.

F :

へえ、そうなんですね。つまり向こうに並んでいる小さな家みたいなもののことですよね？

M : Exactly. Each one of those is a model of an actual Victorian house here in town.

F :

とてもかわいいですよね！ 完璧！ 私のお土産問題は解決しましたよ！

Unit 108 医者との会話
Talking to a Doctor (About an Ailment)

STEP 1 各センテンスをシャドーイングしよう。　CD 2-48

STEP 2 テキストを見ながらスキットを演じてみよう。　CD 2-48

F : I started to feel sick from the third day I came here.

こちらに来た3日目から具合が悪くなり始めました。

* the third day I came here は「私がここに来て3日目」。

M : I see. Do you think it was something that you ate?

そうですか。なにかの食べ物だと思いますか？

F : It might be. Plus, I'm just not used to this weather. It's so hot!

そうかもしれません。それと、単純にこの気候に慣れてないんです。暑すぎますよ！

M : It's common that people get ill when they travel long distances to new places. Let me take your temperature.

新しい場所まで長旅をすると、人が具合を悪くするのはよくあることですよ。体温を測らせてください。

* let me ... は「私に…させて」という意味。

F : I just hope I can feel better soon so I can enjoy this trip!

この旅を楽しめるように、すぐによくなることを願っているだけなんです！

* I just hope (that) ... は「単に…を望んでいる」という意味。

旅行会話 ★★★

STEP 3 　日本語訳を見ながらスキットを演じてみよう。　CD 2-48

F :
こちらに来た3日目から具合が悪くなり始めました。

M : I see. Do you think it was something that you ate?

F :
そうかもしれません。それと、単純にこの気候に慣れてないんです。暑すぎますよ！

M : It's common that people get ill when they travel long distances to new places. Let me take your temperature.

F :
この旅を楽しめるように、すぐによくなることを願っているだけなんです！

Unit 109 警官との会話
Talking to a Police Officer (as a Crime Witness)

STEP 1 各センテンスをシャドーイングしよう。　CD 2-49

STEP 2 テキストを見ながらスキットを演じてみよう。　CD 2-49

M: I understand that you were a witness to what happened?

あなたが出来事の目撃者だったのですね？

＊ I understand that ... は「…ということを理解している」という意味。

F: Yes, officer. I was in the store the whole time.

はい、おまわりさん。私はずっとそのお店にいたんです。

M: I see. And are you certain this was the man?

そうですか。で、これがその男だったというのは確かなんですね？

＊ Are you certain (that) ...? は「…（ということ）は確かですか？」という意味。

F: Yes, no question. He came in to the store and pointed a gun at the owner.

はい、間違いありません。彼が店に入ってきて、オーナーに拳銃を突きつけたんです。

＊ point a gun at ... は「…に銃を向ける」という意味になるフレーズ。

M: Okay, got it. I need to get a witness statement from you. This will take about an hour.

はい、わかりました。あなたから目撃者調書をもらう必要があります。これには1時間ほどかかります。

＊ この文の take ... は「…（時間）がかかる」という意味。

STEP 3 　日本語訳を見ながらスキットを演じてみよう。　CD 2-49

M: I understand that you were a witness to what happened?

F:

はい、おまわりさん。私はずっとそのお店にいたんです。

M: I see. And are you certain this was the man?

F:

はい、間違いありません。彼が店に入ってきて、オーナーに拳銃を突きつけたんです。

M: Okay, got it. I need to get a witness statement from you. This will take about an hour.

Unit 110　Giving Directions to the Station
駅への道を案内する会話

STEP 1 　各センテンスをシャドーイングしよう。　　CD 2-50

STEP 2 　テキストを見ながらスキットを演じてみよう。　　CD 2-50

M: Excuse me. I'm looking for Grand Central Station. Can you tell me how to get there?

すみません。グランド・セントラル駅を探しているんですが。どう行けばいいか教えてもらえますか？

F: Absolutely. It's not very far. You need to walk down this street until you get to the Hilton hotel there.

もちろん。そう遠くはないですよ。あそこのヒルトン・ホテルに着くまで、この通りを進んでください。

M: Is that the tall building down there with the flags out front?

あそこにある正面に旗が立っている高いビルですか？

* with the flags out front「外の正面に旗がある」

F: Yep. Take a right there and walk another four blocks. When you come to the Central Post Office, take a left.

そうです。そこで右に曲がって、あと4ブロック歩いてください。中央郵便局まで来たら左折です。

* take a right/left「右／左折する」　block「区画」

M: Left at the post office ... got it.

郵便局で左折ですね…わかりました。

F: From there you will see the signs for the station. It's between 34th and 35th street.

そこから、駅に向かう標識が見えますよ。34番街と35番街の間になります。

* sign「標識；掲示」　between A and B「AとBの間」

M: Thank you so much for your help!

とても助かりました！

F: My pleasure. If you get turned around, just ask someone and they should be able to help you.

お役に立ててうれしいです。迷ったら、だれかに聞けばわかるはずですから。

* get turned around「迷う」

STEP 3 日本語訳を見ながらスキットを演じてみよう。　CD 2-50

M :

すみません。グランド・セントラル駅を探しているんですが。どう行けばいいか教えてもらえますか？

F : Absolutely. It's not very far. You need to walk down this street until you get to the Hilton hotel there.

M :

あそこにある正面に旗が立っている高いビルですか？

F : Yep. Take a right there and walk another four blocks. When you come to the Central Post Office, take a left.

M :

郵便局で左折ですね…わかりました。

F : From there you will see the signs for the station. It's between 34th and 35th street.

M :

とても助かりました！

F : My pleasure. If you get turned around, just ask someone and they should be able to help you.

Unit 111 駅の構内を案内する会話
Giving Directions at the Station

STEP 1 各センテンスをシャドーイングしよう。　CD 2-51

STEP 2 テキストを見ながらスキットを演じてみよう。　CD 2-51

F: Excuse me. Can you tell me where to go to catch the Green Line train?
すみません。グリーン・ラインの電車に乗るにはどこに行けばいいでしょうか？

M: Do you already have a token? If not, you'll need to buy one at that machine over there.
トークンはもう買いましたか？ もしまだなら、向こうのあの機械で購入する必要がありますよ。

＊ token「トークン；代用硬貨」

F: I've got a weekly pass. I just don't know which platform I need to go to.
1週間使えるパスを持っているんです。ただ、どこのプラットフォームに行けばいいかわからなくて。

M: Are you headed north or south on the Green Line?
グリーン・ラインで北に向かいますか、それとも南ですか？

＊ be headed ...「…に向かう」

F: North, toward upper Manhattan.
北です、アッパー・マンハッタンのほうです。

M: Well then, you can take that escalator over there and follow the signs to platform 5.
では、向こうのあのエスカレーターに乗って5番線方面の標示に従ってください。

F: Thank you. Do you happen to know how often the trains run?
ありがとう。ひょっとして、どのくらいの頻度で電車が走っているかご存知ですか？

＊ happen to ...「たまたま…する」

M: You shouldn't have to wait long, they run about every ten minutes or so.
長く待つ必要はないはずですよ。10分おきくらいに走っていますから。

＊ every ten minutes「10分おきに」　... or so「…かそこいら」

STEP 3 　日本語訳を見ながらスキットを演じてみよう。　CD 2-51

F : [　　　　　　　　　　　　　　　　　　　　　　　]

すみません。グリーン・ラインの電車に乗るにはどこに行けばいいでしょうか？

M : Do you already have a token? If not, you'll need to buy one at that machine over there.

F : [　　　　　　　　　　　　　　　　　　　　　　　]

1週間使えるパスを持っているんです。ただ、どこのプラットフォームに行けばいいかわからなくて。

M : Are you headed north or south on the Green Line?

F : [　　　　　　　　　　　　　　　　　　　　　　　]

北です、アッパー・マンハッタンのほうです。

M : Well then, you can take that escalator over there and follow the signs to platform 5.

F : [　　　　　　　　　　　　　　　　　　　　　　　]

ありがとう。ひょっとして、どのくらいの頻度で電車が走っているかご存知ですか？

M : You shouldn't have to wait long, they run about every ten minutes or so.

Unit 112 ホテルのチェックイン
Checking Into the Hotel

STEP 1 各センテンスをシャドーイングしよう。 CD 2-52

STEP 2 テキストを見ながらスキットを演じてみよう。 CD 2-52

M: We don't have a reservation. Do you have any rooms available?
予約をしていないのですが。利用できる部屋はありますか？

F: We sure do. How many nights are you looking to stay?
ございますよ。何泊のご予定でしょうか？
* look to ... 「…しようとする」

M: Tonight and tomorrow night, checking out on Monday.
今夜と明日の晩で、月曜にチェック・アウトします。

F: Is it just the two of you? Would you like a king bed or two queens?
おふた方だけですか？ ダブルとツインはどちらがよろしいでしょうか？

M: Yes. Just us. A room with a king-size bed would be preferable.
ええ、ふたりだけです。キング・サイズのベッドの部屋のほうがいいのですが。
* preferable 「より好ましい」

F: No problem. Just so you know we offer a hot breakfast buffet between six and ten am.
問題ありません。お伝えしておきますが、午前6時から10時まで温かいビュッフェ・スタイルの朝食をご提供しております。

M: That sounds great.
それはいいですね。

F: Okay, I have you set up in room #222, for two nights. Your total comes to $210.59.
さて、222号室を2泊でお取りしました。お支払合計は210ドル59セントになります。

M: Thank you. Put it on this credit card, please.
ありがとう。このクレジット・カードでお願いします。
* put 「課す；つける」

旅行会話 ★★

STEP 3 日本語訳を見ながらスキットを演じてみよう。 CD 2-52

M :

予約をしていないのですが。利用できる部屋はありますか？

F : We sure do. How many nights are you looking to stay?

M :

今夜と明日の晩で、月曜にチェック・アウトします。

F : Is it just the two of you? Would you like a king bed or two queens?

M :

ええ、ふたりだけです。キング・サイズのベッドの部屋のほうがいいのですが。

F : No problem. Just so you know we offer a hot breakfast buffet between six and ten am.

M :

それはいいですね。

F : Okay, I have you set up in room #222, for two nights. Your total comes to $210.59.

M :

ありがとう。このクレジット・カードでお願いします。

Unit 113 At the Drive-thru
ドライブスルーでの会話

STEP 1 各センテンスをシャドーイングしよう。　CD 2-53

STEP 2 テキストを見ながらスキットを演じてみよう。　CD 2-53

M : Welcome to Burger Heaven. May I take your order?
バーガー・ヘヴンへようこそ。ご注文は？

F : I'd like a chicken sandwich and onion rings combo meal, please.
チキンのサンドイッチとオニオン・リングのコンボをください。

M : Do you want your chicken crispy or grilled?
クリスピー・チキンとグリルド・チキンのどちらにしますか？

* crispy「サクサクした」　grilled「網で焼いた」

F : I'll have it grilled. Also ... no mayonnaise or tomatoes on that please.
グリルド・チキンでお願いします。それと…マヨネーズやトマトは抜いてください。

M : What would you like to drink with that?
ごいっしょになにをお飲みになりますか？

F : A large iced tea with lemon please. Unsweetened, if you have it.
アイス・レモン・ティーのラージをお願いします。あれば、甘みの入ってないもので。

* unsweetened「甘みの入ってない」

M : Anything for desert? Or will that complete your order today?
デザートになにかいかがですか？ それとも、本日のご注文は以上でしょうか？

F : That will do.
それで大丈夫です。

M : Okay ... your total comes to $8.98. Please pull up to the first window.
わかりました…合計金額は8ドル98セントになります。最初の窓口に停車してお待ちください。

F : Thank you.
どうも。

STEP 3 日本語訳を見ながらスキットを演じてみよう。　CD 2-53

M: Welcome to Burger Heaven. May I take your order?

F:

チキンのサンドイッチとオニオン・リングのコンボをください。

M: Do you want your chicken crispy or grilled?

F:

グリルド・チキンでお願いします。それと…マヨネーズやトマトは抜いてください。

M: What would you like to drink with that?

F:

アイス・レモン・ティーのラージをお願いします。あれば、甘みの入ってないもので。

M: Anything for desert? Or will that complete your order today?

F:

それで大丈夫です。

M: Okay ... your total comes to $8.98. Please pull up to the first window.

F:

どうも。

Unit 114 レストランでの注文
Ordering at a Restaurant

STEP 1 各センテンスをシャドーイングしよう。　CD 2-54

STEP 2 テキストを見ながらスキットを演じてみよう。　CD 2-54

F : Are you ready to order or do you need a few more minutes?
ご注文をお伺いいたしましょうか？　それとも、もうしばらくあとにしますか？

M : What is your soup of the day?
今日のスープはなんでしょうか？

F : Today we have beef and vegetable soup and clam chowder.
本日は、ビーフと野菜のスープと、クラム・チャウダーです。
* clam chowder「クラム・チャウダー（スープ）」

M : Hmmm ... I guess I'll just have a hamburger. Can I substitute onion rings for the French fries?
うーん…ハンバーガーだけにしようかな。フライド・ポテトの代わりにオニオン・リングをいただけますか？
* substitute A for B「A を B の代わりに用いる」

F : Sure. And how would you like your burger cooked?
もちろんです。バーガーの焼き具合はどういたしますか？
* like A cooked B「A が B に調理されるのが好き」

M : Make it medium-well, please. Can I get bacon on it also?
ミディアム・ウェルでお願いします。ベーコンもつけてもらえますか？
* make it medium-well「それをミディアム・ウェルにする」

F : Certainly. And what would you like to drink?
かしこまりました。お飲み物はいかがなさいますか？

M : I'll have unsweetened iced tea if you have it.
あれば、砂糖抜きのアイス・ティーを。

旅行会話 ★★★

STEP 3　日本語訳を見ながらスキットを演じてみよう。　CD 2-54

F : Are you ready to order or do you need a few more minutes?

M :

今日のスープはなんでしょうか？

F : Today we have beef and vegetable soup and clam chowder.

M :

うーん…ハンバーガーだけにしようかな。フライド・ポテトの代わりにオニオン・リングをいただけますか？

F : Sure. And how would you like your burger cooked?

M :

ミディアム・ウェルでお願いします。ベーコンもつけてもらえますか？

F : Certainly. And what would you like to drink?

M :

あれば、砂糖抜きのアイス・ティーを。

Unit 115 Vacation Plans 旅先でのスケジュール

STEP 1 　各センテンスをシャドーイングしよう。　CD 2-55

STEP 2 　テキストを見ながらスキットを演じてみよう。　CD 2-55

M: This is the last day of our vacation here. What do you want to do?
今日がここでの休暇の最終日だね。なにがしたい？

* vacation「休暇旅行」

F: Well, it's 9:30 now. How about we have breakfast on the beach?
そうね、いまは9時半よね。ビーチで朝食を食べるのはどう？

M: That's fine. I want to get some golf in this morning before it gets too hot.
いいね。今朝は、あまり暑くなる前にちょっとゴルフがしたいんだ。

* get some golf「ちょっとゴルフをする」

F: While you're playing golf, I am going to spend a few hours at the spa.
あなたがゴルフをしている間、私はスパで数時間過ごすわ。

M: Okay. What do you think about a late lunch at that seafood restaurant we liked?
わかった。僕らの気に入っているあのシーフード・レストランで遅めのランチにするのはどう？

F: That sounds good. I want to do a little shopping this afternoon too.
いいわね。今日の午後はちょっと買い物もしたいの。

M: We won't have too much time. Remember our flight is at six.
あまり時間はたくさんないからね。フライトは6時だよ。

F: As long as we're back to the hotel by four we should be okay.
ホテルに4時までに戻ってくれば大丈夫なはずよ。

旅行会話 ★★★

STEP 3 日本語訳を見ながらスキットを演じてみよう。　CD 2-55

M: This is the last day of our vacation here. What do you want to do?

F:

そうね、いまは9時半よね。ビーチで朝食を食べるのはどう？

M: That's fine. I want to get some golf in this morning before it gets too hot.

F:

あなたがゴルフをしている間、私はスパで数時間過ごすわ。

M: Okay. What do you think about a late lunch at that seafood restaurant we liked?

F:

いいわね。今日の午後はちょっと買い物もしたいの。

M: We won't have too much time. Remember our flight is at six.

F:

ホテルに4時までに戻ってくれば大丈夫なはずよ。

Unit 116　Asking for a Blanket　毛布を頼む

STEP 1 　各センテンスをシャドーイングしよう。　CD 2-56

STEP 2 　テキストを見ながらスキットを演じてみよう。　CD 2-56

M : Miss, suddenly I've become a little cold.
すみません、急に寒くなったんですが。

F : I'm sorry, sir. What can I do for you?
それはいけませんね。どういたしましょう？

M : Can I have another blanket? As you can see, my daughter has stolen half of this one.
毛布をもう1枚いただけますか？ ご覧のとおり、娘がこっちのを半分取っちゃってるんですよ。

F : Ha, ha; she looks sweet! Let me go back to the flight attendant's station to get you an extra blanket. Anything else?
ハハ、彼女かわいいですね！ アテンダント・ステーションに戻ってもう1枚毛布をお持ちします。ほかには、なにかございますか？

M : Yes, I think I'd like something warm to drink. But I also want to sleep.
ええ、なにか温かい飲み物が欲しいんです。でも、眠くもあるんですが。

F : I'm sorry, we don't have decaffeinated coffee. Just the regular kind.
申し訳ありません、カフェイン抜きのコーヒーは置いていないんです。ふつうの種類しか。

＊ decaffeinated coffee「カフェイン抜きのコーヒー」

M : Yeah, I was afraid so. Could you just bring me some warm water?
ええ、そうだと思ってました。白湯だけもってきてもらえますか？

F : Just warm water? I could make you some hot milk.
ただの白湯ですか？ ホット・ミルクもできますが。

M : No, warm water is fine. And thanks!
いいえ、白湯でけっこうです。いろいろ、ありがとう！

STEP 3 日本語訳を見ながらスキットを演じてみよう。　CD 2-56

M :

すみません、急に寒くなったんですが。

F : I'm sorry, sir. What can I do for you?

M :

毛布をもう1枚いただけますか？ ご覧のとおり、娘がこっちのを半分取っちゃってるんですよ。

F : Ha, ha; she looks sweet! Let me go back to the flight attendant's station to get you an extra blanket. Anything else?

M :

ええ、なにか温かい飲み物が欲しいんです。でも、眠くもあるんですが。

F : I'm sorry, we don't have decaffeinated coffee. Just the regular kind.

M :

ええ、そうだと思ってました。白湯だけもってきてもらえますか？

F : Just warm water? I could make you some hot milk.

M :

いいえ、白湯でけっこうです。いろいろ、ありがとう！

Unit 117 Luggage Doesn't Come / 荷物が出てこない

STEP 1 各センテンスをシャドーイングしよう。　CD 2-57

STEP 2 テキストを見ながらスキットを演じてみよう。　CD 2-57

F: I came in on the flight from Brussels. I'm still waiting for my luggage to show up.

ブリュッセルから飛行機に乗ってきたんです。まだ、荷物が出てくるのを待っているんです。

* luggage「荷物」

M: That luggage should definitely have come by now.

そのお荷物は、もう確実に通り過ぎているはずですよ。

F: Yes, exactly. All the other passengers picked up theirs and left.

確かに、そうですよね。ほかの乗客は自分の荷物を取っていきましたし。

M: As far as I know, the luggage came over on the same flight.

私の理解では、お荷物は同じ便で来ていますよ。

F: So that means it's in this airport, right?

ということは、荷物はこの空港にあるということですよね？

M: Well, it definitely should be. May I see your tags, please?

ええ、確実にそのはずです。あなたのタグを拝見できますか？

F: Here you are. It's two matching suitcases. One large and one medium.

これです。ふたつのおそろいのスーツケースなんです。大きいのと中くらいのです。

* two matching suitcases「ふたつのおそろいのスーツケース」

M: And you checked all around the area, right? Sometimes they are off to the side.

で、あなたはエリア中をチェックしたのですよね？ たまに、横に落ちていますから。

F: Oh, yes, I checked thoroughly. They definitely didn't come with the rest.

ええ、全部、見ました。確かに、ほかのとはいっしょに来ませんでした。

M: I'll see what I can do.

なにができるか考えてみますね。

旅行会話 ★★

STEP 3 　日本語訳を見ながらスキットを演じてみよう。　CD 2-57

F :
[　　　　　　　　　　　　　　　　　　　　　　　　]

ブリュッセルから飛行機に乗ってきたんです。まだ、荷物が出てくるのを待っているんです。

M : That luggage should definitely have come by now.

F :
[　　　　　　　　　　　　　　　　　　　　　　　　]

確かに、そうですよね。ほかの乗客は自分の荷物を取っていきましたし。

M : As far as I know, the luggage came over on the same flight.

F :
[　　　　　　　　　　　　　　　　　　　　　　　　]

ということは、荷物はこの空港にあるということですよね？

M : Well, it definitely should be. May I see your tags, please?

F :
[　　　　　　　　　　　　　　　　　　　　　　　　]

これです。ふたつのおそろいのスーツケースなんです。大きいのと中くらいのです。

M : And you checked all around the area, right? Sometimes they are off to the side.

F :
[　　　　　　　　　　　　　　　　　　　　　　　　]

ええ、全部、見ました。確かに、ほかのとはいっしょに来ませんでした。

M : I'll see what I can do.

Unit 118 苦情の電話
Calling with a Complaint

STEP 1 各センテンスをシャドーイングしよう。　CD 2-58

STEP 2 テキストを見ながらスキットを演じてみよう。　CD 2-58

F: This is the front desk. Can I help you?
フロントです。なにかお手伝いできるでしょうか？

M: I hope so. I am having trouble with the water in my room.
そうですね。部屋の水道に問題があるんですよ。

F: Very sorry, sir. What's the problem?
大変申し訳ございません。どういたしましたか？

M: The knob for the hot water is loose, so the temperature keeps changing.
お湯のノブが緩くて、温度が一定にならないんですよ。

F: Oh, I see. Very sorry about that. Would you like to change rooms?
ああ、そうですか。ほんとうに申し訳ありません。お部屋を変更なさいますか？

M: I guess I could do that. Do you think someone could fix it?
それもできるかもと思ってましたが。だれかに直してもらえないですかね？

* fix「修理する」

F: Well, I will certainly send someone. But if it takes time to fix, it might be better to find you a different room.
えー、もちろん確実に人は行かせます。しかし、もし修理に時間がかかるようなら、お客さまに新しいお部屋を探したほうがよいかもしれません。

M: That sounds good; thanks. I will leave soon. Can someone take a look at it while I'm gone?
それで大丈夫ですよ。私はすぐに出かけるので。出かけている間に、だれかに見てもらえますかね？

F: Yes, sir. Right away.
はい、お客さま。すぐに取りかかりますので。

旅行会話 ★★★

STEP 3 　日本語訳を見ながらスキットを演じてみよう。　CD 2-58

F : This is the front desk. Can I help you?

M :

そうですね。部屋の水道に問題があるんですよ。

F : Very sorry, sir. What's the problem?

M :

お湯のノブが緩くて、温度が一定にならないんですよ。

F : Oh, I see. Very sorry about that. Would you like to change rooms?

M :

それもできるかもと思ってましたが。だれかに直してもらえないですかね？

F : Well, I will certainly send someone. But if it takes time to fix, it might be better to find you a different room.

M :

それで大丈夫ですよ。私はすぐに出かけるので。出かけている間に、だれかに見てもらえますかね？

F : Yes, sir. Right away.

Unit 119 おいしいレストランの推薦
Good Restaurant Recommendation

STEP 1 各センテンスをシャドーイングしよう。　CD 2-59

STEP 2 テキストを見ながらスキットを演じてみよう。　CD 2-59

M: Are there some nice restaurants in the area that you can recommend?
地域のおすすめのおいしいレストランはありますか？

F: There are several. Do you have anything in particular in mind?
いくつかございますよ。なにか特別にお考えのものはありますか？

M: I was thinking something Mediterranean. Maybe Spanish or Greek.
なにか地中海っぽいものを考えてたんです。スペインとかギリシャ料理とかかなあ。

F: Well, I haven't seen either of those within walking distance.
えー、どちらも徒歩圏内には見当たりませんね。
＊ walking distance「徒歩圏」

M: Oh, that's okay. Italian would be good as well.
ああ、ならいいです。イタリアンでもいいですから。

F: There is a Bulgarian restaurant a couple blocks from here. I think that's close to Greek.
ここから数ブロックのところにブルガリア料理店がございます。ギリシャ料理に近いと思いますが。

M: That sounds really nice! Something new to try! How do I get there?
それはいいですね！ 新しいものにチャレンジできますよ！ どうやって行けばいいですか？

F: Go out of the hotel, and turn left, and you'll come to 48th Street.
ホテルを出ていただいて、左に曲がって 48 番街まで行ってください。

M: Yes, I got that.
ええ、わかりました。

F: Turn right and walk for two blocks. It's called Petya's. It has lots of flowers in front.
右折して、2 ブロック歩きます。ペトヤズという店です。店先にたくさんのお花がありますよ。

旅行会話 ★★

249

STEP 3 日本語訳を見ながらスキットを演じてみよう。 CD 2-59

M :

地域のおすすめのおいしいレストランはありますか？

F : There are several. Do you have anything in particular in mind?

M :

なにか地中海っぽいものを考えてたんです。スペインとかギリシャ料理とかかなあ。

F : Well, I haven't seen either of those within walking distance.

M :

ああ、ならいいです。イタリアンでもいいですから。

F : There is a Bulgarian restaurant a couple blocks from here. I think that's close to Greek.

M :

それはいいですね！ 新しいものにチャレンジできますよ！ どうやって行けばいいですか？

F : Go out of the hotel, and turn left, and you'll come to 48th Street.

M :

ええ、わかりました。

F : Turn right and walk for two blocks. It's called Petya's. It has lots of flowers in front.

Unit 120 バス・ツアーについてたずねる
Asking About a Bus Tour

STEP 1 各センテンスをシャドーイングしよう。　CD 2-60

STEP 2 テキストを見ながらスキットを演じてみよう。　CD 2-60

F: I noticed the buses with open tops. Do they give a tour of the city?
屋根のないバスを見かけたんですけど。街のツアーをやってるんですか？

M: Yes, they take you all around. You can get off and get on again as often as you like.
はい、いろいろなところに行けますよ。何度でも好きなだけ乗り降りできます。

F: Do they stop close to here?
この近くにも停まりますか？

M: Yes, there is a pick-up point in front of the Continental Hotel, just one block from here.
はい、ここから１ブロックのところにあるコンチネンタル・ホテルの前に停留所があります。

F: So, the bus takes you to all the main sightseeing spots?
で、バスに乗れば、すべてのおもな観光スポットに行けるんですか？

M: Yes. The museum, the ruins, the cathedral, the wharf. All the main spots.
はい。美術館、遺跡、大聖堂、埠頭、おもな場所すべてです。

* ruin「遺跡」　cathedral「大聖堂」　wharf「埠頭；桟橋」

F: That sounds fun! How much does it cost?
それは楽しそう！　おいくらかかるんでしょう？

M: There are three different companies, and I think they all charge about the same. Would you like to see the brochures?
会社が３つあるんです。それで、料金はだいたい同じだと思いますよ。パンフレットをご覧になりますか？

* brochure「パンフレット」

F: Yes, please!
ええ、お願いします！

STEP 3 日本語訳を見ながらスキットを演じてみよう。　CD 2-60

F :

屋根のないバスを見かけたんですけど。街のツアーをやってるんですか？

M : Yes, they take you all around. You can get off and get on again as often as you like.

F :

この近くにも停まりますか？

M : Yes, there is a pick-up point in front of the Continental Hotel, just one block from here.

F :

で、バスに乗れば、すべてのおもな観光スポットに行けるんですか？

M : Yes. The museum, the ruins, the cathedral, the wharf. All the main spots.

F :

それは楽しそう！ おいくらかかるんでしょう？

M : There are three different companies, and I think they all charge about the same. Would you like to see the brochures?

F :

ええ、お願いします！

Chapter 3
異文化交流

レベル3 ★★★ ········ p. 255

Unit 121 Christmas クリスマス

STEP 1 各センテンスをシャドーイングしよう。　CD 3-01

STEP 2 テキストを見ながらスキットを演じてみよう。　CD 3-01

F: Christmas is about a month away! Have you started shopping yet?
クリスマスは約1カ月後だよね！ 買い物はもう始めたの？

M: So early? I probably won't even think about shopping for another three weeks.
そんなに早く？ 僕はあと3週間くらいは買い物のことも考えないよ。

F: I'm almost done with mine! I have to buy a bunch of presents.
私はほぼ終わったわよ！ 山ほどプレゼントを買わなきゃならないのよね。
* be done with ...「…を終える」　a bunch of ...「たくさんの…」

M: Really? You only have two kids, right?
そうなの？ 子どもは、ふたりだけだったよね？

F: Yeah, but I have to buy some for my husband, my mom and dad in America, my brother ...
うん、でも夫にもいくつかあげるし、アメリカの父と母、それに弟の分も…

M: Wow, so many presents! I just have to buy one, for my son. Is it common for Americans to buy so many presents?
へえ、すごい量のプレゼントだね！ 僕は息子にひとつだけ買えばいいんだ。アメリカではふつうそんなにたくさんプレゼントを買うの？

F: Yes, it is. People with big families end up buying dozens of presents!
うん、そうよ。大家族だと何十個も買うことになるわよ！
* dozens of ...「何ダースもの…；たくさんの…」

M: Christmas shopping in America sounds like a nightmare! You must all be exhausted by Christmas eve!
アメリカのクリスマスの買い物って悪夢だね！ クリスマス・イヴまでには、みんなヘトヘトでしょ！
* nightmare「悪夢」　exhausted「疲れきった；ヘトヘトの」

F: Believe me, we are!
まさに、そのとおりよ！

異文化交流 ★★★

STEP 3 　日本語訳を見ながらスキットを演じてみよう。　CD 3-01

F: Christmas is about a month away! Have you started shopping yet?

M:

そんなに早く？ 僕はあと3週間くらいは買い物のことも考えないよ。

F: I'm almost done with mine! I have to buy a bunch of presents.

M:

そうなの？ 子どもは、ふたりだけだったよね？

F: Yeah, but I have to buy some for my husband, my mom and dad in America, my brother ...

M:

へえ、すごい量のプレゼントだね！ 僕は息子にひとつだけ買えばいいんだ。アメリカではふつうそんなにたくさんプレゼントを買うの？

F: Yes, it is. People with big families end up buying dozens of presents!

M:

アメリカのクリスマスの買い物って悪夢だね！ クリスマス・イヴまでには、みんなヘトヘトでしょ！

F: Believe me, we are!

Unit 122 Valentine's Day バレンタイン・デー

STEP 1 各センテンスをシャドーイングしよう。　CD 3-02

STEP 2 テキストを見ながらスキットを演じてみよう。　CD 3-02

F: What are all these signs I see everywhere for 'White Day?'
あらゆる場所にたくさんあるこの「ホワイト・デー」っていう看板はなんのためのもの？

M: White Day is March 14th. It's the male version of Valentine's Day.
ホワイト・デーは3月14日だよ。バレンタイン・デーの男性版なんだ。

F: Wait a second! You're going to have to explain that a little better.
ちょっと待って！ もうちょっとちゃんと説明してくれなきゃ。

M: Ha ha, okay. On Valentine's Day women buy chocolate for the men in their lives.
ハハ、わかったよ。バレンタイン・デーには、身近にいる男性たちに、女性がチョコレートを買うんだ。

* men in their lives「自分の生活で身近にいる男性たち」

F: Oh, I see ... so on White Day the men return the favor? Is that it?
へえ、そうか…で、ホワイト・デーには男性がお返しをするのね？ そういうこと？

M: Yes, but guys give sweets. They also buy special presents for their steady girlfriends.
そう、でも男性はスイーツをあげるんだよ。恋人には特別なプレゼントも買うんだよね。

F: Well, that sounds nice! I'd call that a fair trade for some chocolate!
それはいいわね！ チョコレートのフェア・トレードってところね！

* fair trade「公正な貿易・取引」

M: What's Valentine's Day like in America?
アメリカのバレンタインはどうなの？

* What is A like in ...?「…ではAはどんなふう？」

F: In America on Valentine's Day, lovers exchange presents. It doesn't have to be chocolate.
アメリカでは、バレンタイン・デーに、恋人同士がプレゼントを交換するの。チョコレートである必要はないのよ。

M: Ah, that sounds more romantic.
へえ、そっちのほうがロマンチックな感じだね。

異文化交流 ★★★

STEP 3 　日本語訳を見ながらスキットを演じてみよう。　CD 3-02

F : What are all these signs I see everywhere for 'White Day?'

M :

ホワイト・デーは3月14日だよ。バレンタイン・デーの男性版なんだ。

F : Wait a second! You're going to have to explain that a little better.

M :

ハハ、わかったよ。バレンタイン・デーには、身近にいる男性たちに、女性がチョコレートを買うんだ。

F : Oh, I see ... so on White Day the men return the favor? Is that it?

M :

そう、でも男性はスイーツをあげるんだよ。恋人には特別なプレゼントも買うんだよね。

F : Well, that sounds nice! I'd call that a fair trade for some chocolate!

M :

アメリカのバレンタインはどうなの？

F : In America on Valentine's Day, lovers exchange presents. It doesn't have to be chocolate.

M :

へえ、そっちのほうがロマンチックな感じだね。

Unit 123 National Holidays 祝祭日・休日

STEP 1 各センテンスをシャドーイングしよう。　CD 3-03

STEP 2 テキストを見ながらスキットを演じてみよう。　CD 3-03

M: I tried to go to the post office today, but it was closed. Is today a holiday?

今日、郵便局に行こうとしたんだけど、閉まってたんだ。今日は祝日なの？

F: Yes, this is 'Ocean Day.' We have a lot of national holidays in Japan. About one a month.

うん、今日は「海の日」だよ。日本にはたくさん祭日があるのよ。だいたい毎月1回くらいね。

＊ a month「1カ月に」

M: I bet you really like having those days off.

絶対に日本人はそういうお休みが大好きだよね。

F: Well, we work so hard, and our vacations tend to be short. So one way we make up for it is the frequent holidays.

うん、一生懸命働くし、休暇が短いからね。それを補うひとつの方法が、多くの祝日を作ることなのよ。

＊ make up for ...「…を補う；補償する」

M: And do a lot of them fall on Mondays?

で、その多くが月曜に当たるんだよね？

＊ fall on ...「…（曜日など）に当たる」

F: Well, yeah, or Friday, so that people get a three-day weekend.

うん、そうね、あるいは金曜かな。みんなが3連休を取れるようにね。

＊ three-day weekend「3連休」

M: We have a few holidays like that. Labor Day and Memorial Day, for example.

アメリカでもそういう祝日は少しあるよ。例えば、労働祭と戦没者追悼記念日とかね。

F: Yes, plus it seems like you all get two weeks or more vacation time. I'm so jealous!

そうね。それに加えて、あなたたちはみんな2週間とか、それ以上のバケーションがもらえるみたいよね。すごくうらやましいわ！

STEP 3 日本語訳を見ながらスキットを演じてみよう。　CD 3-03

M: I tried to go to the post office today, but it was closed. Is today a holiday?

F:

うん、今日は「海の日」だよ。日本にはたくさん祭日があるのよ。だいたい毎月 1 回くらいね。

M: I bet you really like having those days off.

F:

うん、一生懸命働くし、休暇が短いからね。それを補うひとつの方法が、多くの祝日を作ることなのよ。

M: And do a lot of them fall on Mondays?

F:

うん、そうね、あるいは金曜かな。みんなが 3 連休を取れるようにね。

M: We have a few holidays like that. Labor Day and Memorial Day, for example.

F:

そうね。それに加えて、あなたたちはみんな 2 週間とか、それ以上のバケーションがもらえるみたいよね。すごくうらやましいわ！

Unit 124 Life-work Balance ライフ・ワーク・バランス

STEP 1 各センテンスをシャドーイングしよう。　CD 3-04

STEP 2 テキストを見ながらスキットを演じてみよう。　CD 3-04

F : I hear that it's not unusual for workers in Tokyo to work until midnight! Is that true?

東京の労働者たちは深夜まで働くこともめずらしくないって聞くけど、ホント？

M : Yes, or even later, unfortunately. Some people miss the last train and have to take taxis home.

うん、あるいは、残念ながらもっと遅いこともあるよ。終電を逃してタクシーで帰宅する人もいるし。

* even「までも」 unfortunately「残念ながら；不幸なことだが」

F : Sorry, but that seems wrong to me. Work ends up being your whole life!

悪いけど、それは間違ってると思うわ。結局、仕事が人生のすべてになっちゃうじゃない！

M : Well, it's not like that for everybody, but I see your point. It's different in America?

うーん、みんながみんなそうではないけど、君の言いたいことはわかるよ。アメリカでは違うの？

* it's not like ...「…のようではない」 point「要点；言いたいこと」

F : Yeah, a little different. I would guess most Americans are back home by eight p.m.

うん、ちょっと違うわね。ほとんどのアメリカ人は午後 8 時までには帰宅してると思うわ。

M : That's not fair! But I think outside the big cities in Japan it's the same.

それはずるいなあ！ でも、日本の大都市以外でも、そんな感じだと思うよ。

F : Well, yeah. Isn't that the way it should be? To Americans, life-work balance is very important.

うんそうよ。そうあるべきなんじゃないかな？ アメリカ人にとって、ライフ・ワーク・バランスはとても重要なの。

M : I wish that concept would catch on with Japanese companies. They make people work too hard!

日本の企業にもそのコンセプトが受け入れられるといいんだけどね。日本の企業は社員を働かせすぎてるよ！

* concept「概念；観念」 catch on with ...「…に受け入れられる；理解される」

異文化交流 ★★★

STEP 3 　日本語訳を見ながらスキットを演じてみよう。　CD 3-04

F : I hear that it's not unusual for workers in Tokyo to work until midnight! Is that true?

M :

うん、あるいは、残念ながらもっと遅いこともあるよ。終電を逃してタクシーで帰宅する人もいるし。

F : Sorry, but that seems wrong to me. Work ends up being your whole life!

M :

うーん、みんながみんなそうではないけど、君の言いたいことはわかるよ。アメリカでは違うの？

F : Yeah, a little different. I would guess most Americans are back home by eight p.m.

M :

それはずるいなあ！でも、日本の大都市以外でも、そんな感じだと思うよ。

F : Well, yeah. Isn't that the way it should be? To Americans, life-work balance is very important.

M :

日本の企業にもそのコンセプトが受け入れられるといいんだけどね。日本の企業は社員を働かせすぎてるよ！

Unit 125 Salaryman Lifestyle サラリーマンの生活

STEP 1 各センテンスをシャドーイングしよう。　CD 3-05

STEP 2 テキストを見ながらスキットを演じてみよう。　CD 3-05

M: What is your impression of the Japanese 'salaryman?'

日本の「サラリーマン」の印象はどう？

F: Ha ha! Well, I guess I picture an army of men holding briefcases and walking to work in dark blue suits.

ハハ！ そうね、ブリーフケースを抱えてダーク・ブルーのスーツで歩いて出勤していく男性の軍隊を想像するかなあ。

M: Yeah, I guess that's our image too. But other countries have the same thing, right?

うん、それは日本人の抱くイメージと同じだね。でも、ほかの国も同じなんじゃないの？

F: Well, it's kind of an outdated image for American workers. It's like our image of the 1950s.

うーん、アメリカの労働者にとっては、それは古くさいイメージよ。アメリカの50年代の感じかな。

＊ kind of ... 「なんなく…；ある種…」 outdated「古くさい」

M: In Japan, that image will never change. At least it makes it easy to decide what to wear to work!

日本では、そのイメージは変わらないと思うよ。少なくとも、仕事になにを着ていくか決めるのがかんたんだからね！

F: Hmmm, seems like Japanese business people are very conservative!

ふーん、日本のビジネスマンはかなり保守的みたいね！

＊ conservative「保守的な」

M: We're used to dressing the same. After all, we wore uniforms all through our school years.

日本人は同じ服装をするのに慣れてるんだよ。そもそも、学校ではずっと制服を着てきたからね。

＊ After all, ... 「そもそも…だから」 all through ... 「…の間中ずっと」

F: In America, the 1960s was the turning point. Now, even some executives wear jeans to work!

アメリカでは60年代が転換期だったのよ。いまでは、ジーンズで会社に来る重役もいるのよね！

＊ executive「重役；取締役」

STEP 3 　日本語訳を見ながらスキットを演じてみよう。　CD 3-05

M :

日本の「サラリーマン」の印象はどう？

F : Ha ha! Well, I guess I picture an army of men holding briefcases and walking to work in dark blue suits.

M :

うん、それは日本人の抱くイメージと同じだね。でも、ほかの国も同じなんじゃないの？

F : Well, it's kind of an outdated image for American workers. It's like our image of the 1950s.

M :

日本では、そのイメージは変わらないと思うよ。少なくとも、仕事になにを着ていくか決めるのがかんたんだからね！

F : Hmmm, seems like Japanese business people are very conservative!

M :

日本人は同じ服装をするのに慣れてるんだよ。そもそも、学校ではずっと制服を着てきたからね。

F : In America, the 1960s was the turning point. Now, even some executives wear jeans to work!

Unit 126 Drinking 飲酒

STEP 1 各センテンスをシャドーイングしよう。　CD 3-06

STEP 2 テキストを見ながらスキットを演じてみよう。　CD 3-06

M: Don't Americans go out for drinks with their coworkers very often?
アメリカ人はあまり同僚とお酒を飲みにいかないの？

F: Not all that often. Americans tend to leave in time for dinner on most nights.
そんなに頻繁にはね。アメリカ人はほとんど毎晩、夕食に間に合うように帰る傾向にあるわよ。

M: I see. In Japan, we work late, so a drink or two after work is our way to wind down.
そうか。日本では遅くまで働くから、仕事のあとの1、2杯はリラックスするためのひとつの方法なんだよね。
* wind down「(解放されて) リラックスする」

F: Yeah, when my husband worked for a Japanese company, he did that. And also with customers.
そうね、夫が日本企業で働いていた頃は、そうしていたわね。それと、顧客といっしょにもね。

M: Yes. Taking clients or customers out for drinks is a part of our business culture. But less so recently.
うん、お客さんたちを飲みに連れていくのも、日本のビジネス文化の一部なんだ。でも、最近は減っているよ。

F: Really? Why have things changed?
そうなの？ どうして変わってきているの？

M: Mostly because of budget cuts. And also because it's uncomfortable for some people, especially women.
ほとんどは予算の削減が理由だよ。それに一部の人には居心地がよくないしね。特に女性たちには。
* uncomfortable「不快な」

F: Yes, I can certainly understand that. We have that same problem in the United States, as well.
ええ、それはよくわかるわ。アメリカでも同じ問題があるのよ。
* as well「同様に」

異文化交流 ★★★

STEP 3 　日本語訳を見ながらスキットを演じてみよう。　CD 3-06

M :

アメリカ人はあまり同僚とお酒を飲みにいかないの？

F : Not all that often. Americans tend to leave in time for dinner on most nights.

M :

そうか。日本では遅くまで働くから、仕事のあとの1、2杯はリラックスするためのひとつの方法なんだよね。

F : Yeah, when my husband worked for a Japanese company, he did that. And also with customers.

M :

うん、お客さんたちを飲みに連れていくのも、日本のビジネス文化の一部なんだ。でも、最近は減っているよ。

F : Really? Why have things changed?

M :

ほとんどは予算の削減が理由だよ。それに一部の人には居心地がよくないしね。特に女性たちには。

F : Yes, I can certainly understand that. We have that same problem in the United States, as well.

Unit 127 Radio Exercise ラジオ体操

STEP 1 各センテンスをシャドーイングしよう。 CD 3-07

STEP 2 テキストを見ながらスキットを演じてみよう。 CD 3-07

F : Did you see those people back there? What were they doing?
後ろのあの人たち見た？ みんなで、なにをしていたの？

M : Back in the park? Oh, they were doing calisthenics.
後ろの公園の？ ああ、体操してたんだよ。

＊ calisthenics「(柔軟) 体操」

F : Were they warming up for some game or something?
なにかの試合かなにかのために、ウォーミング・アップとかをしてたのかな？

＊ warm up「(運動の準備に) 体を温める」 ... or something「…かなにか」

M : No, just stretching for fitness. People do that all over Japan. It's called 'radio exercise.'
いやあ、健康のためのただのストレッチだよ。日本中であれをやってるんだよ。「ラジオ体操」っていうんだ。

F : So THAT'S how Japanese stay so fit, huh? It looked like a military drill.
ということは、あれが日本人が健康な秘訣なの？ 軍隊の訓練みたいに見えたけど。

M : It IS similar. Traditional Japanese companies do it too. We Japanese like to do things in groups.
似てはいるよね。歴史の古い日本企業もやっているよ。僕ら日本人はグループでなにかをするのが好きなんだよ。

F : In America lots of people come together in parks to do yoga, so it's kind of similar.
アメリカでは、たくさんの人が集まって公園でヨガをやるわよ。ちょっと似てるかもね。

＊ come together「集まる」

M : Yoga is getting more and more popular here, too. I think 'radio exercise' is more for the older generation.
ヨガは日本でもどんどん人気が出ているよ。「ラジオ体操」は年齢が上の人たち向けだと思うな。

＊ more for ...「もっと…のための；…向きの」 generation「世代」

異文化交流 ★★★

STEP 3 日本語訳を見ながらスキットを演じてみよう。　　CD 3-07

F : Did you see those people back there? What were they doing?

M :

後ろの公園の？ ああ、体操してたんだよ。

F : Were they warming up for some game or something?

M :

いやあ、健康のためのただのストレッチだよ。日本中であれをやってるんだよ。「ラジオ体操」っていうんだ。

F : So THAT'S how Japanese stay so fit, huh? It looked like a military drill.

M :

似てはいるよね。歴史の古い日本企業もやっているよ。僕ら日本人はグループでなにかをするのが好きなんだよ。

F : In America lots of people come together in parks to do yoga, so it's kind of similar.

M :

ヨガは日本でもどんどん人気が出ているよ。「ラジオ体操」は年齢が上の人たち向けだと思うな。

Unit 128 Women in the Workplace 女性と仕事

STEP 1 各センテンスをシャドーイングしよう。　CD 3-08

STEP 2 テキストを見ながらスキットを演じてみよう。　CD 3-08

F: Do women have the same opportunities as men in America, in terms of jobs?

アメリカでは、仕事の面では女性に男性と同じ機会が与えられているの？

＊ same A as B「Bと同じA」　opportunity「機会」　in terms of ...「…の点で」

M: Well, we've made a lot of progress, but still have a long way to go. How about Japan?

うーん、だいぶ進歩はしたけど、まだまだだよ。日本ではどう？

＊ progress「進歩」　still have a long way to go「(達成までの)進むべき道のりはまだ長い」

F: The situation is not very fair. I read that we aren't even in the top 100 countries in terms of equality.

あまり公平ではないわ。男女の平等に関しては、日本はトップ100にも入ってないって、記事で読んだわ。

＊ situation「状況」　fair「公平な」　equality「平等；機会均等」

M: Really? I'm pretty sure America would be pretty close to the top of that list. There are many women CEOs, even of big companies, for example.

そうなの？ きっと、アメリカはそのリストのトップに近いところにいると思うな。例えば、大企業でさえ、女性のCEOがたくさんいるしね。

＊ the top of ...「…の最上位」

F: Executive positions are almost always men in Japan. Unless it's a company that makes products for women.

重役の地位は、日本ではほぼ男性が占めているわ。女性用の製品を作っている会社ででもなければね。

＊ executive position「重役の地位」　almost always「ほとんどいつも」

M: Like I said, America still has inequality. We've never had a woman president, for example. And I'm pretty sure the figure for executives is under 20%.

繰り返しになるけど、アメリカにもまだ不平等はあるよ。例えば、女性の大統領はまだいないんだ。それに、きっと重役の数も20%よりも低いだろうね。

＊ inequality「不平等」　president「大統領」　figure「数字；数値」

異文化交流 ★★★

STEP 3 　日本語訳を見ながらスキットを演じてみよう。　　CD 3-08

F :

アメリカでは、仕事の面では女性に男性と同じ機会が与えられているの？

M : Well, we've made a lot of progress, but still have a long way to go. How about Japan?

F :

あまり公平ではないわ。男女の平等に関しては、日本はトップ100にも入ってないって、記事で読んだわ。

M : Really? I'm pretty sure America would be pretty close to the top of that list. There are many women CEOs, even of big companies, for example.

F :

重役の地位は、日本ではほぼ男性が占めているわ。女性用の製品を作っている会社ででもなければね。

M : Like I said, America still has inequality. We've never had a woman president, for example. And I'm pretty sure the figure for executives is under 20%.

Unit 129 Housework 家事

STEP 1 各センテンスをシャドーイングしよう。　CD 3-09

STEP 2 テキストを見ながらスキットを演じてみよう。　CD 3-09

M: How do you divide up your household chores?
おたくでは、家事はどうやって分担しているの？
* divide up「(分担などを) 分ける」　household chores「家事」

F: Well, unfortunately, my husband doesn't do much. He's old-fashioned that way.
うん、残念ながら、うちの夫はあまりやらないのよ。その点、彼は古くさくって。

M: That IS old-fashioned! You mean he thinks housework is 'women's work?'
ものすごく古くさいよ！ 彼は家事を「女性の仕事」だと思ってるってことなの？

F: Basically, yes. The most he usually does is take the kids out so they won't be in my way while I clean.
基本的にはそうね。いちばんやってくれても、いつも子どもを外に連れ出すくらいよ。子どもが掃除の邪魔にならないようにね。
* so ...「…なように」　while ...「…の間」

M: No fair! Although, in a way I can see how that's helpful.
不公平だよ！ ある意味、それも助けになるのはわかるけど。

F: How about in America? Do most American husbands feel a responsibility to do housework.
アメリカではどうなの？ ほとんどのアメリカの夫は家事をする責任を感じてる？

M: I would say yes, recently. And guys usually do things like mow the lawn, take out trash, fix things, etc.
最近はそうだと思うよ。で、男性はたいてい芝刈りやゴミ出しとか修繕とかをやってるよ。
* I would say ...「…だろうと思う」断言を避ける表現。　things like ...「…といったこと」
　mow the lawn「芝刈りをする」

F: Hardly any Japanese homes have lawns. But my husband would probably expect ME to mow it!
日本の家にはほとんど芝はないわよ。でも、うちの夫は、おそらく私が芝刈りをするのを期待するでしょうね！
* hardly any ...「ほとんど…ない」

異文化交流 ★★★

271

STEP 3 日本語訳を見ながらスキットを演じてみよう。 CD 3-09

M : How do you divide up your household chores?

F :

うん、残念ながら、うちの夫はあまりやらないのよ。その点、彼は古くさくって。

M : That IS old-fashioned! You mean he thinks housework is 'women's work?'

F :

基本的にはそうね。いちばんやってくれても、いつも子どもを外に連れ出すくらいよ。子どもが掃除の邪魔にならないようにね。

M : No fair! Although, in a way I can see how that's helpful.

F :

アメリカではどうなの？ ほとんどのアメリカの夫は家事をする責任を感じてる？

M : I would say yes, recently. And guys usually do things like mow the lawn, take out trash, fix things, etc.

F :

日本の家にはほとんど芝はないわよ。でも、うちの夫は、おそらく私が芝刈りをするのを期待するでしょうね！

Unit 130 College Life 大学生活

STEP 1 各センテンスをシャドーイングしよう。　CD 3-10

STEP 2 テキストを見ながらスキットを演じてみよう。　CD 3-10

F : I heard that many Japanese college students focus more on their circles than on studies. Is that true?

日本の学生の多くが勉強よりもサークルに力を入れているって聞いたけど。ほんとうなの？

* focus on ...「…に打ち込む」

M : Yes, that's pretty common. Japanese universities tend not to make a big deal about attendance and assignments, especially private ones.

うん、けっこう一般的だね。日本の大学は出席や課題などにあまりうるさくない傾向があるんだ。特に私立大学はね。

F : But I thought Japanese people studied all the time.

でも、私は日本人はいつも勉強しているものだと思ってたわ。

M : Not exactly. College for us is sort of like an oasis. It's a period in our life where we get to play, and discover ourselves more.

そうでもないよ。僕らにとって大学は一種のオアシスなんだ。遊んだり自分のことをもっと知ったりするチャンスがある時期なんだよ。

* sort of like ...「ある種…のような」　oasis「オアシス」　get to ...「…する機会がある」
  discover「発見する」

F : I see. I guess that's true for some American students as well. Some study hard, but others don't.

そうなんだ。アメリカの学生にも同じような人たちはいるかもね。懸命に勉強する人もいるし、そうでもない人もいるわ。

* as well「同様に」

M : One thing is that in Japan, parents are generally expected to pay for college tuition. So students don't take their studies as seriously.

日本では、概して両親が大学の学費を払ってくれると考えられているのもあるかな。だから、学生は学業をそれほど真剣に考えないんd。

* be expected to ...「…することを期待される」　college tuition「大学の学費」

F : I think it's a good thing that many Americans put themselves through school.

アメリカ人の多くが自力で学校を卒業するのはいいことだと思うわね。

* put oneself through ...「自力で…を卒業する」

異文化交流 ★★★

STEP 3　日本語訳を見ながらスキットを演じてみよう。　CD 3-10

F: I heard that many Japanese college students focus more on their circles than on studies. Is that true?

M:

うん、けっこう一般的だね。日本の大学は出席や課題などにあまりうるさくない傾向があるんだ。特に私立大学はね。

F: But I thought Japanese people studied all the time.

M:

そうでもないよ。僕らにとって大学は一種のオアシスなんだ。遊んだり自分のことをもっと知ったりするチャンスがある時期なんだよ。

F: I see. I guess that's true for some American students as well. Some study hard, but others don't.

M:

日本では、概して両親が大学の学費を払ってくれると考えられているのもあるかな。だから、学生は学業をそれほど真剣に考えないんだ。

F: I think it's a good thing that many Americans put themselves through school.

Unit 131 Adult Education 生涯教育

STEP 1 各センテンスをシャドーイングしよう。　CD 3-11

STEP 2 テキストを見ながらスキットを演じてみよう。　CD 3-11

M: I have three American friends who are back in college.
大学に戻ってるアメリカ人の友人が3人いるんだよね。

F: Furthering one's education is very common in the States. How about in Japan?
アメリカでは、自分の教育をさらに深めるのは一般的なのよ。日本はどうなの？

M: It's not common at all. You never see an older person in a college classroom.
まったく一般的ではないね。大学の教室では年齢が上の人は見かけないよ。

F: Don't Japanese people believe in lifelong education?
日本人は生涯教育の価値を認めていないの？

M: Well, in Japan once you join the business world, you pretty much feel like you should stay there.
うーん、日本ではいったんビジネスの世界に入ると、けっこうそこに留まるべきだって感じるんだよね。

F: That's a different attitude than America. Going back for a new degree is a common option.
アメリカ人とは違った姿勢ね。新しい学位のために大学に戻ることが一般的な選択肢よ。

＊ attitude「姿勢；態度；判断」　degree「学位」　option「選択肢」

M: Japanese adults would feel too embarrassed to sit in a classroom with a bunch of kids.
日本の大人は、大勢の子どもたちといっしょにクラスにいるのがとても決まりが悪く感じるんだろうね。

＊ embarrassed「決まりの悪い；恥ずかしい」　bunch of ...「たくさんの…」

F: In America, it is so common that there is nothing to be embarrassed about.
アメリカでは、ものすごくふつうだから、恥ずかしがることなんか全然ないのよね。

＊ there is nothing to ...「…することはなにもない」

M: I wonder if Japan will become like that. Frankly, I don't see that happening.
日本はそんなふうになるかなあ？ 正直、それはなさそうだなあ。

＊ I don't see that happening.「そうはならないだろうね」直訳は「それが将来的に起こるのを私は見ない」。

異文化交流 ★★★

STEP 3 　日本語訳を見ながらスキットを演じてみよう。　CD 3-11

M :

大学に戻ってるアメリカ人の友人が3人いるんだよね。

F : Furthering one's education is very common in the States. How about in Japan?

M :

まったく一般的ではないね。大学の教室では年齢が上の人は見かけないよ。

F : Don't Japanese people believe in lifelong education?

M :

うーん、日本ではいったんビジネスの世界に入ると、けっこうそこに留まるべきだって感じるんだよね。

F : That's a different attitude than America. Going back for a new degree is a common option.

M :

日本の大人は、大勢の子どもたちといっしょにクラスにいるのがとても決まりが悪く感じるんだろうね。

F : In America, it is so common that there is nothing to be embarrassed about.

M :

日本はそんなふうになるかなあ？ 正直、それはなさそうだなあ。

Unit 132 Uniforms 制服

STEP 1 各センテンスをシャドーイングしよう。　CD 3-12

STEP 2 テキストを見ながらスキットを演じてみよう。　CD 3-12

F : My silly daughter actually said her uniform is the main reason she chose her high school!

実は、うちのバカ娘がね、高校を選んだいちばんの理由が制服なんだって言ってたの。

M : You're ... kidding, right?

冗談だよね？

F : No, it's true! Uniforms are a huge thing for junior-high and high school girls. They want to look cute.

いいえ、ホントのことよ！ 女子中高生は制服にすごく関心が強いの。かわいく見せたいのよね。

M : How funny! Do all the schools require uniforms?

変なの！ どの学校でも制服が必要なの？

F : Basically, except for Tokyo's public schools. How about in the States?

東京の公立校を除いて、基本的にはね。アメリカではどうなの？

M : Only a few exclusive schools make kids wear uniforms. But I don't think kids particularly like them.

子どもに制服を着せるのは、ほんの一部の有名校だけだよ。でも、子どもたちが特にそれを好きだとは思わないけど。

* exclusive「特権階級に限定された」　particularly「特別に；特に」

F : Well, in Japan, even a lot of companies have uniforms for their non-service employees.

うん、日本では、会社の多くでも、非サービス部門の社員には制服があるのよ。

* even ...「…でさえ」　non-service「非サービス（部門）の」

M : Fascinating. I guess it helps you feel like part of a team, then?

それは、おもしろいね。そうすると、チームの一員になったような感じがするんでしょ？

* fascinating「(話などが) おもしろい」
  help someone feel like ...「(人) が…のように感じるのに役立つ」

F : It depends on the person. Some people don't like them. But at least it keeps cleaning bills down.

それは人によるわよ。好きじゃない人もいるしね。でも、少なくとも、クリーニング代は抑えられるわね。

異文化交流 ★★★

STEP 3 日本語訳を見ながらスキットを演じてみよう。　CD 3-12

F :
実は、うちのバカ娘がね、高校を選んだいちばんの理由が制服なんだって言ってたの。

M : You're ... kidding, right?

F :
いいえ、ホントのことよ！ 女子中高生は制服にすごく関心が強いの。かわいく見せたいのよね。

M : How funny! Do all the schools require uniforms?

F :
東京の公立校を除いて、基本的にはね。アメリカではどうなの？

M : Only a few exclusive schools make kids wear uniforms. But I don't think kids particularly like them.

F :
うん、日本では、会社の多くでも、非サービス部門の社員には制服があるのよ。

M : Fascinating. I guess it helps you feel like part of a team, then?

F :
それは人によるわよ。好きじゃない人もいるしね。でも、少なくとも、クリーニング代は抑えられるわね。

Unit 133 Public Transportation 公共交通機関

STEP 1 各センテンスをシャドーイングしよう。　CD 3-13

STEP 2 テキストを見ながらスキットを演じてみよう。　CD 3-13

M: In Tokyo you can take a train to anyplace you want to go! It's great! Are other Japanese cities like this too?

東京では、どこでも行きたいところに電車に乗っていけるね！　すばらしいよ！　ほかの日本の都市もこんな感じなの？

＊ to anyplace「どこにでも」

F: Well, Tokyo has the most public transportation, but all major cities here have trains or subways.

うーん、公共交通機関は東京がいちばん発達してるけど、すべての大都市に電車や地下鉄があるわ。

＊ public transportation「公共交通機関」

M: That's really cool. In America maybe only two or three cities have decent public transportation.

すごいよね。アメリカでは、おそらく2、3の都市にしか、ちゃんとした公共交通機関がないよ。

＊ decent「ちゃんとした」

F: I heard that if you live in Los Angeles you can't go anywhere without a car.

もし、ロサンゼルスに住んでいたら、自動車がないとどこにも行けないって聞いたわ。

＊ not ... anywhere「どこにも…ない」　without ...「…なしでは」

M: It's true! But most American cities are like that. You need a car for just about everything you do.

そうなんだよ！　でもほとんどのアメリカの都市はそんなふうだよ。やることのほとんど全部に自動車が必要なんだ。

＊ just about everything「ほとんどすべてのこと」

F: In Japanese cities, if you live near a station, you can get most things you need in your own neighborhood.

日本の都会では、駅の近くに住んでいれば、近所を回れば必要な物がほとんど手に入るわよ。

M: That must be really nice. We don't really have anything like that. I wish we did.

それはいいだろうね。アメリカではそんなこと全然ないよ。そうだったらいいのになあ。

異文化交流 ★★★

279

STEP 3　日本語訳を見ながらスキットを演じてみよう。　CD 3-13

M: In Tokyo you can take a train to anyplace you want to go! It's great! Are other Japanese cities like this too?

F:

うーん、公共交通機関は東京がいちばん発達してるけど、すべての大都市に電車や地下鉄があるわ。

M: That's really cool. In America maybe only two or three cities have decent public transportation.

F:

もし、ロサンゼルスに住んでいたら、自動車がないとどこにも行けないって聞いたわ。

M: It's true! But most American cities are like that. You need a car for just about everything you do.

F:

日本の都会では、駅の近くに住んでいれば、近所を回れば必要な物がほとんど手に入るわよ。

M: That must be really nice. We don't really have anything like that. I wish we did.

Unit 134　Cars　自動車

STEP 1　各センテンスをシャドーイングしよう。　CD 3-14

STEP 2　テキストを見ながらスキットを演じてみよう。　CD 3-14

M: I think Japanese people must wash their cars every other day!

日本人は 2 日に 1 回、自動車を洗ってるに違いないよね！

＊ every other day「1 日おきに」

F: Not quite. But it's considered very shameful to drive around in a dirty car.

そこまでじゃないわ。でも、汚い自動車で走り回るのは、恥ずかしいことだと考えられてるわね。

＊ not quite「必ずしも…ではない；完全には…ではない」

M: And the cars all look so new. I never see anyone driving around in an old clunker.

それに、自動車は全部すごく新しく見えるよ。ポンコツに乗って走ってる人なんて見たこともないよ。

＊ clunker「おんぼろ車」

F: That's true. Japanese, especially men, love cars, and take pride in them.

そうね。日本人、特に男性は自動車が大好きで、誇りをもってるの。

＊ especially「特に」　take pride in ...「…に誇りをもつ」

M: That's interesting. You have a lot of really big car companies.

それは興味深いね。日本にはたくさん大手の自動車会社があるよね。

F: Yes, and also many Japanese don't have big homes that we can show off and care for. So taking good care of your car is a good 'subsitute.'

ええ、それに多くの日本人は、自慢したり大事にするための大きな家を持ってないのよ。だから、自分の車を大事にするのが、ちょうどいい代用になるの。

＊ show off「自慢する；見せびらかす」　subsitute「代用（品）」

M: I see! Of course, some Americans are the same way, but some people seem to never clean their cars!

そうか！ もちろん、アメリカ人にも同じような人はいるけど、決して自動車を洗わない感じの人もいるんだよね！

＊ clean「掃除する」

STEP 3 　日本語訳を見ながらスキットを演じてみよう。　CD 3-14

M: I think Japanese people must wash their cars every other day!

F:

そこまでじゃないわ。でも、汚い自動車で走り回るのは、恥ずかしいことだと考えられてるわね。

M: And the cars all look so new. I never see anyone driving around in an old clunker.

F:

そうね。日本人、特に男性は自動車が大好きで、誇りをもってるの。

M: That's interesting. You have a lot of really big car companies.

F:

ええ、それに多くの日本人は、自慢したり大事にするための大きな家を持ってないのよ。だから、自分の車を大事にするのが、ちょうどいい代用になるの。

M: I see! Of course, some Americans are the same way, but some people seem to never clean their cars!

Unit 135 Announcement 街角の放送

STEP 1 各センテンスをシャドーイングしよう。 CD 3-15

STEP 2 テキストを見ながらスキットを演じてみよう。 CD 3-15

F: In my neighborhood in Tokyo, it seemed like there were always trucks driving around with speakers on top!

うちの東京の近隣では、いつも屋根にスピーカーをつけたトラックが走り回っていたように思うわ。

* it seemed like ...「…のように思えた」 with speakers on top「屋根の上にスピーカーをつけて」

M: Ha ha, yes! Japanese neighborhoods can get pretty noisy, I guess!

ハハ、そうだね！ 日本の住宅街はけっこううるさくなることがあるかもね！

F: American suburban neighborhoods are much more quiet.

アメリカの郊外の住宅地はずっと静かよ。

M: In Japan, trucks go around collecting appliances people don't want, or selling hot sweet potatoes.

日本では、いらなくなった器具を集めたり、石焼き芋を売ったりしながら、トラックが走り回ってるんだ。

F: Ah, yes, I remember the sweet potatoes! It was like a song.

そうそう、サツマイモは覚えているわ！ 歌みたいだったわ。

M: Yes, that's right. And there are also politicians going around during election season.

うん、そのとおり。それに、選挙シーズンには政治家もぐるぐる回っているよ。

* politician「政治家」 during election season「選挙期間中」

F: Yes! Those were the worst! They just go around shouting out their names again and again!

そうよ！ あれは最悪だった！ ただ何度も自分の名前を叫びながら回るのよね！

M: I agree that it's very annoying. And of course, there are all the announcements on trains.

とてもうっとうしいのは認めるよ。それに、もちろん、電車でもさんざん放送が流れるんだよね。

F: I like those! I would have been lost without them!

それは好きよ！ 車内放送がなければ、迷っちゃってたと思うわ！

* would have been lost「迷っていただろう」仮定法過去完了。過去の事実に反する想像を表す。

STEP 3 　日本語訳を見ながらスキットを演じてみよう。　CD 3-15

F: In my neighborhood in Tokyo, it seemed like there were always trucks driving around with speakers on top!

M:

ハハ、そうだね！日本の住宅街はけっこううるさくなることがあるかもね！

F: American suburban neighborhoods are much more quiet.

M:

日本では、いらなくなった器具を集めたり、石焼き芋を売ったりしながら、トラックが走り回ってるんだ。

F: Ah, yes, I remember the sweet potatoes! It was like a song.

M:

うん、そのとおり。それに、選挙シーズンには政治家もぐるぐる回っているよ。

F: Yes! Those were the worst! They just go around shouting out their names again and again!

M:

とてもうっとうしいのは認めるよ。それに、もちろん、電車でもさんざん放送が流れるんだよね。

F: I like those! I would have been lost without them!

Unit 136 混雑と渋滞
Crowded Trains and Traffic Jams

STEP 1 各センテンスをシャドーイングしよう。　CD 3-16

STEP 2 テキストを見ながらスキットを演じてみよう。　CD 3-16

F: On today's rush hour train, I felt like one more person would have made the train explode!

今日のラッシュ・アワーの電車は、もうひとり乗っかると電車が爆発するかもって感じたわ！

M: Oh, gosh, that sounds awful! How do people stand it?

ああ、それはひどいね！　どうしてみんな我慢できるの？

* Oh, gosh.「それはひどい」gosh は god への言及を避けるための単語。　stand「我慢する」

F: We just get used to it, even though we hate it! Even Japanese outside of Tokyo are shocked when they experience it.

単に慣れているだけよ。でも、大嫌いだけどね！　東京の外から来る日本人も、体験するとショックを受けるわ。

M: New York subways get crowded too, but not as bad. What WE hate with a passion is getting stuck in traffic!

ニューヨークの地下鉄も混雑するけど、それほどひどくはないよ。僕らがホントに嫌いなのは、交通渋滞に巻き込まれることさ。

* with a passion「(怒りなどの)激情をもって」　get stuck in traffic「渋滞にはまる」

F: Traffic jams are a problem in Japan, too. But I guess they are more a feature of American commuting?

渋滞は日本でも問題よ。でも、渋滞は日本よりもアメリカの通勤の特色でしょう？

* feature「特徴；特色」　commuting「通勤」

M: I think so. Every major city has to deal with them. Delays from accidents or road damage happen a lot, and then your car just crawls. It is so frustrating!

そうだと思うよ。どの大都市も取り組まなければいけない問題だよ。事故や道路の破損による遅れがたくさん起こるんだよ。で、車はのろのろ運転さ。ホントにイライラするよ！

* deal with ...「…に対処する」　crawl「のろのろ進む」　frustrating「イライラさせる」

F: But at least in your car, you have your own space.

でも少なくとも車に乗っていれば、自分のスペースはあるわよね。

M: Yeah, that's true.

まあ、それはそうだね。

異文化交流 ★★★

STEP 3 日本語訳を見ながらスキットを演じてみよう。 CD 3-16

F : [　　　　　　　　　　　　　　　　　　　　]

今日のラッシュ・アワーの電車は、もうひとり乗っかると電車が爆発するかもって感じたわ！

M : Oh, gosh, that sounds awful! How do people stand it?

F : [　　　　　　　　　　　　　　　　　　　　]

単に慣れているだけよ。でも、大嫌いだけどね！ 東京の外から来る日本人も、体験するとショックを受けるわ。

M : New York subways get crowded too, but not as bad. What WE hate with a passion is getting stuck in traffic!

F : [　　　　　　　　　　　　　　　　　　　　]

渋滞は日本でも問題よ。でも、渋滞は日本よりもアメリカの通勤の特色でしょう？

M : I think so. Every major city has to deal with them. Delays from accidents or road damage happen a lot, and then your car just crawls. It is so frustrating!

F : [　　　　　　　　　　　　　　　　　　　　]

でも少なくとも車に乗っていれば、自分のスペースはあるわよね。

M : Yeah, that's true.

Unit 137　Streets　街路

STEP 1 　各センテンスをシャドーイングしよう。　CD 3-17

STEP 2 　テキストを見ながらスキットを演じてみよう。　CD 3-17

F : I often see foreigners taking pictures or videos of the big crossing in Shibuya.

渋谷の大きな交差点を写真やビデオに撮っている外国人をよく見かけるわ。

M : Yeah, we are fascinated by it! A giant sea of people coming together and then moving apart!

うん、魅了されちゃうんだよね！　人の大きな波が集まってきて、そして離れていくんだもん！

＊ sea of people「人の海」　come together and move apart「集合・離散する」

F : Don't you have anything similar in America?

アメリカには似たものはないの？

M : Actually, I don't think so. Those scramble crossings aren't common because our cities are built on grids.

うーん、ないんじゃないかと思うな。アメリカの都市は碁盤の目の上にできているから、スクランブル交差点は一般的じゃないんだよ。

＊ be built on grids「碁盤の目の上に建てられている」受動態表現。

F : Some of ours are too, like Kyoto and Sapporo. But Tokyo has lots of those kinds of crossings.

日本のいくつかの都市もそうよ。京都とか札幌とか。でも、東京にはああいった交差点がたくさんあるわ。

M : In American suburbs, we have lots of 'cul-de-sacs.' That's a street off a main road that goes in a loop.

アメリカの郊外には、たくさんの袋小路があるよ。主要な道路から外れたループ状の通りなんだよ。

＊ suburbs「郊外」　cul-de-sac「袋小路」　off a main road「メインの道路を離れた」

F : That's interesting. What's the point of a street like that?

おもしろいわね。そういった通りをどうして作ってるの？

M : Well, the street is lined with a group of houses or condos. It's like a little village.

通りには家やマンションのグループが並んでいるんだけど、それが小さな村みたいな感じなんだよ。

＊ condo「分譲マンション」

異文化交流 ★★★

STEP 3　日本語訳を見ながらスキットを演じてみよう。　CD 3-17

F:
渋谷の大きな交差点を写真やビデオに撮っている外国人をよく見かけるわ。

M: Yeah, we are fascinated by it! A giant sea of people coming together and then moving apart!

F:
アメリカには似たものはないの？

M: Actually, I don't think so. Those scramble crossings aren't common because our cities are built on grids.

F:
日本のいくつかの都市もそうよ。京都とか札幌とか。でも、東京にはああいった交差点がたくさんあるわ。

M: In American suburbs, we have lots of 'cul-de-sacs.' That's a street off a main road that goes in a loop.

F:
おもしろいわね。そういった通りをどうして作ってるの？

M: Well, the street is lined with a group of houses or condos. It's like a little village.

Unit 138 エアコンとヒーター
Home AC and Heating Devices

STEP 1 各センテンスをシャドーイングしよう。　CD 3-18

STEP 2 テキストを見ながらスキットを演じてみよう。　CD 3-18

M: I come from way up north in America, but I feel colder in Japan than back home!
アメリカのかなり北の方から来たんだけど、家よりも日本のほうが寒く感じるよ！
* way up north「かなり北方」　colder than ...「…より寒い」

F: Really? Why?
そうなの？どうして？

M: Because my room takes so long to get warm. Why do they put those things near the ceiling?
だって、部屋が暖まるのに、かなりの時間がかかるんだよ。どうして、エアコンを天井近くに取りつけちゃうんだろう？

F: We put them where they don't take up space.
日本では、場所を取らないところに取りつけてるだけよ。
* take up space「場所を取る」

M: Yeah, but don't you realize that heat flows UP?
うん、でも君たちは熱が上に流れるってことを知らないのかい？

F: Well, they have fans that blow the air down, but I know what you mean.
うーん、機械には空気を下に吹かせるファンがついているんだけど、あなたの言いたいこともわからなくはないわ。
* fan「羽根」　blow the air down「空気を下に吹きつける」

M: Most American homes have a central heating system.
ほとんどのアメリカの家にはセントラル・ヒーティングがついているんだよね。

F: Hokkaido is like that. But in Tokyo we have the units that blow warm AND cool air.
北海道はそんな感じよ。でも、東京では、暖かい空気と冷たい空気を出す機械があるのよね。

M: So interesting. Back home, we have separate units for AC in the summer.
おもしろいね。アメリカでは、夏には空調のための別の機械があるんだよ。
* back home「故郷では」　separate「分かれた；分離した」　AC = air conditioning「空調」

F: It must be really nice to have so much space in your homes!
家にたくさんスペースがあるっていうのは、きっとすごくいいでしょうね！

異文化交流 ★★★

STEP 3 　日本語訳を見ながらスキットを演じてみよう。　CD 3-18

M: I come from way up north in America, but I feel colder in Japan than back home!

F:

そうなの？ どうして？

M: Because my room takes so long to get warm. Why do they put those things near the ceiling?

F:

日本では、場所を取らないところに取りつけてるだけよ。

M: Yeah, but don't you realize that heat flows UP?

F:

うーん、機械には空気を下に吹かせるファンがついているんだけど、あなたの言いたいこともわからなくはないわ。

M: Most American homes have a central heating system.

F:

北海道はそんな感じよ。でも、東京では、暖かい空気と冷たい空気を出す機械があるのよね。

M: So interesting. Back home, we have separate units for AC in the summer.

F:

家にたくさんスペースがあるっていうのは、きっとすごくいいでしょうね！

Unit 139 Hobbies 趣味

STEP 1 各センテンスをシャドーイングしよう。　CD 3-19

STEP 2 テキストを見ながらスキットを演じてみよう。　CD 3-19

M : It seems like Japanese people really take their hobbies seriously!
日本人は趣味をとても真剣に捉えているようだよね！
* take ... seriously「…を真剣に受け取る；考える」

F : What do you mean, exactly?
厳密にはどういう意味で言ってるの？

M : Well, for example, the cyclists in my neighborhood all dress like they're in the Tour de France!
うん、例えばね、うちの近所で自転車に乗ってる人はみんなツール・ド・フランスに出ているような服装なんだよ！

F : Ha ha! Oh, I see. Yeah, I notice how Americans are much more casual about such things.
ハハ！ そうよね。アメリカ人は、そういうことに関しては、はるかに無頓着よね。
* casual「カジュアルな；無頓着な」

M : Yeah, we just put on shorts and a T-shirt! Why do you think it's so important in your culture?
うん、僕らは半ズボンとTシャツを着るだけさ！ どうして日本文化ではそんなに重要なのかな？

F : I think it's because of our traditional 'hobbies,' like tea ceremony. We feel that when doing something, there is a 'right' way to do it.
茶道のような伝統的な趣味が理由だと思うわ。私たちは、なにかをするときには、それを行う作法があると感じるのよ。

M : Hmmm ... so you mean, even when doing western hobbies, there is a kind of formality involved?
ふーーん…で、君の意見では、西洋の趣味をやるときにも、ある種の作法が入り込んでくるということなんだね？
* even when ...「…のときでさえ」　formality「形式；作法」　involved「入り込んで」

F : Yes. We love having fun, but it's not like we're just 'goofing off.'
ええ。私たちは楽しむのが好きだけど、それは適当にやるだけって感じではないのよ。
* goof off「適当にやって時間を無駄に使う；ふざける；怠ける；遊ぶ」

異文化交流 ★★★

STEP 3 　　日本語訳を見ながらスキットを演じてみよう。　　CD 3-19

M: It seems like Japanese people really take their hobbies seriously!

F:

厳密にはどういう意味で言ってるの？

M: Well, for example, the cyclists in my neighborhood all dress like they're in the Tour de France!

F:

ハハ！そうよね。アメリカ人は、そういうことに関しては、はるかに無頓着よね。

M: Yeah, we just put on shorts and a T-shirt! Why do you think it's so important in your culture?

F:

茶道のような伝統的な趣味が理由だと思うわ。私たちは、なにかをするときには、それを行う作法があると感じるのよ。

M: Hmmm ... so you mean, even when doing western hobbies, there is a kind of formality involved?

F:

ええ。私たちは楽しむのが好きだけど、それは適当にやるだけって感じではないのよ。

Unit 140 Pro Sports プロ・スポーツ

STEP 1 各センテンスをシャドーイングしよう。　CD 3-20

STEP 2 テキストを見ながらスキットを演じてみよう。　CD 3-20

F: I don't like Major League baseball! I wish you would stop stealing our best players!

私はメジャー・リーグの野球が好きじゃないわ！ アメリカが、日本のいい選手たちを盗まなければいいのに！

* Major League「メジャー・リーグ」　steal「盗む」

M: Ha ha! It's hardly 'stealing.' You need to pay your guys better!

ハハ！「盗み」なんてほど遠いよ。日本は、もっと報酬を出さなきゃダメだよ！

* hardly「ほとんど…ではない」　guy「男性；人」ここでは選手を指す。

F: Our players make a lot of money. They just want to prove themselves at a higher level.

日本でも選手はたくさん稼いでいるわ。選手たちは高いレベルで自分の力を試したいだけよ。

* prove oneself「自分の力量を証明する」

M: I agree, but the pay scale IS a factor. It's crazy how much American pro athletes make.

そうだね。でも、報酬の規模も一因ではあるよ。アメリカのプロ運動選手が稼ぐ額はまともじゃないんだ。

F: Why is that? Where does all that money come from?

どうしてそうなってるの？ そんなにたくさんのお金がどこから出てくるのよ？

M: Sports are huge in America. Companies pay millions to advertise during big games.

アメリカのスポーツ産業は巨大なんだよ。大きな試合で宣伝するために、企業は何百万も支払うのさ。

F: Japanese like pro sports too. But it's mostly baseball, and recently soccer.

日本人もプロ・スポーツは好きよ。でも、ほとんどは野球よ、最近はサッカーもだけど。

M: In America, some cities have pro teams playing baseball, football, basketball and hockey.

アメリカでは、いくつかの都市は、野球とアメフト、バスケットにホッケーのプロ・チームをもっているよ。

F: Wow, Americans really are sports crazy!

うひゃ〜、アメリカ人って、ホントにスポーツ超大好き国民よね！

異文化交流 ★★★

STEP 3 日本語訳を見ながらスキットを演じてみよう。 CD 3-20

F :

私はメジャー・リーグの野球が好きじゃないわ！ アメリカが、日本のいい選手たちを盗まなければいいのに！

M : Ha ha! It's hardly 'stealing.' You need to pay your guys better!

F :

日本でも選手はたくさん稼いでいるわ。選手たちは高いレベルで自分の力を試したいだけよ。

M : I agree, but the pay scale IS a factor. It's crazy how much American pro athletes make.

F :

どうしてそうなってるの？ そんなにたくさんのお金がどこから出てくるのよ？

M : Sports are huge in America. Companies pay millions to advertise during big games.

F :

日本人もプロ・スポーツは好きよ。でも、ほとんどは野球よ、最近はサッカーもだけど。

M : In America, some cities have pro teams playing baseball, football, basketball and hockey.

F :

うひゃ〜、アメリカ人って、ホントにスポーツ超大好き国民よね！

Unit 141 Animation アニメ

STEP 1 各センテンスをシャドーイングしよう。　CD 3-21

STEP 2 テキストを見ながらスキットを演じてみよう。　CD 3-21

M: Like many Americans, I love Japanese animation! Is American animation popular in Japan?

アメリカ人の多くと同じで、僕は日本のアニメが大好きなんだ！ アメリカのアニメは日本では人気がある？

F: Only the movies. I've never seen American animated TV programs.

映画だけね。アメリカのアニメのテレビ番組は観たことがないわ。

*animated TV program「アニメのテレビ番組」

M: In America, the TV shows are done on a cheap budget for kids.

アメリカでは、テレビ番組は、子ども向けに安い予算で作られているんだよ。

*on a cheap budget「低予算で」

F: In Japan, the technical quality is very important. I think it's one of the industries where we still lead the world.

日本では、技術的なクオリティーがすごく重要ね。アニメは、まだ、世界をリードしている産業のひとつだと思うわ。

M: Maybe it's the audience. In America, cartoons are pretty much limited to kids.

たぶん視聴者の問題だね。アメリカでは、マンガはかなり子どもたち限定だから。

*audience「(テレビの) 視聴者；聴衆」

F: Yeah, whereas in Japan it's one of our most important art forms.

うん、一方、日本では重要な芸術形式のひとつになっているわ。

*whereas「一方」

M: Yes, they are beautiful! Many have become popular in the States.

そうだね、すごくきれいだよね！ たくさんの作品がアメリカでも有名になったよ。

F: I always feel proud when I hear that a Japanese animated film has won an international award!

日本のアニメ映画が国際的な賞を受賞したと聞くと、いつも誇りに感じるのよね。

異文化交流 ★★★

STEP 3 日本語訳を見ながらスキットを演じてみよう。 CD 3-21

M : Like many Americans, I love Japanese animation! Is American animation popular in Japan?

F :

映画だけね。アメリカのアニメのテレビ番組は観たことがないわ。

M : In America, the TV shows are done on a cheap budget for kids.

F :

日本では、技術的なクオリティーがすごく重要ね。アニメは、まだ、世界をリードしている産業のひとつだと思うわ。

M : Maybe it's the audience. In America, cartoons are pretty much limited to kids.

F :

うん、一方、日本では重要な芸術形式のひとつになっているわ。

M : Yes, they are beautiful! Many have become popular in the States.

F :

日本のアニメ映画が国際的な賞を受賞したと聞くと、いつも誇りに感じるのよね。

Unit 142 Movies 映画

STEP 1 各センテンスをシャドーイングしよう。　CD 3-22

STEP 2 テキストを見ながらスキットを演じてみよう。　CD 3-22

F : It seems like all American movies are big budget action movies with explosions!
アメリカの映画は全部、大規模な予算で爆破だらけのアクション映画ばかりみたいだよね！
* big budget「大規模な予算」　explosions「爆発」

M : We have a lot of kinds of movies! But the action ones are the most popular, so they come to Japan.
いろいろな種類の映画があるよ！　でも、アクションものがいちばん人気なんだ。だからそれが日本に来るんだよ。
* a lot of kinds of ...「多種多様な…」

F : It seems like Americans really love to watch things blow up and get destroyed!
アメリカ人って、物が爆発して破壊されるのを観るのがホントに大好きみたいだわ。

M : That sounds funny! After all, it was Japan that created the Godzilla movies!
それはおかしいよ！　だって、そもそもゴジラ映画を作ったのは日本だったじゃないの！
* funny「変な；おかしな」　After all, ...「だってそもそも…だよね」

F : True, but we don't make very many movies like that anymore. Most of our movies are romances and dramas.
そうね、でも、日本ではああいった映画はもうあまり作ってないわ。日本映画のほとんどはロマンスやドラマチックな映画よ。
* not ... anymore「もはや…ない」　most of ...「…のほとんど」

M : We make those kinds of movies too! The problem is that in America, the biggest audience for movies is teenagers.
アメリカでもそういう映画を作ってはいるよ！　問題は、アメリカでは映画の最大の観客が10代の若者だってことさ。

F : I see. And of course they love all the action and special effects.
そうか。それで、もちろん彼らはアクションや特撮だらけの映画が好きなのよね。

異文化交流 ★★★

297

STEP 3 日本語訳を見ながらスキットを演じてみよう。 CD 3-22

F :

アメリカの映画は全部、大規模な予算で爆破だらけのアクション映画ばかりみたいだよね！

M : We have a lot of kinds of movies! But the action ones are the most popular, so they come to Japan.

F :

アメリカ人って、物が爆発して破壊されるのを観るのがホントに大好きみたいだわ。

M : That sounds funny! After all, it was Japan that created the Godzilla movies!

F :

そうね、でも、日本ではああいった映画はもうあまり作ってないわ。日本映画のほとんどはロマンスやドラマチックな映画よ。

M : We make those kinds of movies too! The problem is that in America, the biggest audience for movies is teenagers.

F :

そうか。それで、もちろん彼らはアクションや特撮だらけの映画が好きなのよね。

Unit 143 Fashion ファッション

STEP 1 各センテンスをシャドーイングしよう。 CD 3-23

STEP 2 テキストを見ながらスキットを演じてみよう。 CD 3-23

F: Department stores in Tokyo have really nice fashion things for men! Lots of designer brands!
東京のデパートにはホントにいい男性ファッションの品物が置いてあるよね。すごい数のデザイナー・ブランドがあるし！

M: Don't you have those in American stores?
アメリカのお店にはそういうものはないの？

F: Not so many. There isn't as much demand. Americans in general, and especially men, dress very casually.
そんなに多くはないわ。あまり需要がないからね。一般的にアメリカ人、特に男性はとてもカジュアルな服装なのよ。
* demand「需要」

M: But what about for parties and concerts and things? Don't you dress up?
でも、パーティーやコンサートとかはどうなの？ ドレス・アップしないわけ？
* ... and things「…など；…とか」 dress up「着飾る；ドレス・アップする」

F: Not that much, to be honest. For guys, a pullover sweater and slacks is pretty much the whole deal!
正直、それほどはね。男性には、プルオーバーのセーターとスラックスがほぼすべてなのよ！
* pretty much the whole deal「ほぼ全部」直訳は「ほぼすべての取引」。

M: That seems kind of boring. In Japanese cities, lots of women AND men take fashion pretty seriously.
それは、なんだかつまらないね。日本の都会では、多くの女性に加えて男性もファッションを真剣に考えてるよ。

F: Yeah, and they look great. I would love to see American guys dress up more.
うん、それにみんなすてきよね。アメリカの男性ももっとドレス・アップすればいいのに。

M: Why do you suppose they don't?
どうして、そうしないんだと思う？
* suppose「思う；考える」

F: Well, it's just our culture to wear clothes that we feel really comfortable in.
うん、着ていて心地よい洋服を身につけるのが、単純に私たちの文化なのよ。

STEP 3 日本語訳を見ながらスキットを演じてみよう。　CD 3-23

F : Department stores in Tokyo have really nice fashion things for men! Lots of designer brands!

M :

アメリカのお店にはそういうものはないの？

F : Not so many. There isn't as much demand. Americans in general, and especially men, dress very casually.

M :

でも、パーティーやコンサートとかはどうなの？ ドレス・アップしないわけ？

F : Not that much, to be honest. For guys, a pullover sweater and slacks is pretty much the whole deal!

M :

それは、なんだかつまらないね。日本の都会では、多くの女性に加えて男性もファッションを真剣に考えてるよ。

F : Yeah, and they look great. I would love to see American guys dress up more.

M :

どうして、そうしないんだと思う？

F : Well, it's just our culture to wear clothes that we feel really comfortable in.

Unit 144 Subcultures サブカルチャー

STEP 1 各センテンスをシャドーイングしよう。　CD 3-24

STEP 2 テキストを見ながらスキットを演じてみよう。　CD 3-24

F: This is Akihabara. This is the center of our 'geek culture.' In Japan they are known as 'otaku.'

ここが秋葉原よ。日本のギーク文化の中心なのよ。日本では「オタク」と言われているけどね。

* center「中心」　geek「オタク」

M: Interesting! So what happens here?

おもしろいね！ で、ここではどんなことが行われてるの？

F: Well, they love anime, and other fantasy-related things. They can pick up gadgets and costumes here.

えーとね、オタクの人はアニメとかファンタジー関連のものが大好きなの。ここでは細かな品物やコスチュームが買えるのよ。

* fantasy-related「ファンタジーに関連した」　gadgets「気の利いた小道具」

M: Wow! And do they have performances?

へえ！ それで、パフォーマンスもやるのかな？

F: Maybe not so much. That's more likely to happen in Yoyogi Park, on Sundays. People wear crazy costumes and perform or just pose for photos.

おそらく、それほどでもないと思うわ。それなら、日曜日の代々木公園のほうがやってそうね。みんな、ものすごい衣装を着てパフォーマンスしたり、単に写真用にポーズを取ったりしてるわ。

M: Hmmm ... I wonder if that's anything like Venice Beach in Los Angeles. That's where OUR eccentrics hang out!

うーーん、それって、ロスのヴェニス・ビーチみたいなものなのかなあ？ ヴェニス・ビーチにはアメリカの変わり者が集まるんだ！

* eccentric「奇人；変人」　hang out「頻繁に行く；ぶらつく」

F: Really? Are they like Japanese geeks?

そうなの？ 日本のオタクみたいなもの？

M: In Venice, folks just want to show off their individuality. They go around almost naked, paint their bodies, things like that.

ヴェニスの人たちは自分の個性を自慢したいだけなんだ。ほとんど裸で歩き回ったり、カラダにペイントしたり、そんなことをしてるよ。

* folks「人々」　show off「見せびらかす；誇示する」　go around naked「裸でうろつく」

異文化交流 ★★★

301

STEP 3 日本語訳を見ながらスキットを演じてみよう。　CD 3-24

F :

ここが秋葉原よ。日本のギーク文化の中心なのよ。日本では「オタク」と言われているけどね。

M : Interesting! So what happens here?

F :

えーとね、オタクの人はアニメとかファンタジー関連のものが大好きなの。ここでは細かな品物やコスチュームが買えるのよ。

M : Wow! And do they have performances?

F :

おそらく、それほどでもないと思うわ。それなら、日曜日の代々木公園のほうがやってそうね。みんな、ものすごい衣装を着てパフォーマンスしたり、単に写真用にポーズを取ったりしてるわ。

M : Hmmm ... I wonder if that's anything like Venice Beach in Los Angeles. That's where OUR eccentrics hang out!

F :

そうなの？ 日本のオタクみたいなもの？

M : In Venice, folks just want to show off their individuality. They go around almost naked, paint their bodies, things like that.

Unit 145　Sightseeing Spots　観光スポット

STEP 1 　各センテンスをシャドーイングしよう。　　CD 3-25

STEP 2 　テキストを見ながらスキットを演じてみよう。　　CD 3-25

F: We Japanese love to visit historic places, particularly Kyoto.

日本人は歴史的な場所を訪れるのが大好きなの、特に京都ね。

M: I bet! In America, our history is much shorter. But people like to visit historical places.

そうだろうね！ アメリカは、歴史が短いんだ。でも、みんな歴史的な場所に行くのは好きだよ。

F: Where do they like to go?

どこに行くのが好きなの？

M: Well, for example, New England. Some buildings there date back to our colonial days.

うん、例えば、ニュー・イングランドだね。そこの建物のいくつかは植民地時代にまで歴史が遡るんだ。

* date back to ...「…（時代）に遡る」　colonial days「植民地時代」

F: Wow, that's older than I imagined! But we have shrines and temples that are much older. The Kamakura Great Buddha is about eight hundred years old.

へえ、私の想像よりも古いわ！ でも、日本にはもっと古い神社やお寺があるわよ。鎌倉の大仏はだいたい8百歳なのよ。

* shrines and temples「寺社」

M: That's old! For Americans, our national parks are our biggest attraction.

それは古いね！ アメリカ人にとっては国立公園こそが最大の魅力なんだよね。

* attraction「魅力；ひきつけるもの」

F: We have national parks, but they are much smaller. I imagine American parks are enormous.

日本にも国定公園はあるけど、ずっと規模が小さいわ。アメリカの公園は巨大なんでしょうね。

M: Indeed, and spectacular. Lots of people know Yellowstone, Yosemite and The Grand Canyon. But there are many others just as gorgeous.

そうなんだ、それに壮大な眺めなんだよ。イエローストーンとヨセミテ、グランド・キャニオンは多くの人に知られているよ。でも、同じくらいすごいところがほかにもたくさんあるんだよ。

* spectacular「目を見張る；壮観な」

異文化交流 ★★★

303

STEP 3 　日本語訳を見ながらスキットを演じてみよう。　CD 3-25

F :

日本人は歴史的な場所を訪れるのが大好きなの、特に京都ね。

M : I bet! In America, our history is much shorter. But people like to visit historical places.

F :

どこに行くのが好きなの？

M : Well, for example, New England. Some buildings there date back to our colonial days.

F :

へえ、私の想像よりも古いわ！　でも、日本にはもっと古い神社やお寺があるわよ。鎌倉の大仏はだいたい8百歳なのよ。

M : That's old! For Americans, our national parks are our biggest attraction.

F :

日本にも国定公園はあるけど、ずっと規模が小さいわ。アメリカの公園は巨大なんでしょうね。

M : Indeed, and spectacular. Lots of people know Yellowstone, Yosemite and The Grand Canyon. But there are many others just as gorgeous.

Unit 146 Comedians コメディアン

STEP 1 各センテンスをシャドーイングしよう。 CD 3-26

STEP 2 テキストを見ながらスキットを演じてみよう。 CD 3-26

F: Have you ever seen a rakugo comedy performance?
落語は見たことある？
* rakugo comedy performance「落語」

M: Is it like a stand-up comedy act?
それって、スタンダップ・コメディーみたいなものかな？
* stand-up comedy「スタンダップ・コメディー」立って行うコメディー。

F: No, the opposite! It's a 'sit-down' comedy act, because the performers always sit!
いや、逆よ！ 落語は「シッダウン」コメディーなのよ、演者がずっと座っているから！
* opposite「正反対の」 performer「演者」

M: Oh, interesting. Our comedians always stand so they can use body language.
へえ、おもしろいね。アメリカ人のコメディアンは、ボディー・ランゲージが使えるように、いつも立っているよ。

F: Rakugo performers use a folding fan and a hand towel as props.
落語家は扇子や手ぬぐいを小道具として使うのよね。
* folding fan「扇子」 hand towel「手ぬぐい」 props「小道具」

M: Interesting! Do you also have stand-up comedy?
おもしろい！ 日本にはスタンダップ・コメディーもあるの？

F: Yes, but it's different. In America, it is usually one person, right?
ええ、でも、違うものね。アメリカではいつもひとりでやるんでしょ？

M: Yes, almost always. One person telling jokes for an hour or so.
うん、ほとんどそうだね。ひとりの人が１時間くらいジョークを飛ばし続けるんだよ。

F: Our 'stand-up' comedians usually work in pairs, called 'manzai,' performing short skits.
日本の「スタンダップ」コメディアンは、たいていペアでやるの。「漫才」といって、寸劇をやるのよ。

M: We call that type of performance 'vaudeville.' But it's mostly gone.
アメリカではそういうタイプの芸を「ボードビル」って呼ぶんだ。でも、ほとんどなくなっちゃったけど。

異文化交流 ★★★

STEP 3 　日本語訳を見ながらスキットを演じてみよう。　CD 3-26

F :

落語は見たことある？

M : Is it like a stand-up comedy act?

F :

いや、逆よ！ 落語は「シッダウン」コメディーなのよ、演者がずっと座っているから！

M : Oh, interesting. Our comedians always stand so they can use body language.

F :

落語家は扇子や手ぬぐいを小道具として使うのよね。

M : Interesting! Do you also have stand-up comedy?

F :

ええ、でも、違うものね。アメリカではいつもひとりでやるんでしょ？

M : Yes, almost always. One person telling jokes for an hour or so.

F :

日本の「スタンダップ」コメディアンは、たいていペアでやるの。「漫才」といって、寸劇をやるのよ。

M : We call that type of performance 'vaudeville.' But it's mostly gone.

Unit 147 スターとアイドル
Stars and Idols

STEP 1 各センテンスをシャドーイングしよう。　CD 3-27

STEP 2 テキストを見ながらスキットを演じてみよう。　CD 3-27

F: It's surprising to me to see your singers acting in movies and having TV shows.
日本の歌手が映画で演技したり、テレビ番組に出ていたりするのを見ると驚いちゃうわ。

M: That's not common in America?
それってアメリカではあまりないの？

F: It's pretty rare. Some of the biggest female singers make movies, but that's about it.
かなり稀よ。大物の女性歌手がいくらか映画を作っているけど、だいたいそのくらいよ。
* rare「稀な」　that's about it「まあ、そんなところだ」

M: Our more 'serious' musical artists don't do that, but our 'idols' are expected to do it all.
日本でも、もっと真剣な音楽アーティストは、それはしないけど、アイドルたちにはそういうのを全部やることが望まれているのさ。

F: It must be exhausting for them!
すごく疲れるでしょうね！

M: It's tiring, but it's what they want. They are loved by millions of Japanese.
それは骨が折れるよね。でも、それはアイドルが望んでいることだから。何百万もの日本人に愛されているしね。

F: American stars want to be famous, but then complain about paparazzi!
アメリカのスターは有名にはなりたがるけど、パパラッチに関して不平を言うのよね！
* complain about ...「…について不平を言う」　paparazzi「パパラッチ」

M: Japanese stars are expected not to complain about their jobs. They may be punished by the media if they do.
日本のスターたちは、仕事で文句を言わないことが望まれているよ。文句を言えば、メディアに叩かれちゃうかもしれないね。
* punish「罰する」

F: In America, when stars complain it becomes a new gossip story, but it doesn't hurt their popularity.
アメリカでは、スターが文句を言うと、新しいゴシップになるわ。でも、それがスターの人気を損なったりはしないの。
* gossip「噂話」　hurt「傷つける；損なう」

異文化交流 ★★★

STEP 3 日本語訳を見ながらスキットを演じてみよう。 CD 3-27

F : It's surprising to me to see your singers acting in movies and having TV shows.

M :

それってアメリカではあまりないの？

F : It's pretty rare. Some of the biggest female singers make movies, but that's about it.

M :

日本でも、もっと真剣な音楽アーティストは、それはしないけど、アイドルたちにはそういうのを全部やることが望まれているのさ。

F : It must be exhausting for them!

M :

それは骨が折れるよね。でも、それはアイドルが望んでいることだから。何百万もの日本人に愛されているしね。

F : American stars want to be famous, but then complain about paparazzi!

M :

日本のスターたちは、仕事で文句を言わないことが望まれているよ。文句を言えば、メディアに叩かれちゃうかもしれないね。

F : In America, when stars complain it becomes a new gossip story, but it doesn't hurt their popularity.

Unit 148　TV Styles テレビ番組のスタイル

STEP 1 　各センテンスをシャドーイングしよう。　CD 3-28

STEP 2 　テキストを見ながらスキットを演じてみよう。　CD 3-28

M: Every time I turn on the TV in Japan I see somebody eating something!
日本でテレビをつけるたびに、だれかがなにかを食べているところを見かけるよ！
* Every time ...「…するといつも；するたびに」

F: Ha ha! Yes, we love to learn about cooking and restaurants.
ハハ！　日本人は料理やレストランについて知るのが大好きなのよね。

M: That's very different from American TV.
アメリカのテレビとは大違いだね。

F: Well, I've never seen someone eating or cooking in your movies or TV programs!
そうね、アメリカの映画やテレビ番組で、だれかが食事や料理をしているところは観たことがないわ。

M: I guess we just think those things are so natural that they don't need to be shown.
おそらく、そういったことはとても自然だから、映される必要がないんだろうね。
* be shown「映し出される」

F: On the other hand, we enjoy seeing people sharing meals because it makes them seem more real to us.
一方で、日本人はみんながいっしょに食事をしているところを観るのが好きよね。そのおかげでずっとリアルに見えるのよね。
* on the other hand, ...「一方で…」　real「リアルな；真に迫った」

M: Usually if someone is shown eating in American TV or movies, it is part of a gag, or the beginning of a romantic moment.
アメリカのテレビや映画でだれかが食べているところが出てきたら、それはたいていギャグの一部としてだよ。あるいはロマンチックな瞬間の始まりだね。
* part of ...「…の一部」　the beginning of ...「…の始まり」

F: Not in Japan. Watching our favorite characters eating makes them seem like members of our family.
日本では違うわね。お気に入りのキャラクターが食べているところを観ると、その人たちを家族の一員のように感じるのよ。

異文化交流 ★★★

STEP 3 日本語訳を見ながらスキットを演じてみよう。　CD 3-28

M: Every time I turn on the TV in Japan I see somebody eating something!

F:

ハハ！ 日本人は料理やレストランについて知るのが大好きなのよね。

M: That's very different from American TV.

F:

そうね、アメリカの映画やテレビ番組で、だれかが食事や料理をしているところは観たことがないわ。

M: I guess we just think those things are so natural that they don't need to be shown.

F:

一方で、日本人はみんながいっしょに食事をしているところを観るのが好きよね。そのおかげでずっとリアルに見えるのよね。

M: Usually if someone is shown eating in American TV or movies, it is part of a gag, or the beginning of a romantic moment.

F:

日本では違うわね。お気に入りのキャラクターが食べているのを観ると、その人たちを家族の一員のように感じるのよ。

Unit 149 主食
Food Staples

STEP 1 各センテンスをシャドーイングしよう。　CD 3-29

STEP 2 テキストを見ながらスキットを演じてみよう。　CD 3-29

F: For most Japanese, the basis of a meal is rice, fish and miso soup. And maybe pickles.

多くの日本人にとって、食事の基本はお米と魚、それに味噌汁なの。それとおそらくお漬け物ね。

M: Hmmm. In America, many people think about meat and potatoes the same way. And a vegetable.

うーん。アメリカでは、多くの人が肉とポテトを同じふうに考えているよ。それと野菜だね。

F: I see. So potatoes are to Americans what rice is to Japanese?

そうか。ということは、日本人がお米を食べるように、アメリカ人はポテトを食べるわけね。

＊ A is to ... what B is to ...「…にとってのAは、…にとってのBと同じだ」

M: I guess you could say that. But not everybody. Some people might prefer bread or pasta.

そうとも言えるかな。でも、みんなではないんだ。パンやパスタのほうを好む人もいるからね。

F: We like those too. But many Japanese just don't feel satisfied without a bowl of rice.

私たちもそれは好きだよ。でも、多くの日本人は、1杯のご飯がないと満足しないと思うな。

＊ feel satisfied「満足する」　a bowl of ...「茶碗1杯の…」

M: That's different from Americans. As long as we have some starchy food, we feel full.

そこはアメリカ人とは違うね。デンプン質の食べ物がありさえすれば、満足するからね。

＊ be different from ...「…とは異なる」　starchy「デンプン質の」

F: And how about meat? Can it be any kind, including fish?

で、お肉はどうなの？　それって、魚も含めてどんなものでもいいのかな？

M: Yes. But recently vegetarianism is becoming more and more popular too. Most people are cutting down on red meat.

うん。でも、最近は菜食主義もどんどん人気になっているんだ。ほとんどの人が赤肉を減らしているよ。

＊ vegetarianism「菜食（主義）」　cut down on ...「…を減らす」
　red meat「赤肉」牛肉や羊肉など赤身の肉。

異文化交流 ★★★

STEP 3 　日本語訳を見ながらスキットを演じてみよう。　CD 3-29

F : _____

多くの日本人にとって、食事の基本はお米と魚、それに味噌汁なの。それとおそらくお漬け物ね。

M : Hmmm. In America, many people think about meat and potatoes the same way. And a vegetable.

F : _____

そうか。ということは、日本人がお米を食べるように、アメリカ人はポテトを食べるわけね。

M : I guess you could say that. But not everybody. Some people might prefer bread or pasta.

F : _____

私たちもそれは好きだよ。でも、多くの日本人は、1杯のご飯がないと満足しないと思うな。

M : That's different from Americans. As long as we have some starchy food, we feel full.

F : _____

で、お肉はどうなの？ それって、魚も含めてどんなものでもいいのかな？

M : Yes. But recently vegetarianism is becoming more and more popular too. Most people are cutting down on red meat.

Unit 150 Noodles and Bread 麺類とパン

STEP 1 各センテンスをシャドーイングしよう。　CD 3-30

STEP 2 テキストを見ながらスキットを演じてみよう。　CD 3-30

F: We Japanese love noodles! Ramen, udon, soba, soumen, etc.
日本人は麺類が大好きなの！ ラーメン、うどん、そば、そうめんとかね。

M: Well, noodles are great! We Americans have to have our pasta!
うん、麺類はいいよね！ 僕らアメリカ人はパスタがなきゃダメ！
* have to have ...「…がなければダメだ」

F: We love pasta too! But most Asian noodle dishes serve the noodles in a soup.
日本人もパスタ好きだよ！ でも、ほとんどのアジアの麺料理は麺をスープに入れて出すのよ。

M: Yes, so yummy! I love ramen too.
うん、すごくおいしいよね！ 僕もラーメンが大好きなんだ。

F: Do Americans have a similar love of some kind of food?
アメリカ人はなにかの食べ物を似たように気に入っているのかな？
* similar love「似たような愛着・好み」

M: Well, there's pasta. And I guess I would say bread. We have many kinds, like bagels, sourdough bread, etc. And pizza, which is basically bread with sauce on top.
うん、パスタだよね。それと、パンだろうね。いろんな種類があるんだよ。ベーグルとか、サワードウ・ブレッドとかね。それから、ピザ。これは基本的には上にソースを塗ったパンだよね。
* I guess I would say ...「おそらく…かなあ」

F: That's true! When a pizza crust is well done, it's like eating delicious bread.
そうね！ ピザの皮が上手に焼けると、おいしいパンを食べている感じよね。

M: Exactly! And freshly baked!
そのとおり！ 焼きたてのね！

F: I agree. But I like pulling delicious noodles out of a hot broth even better!
そうよね。でも、私は熱々のスープからおいしい麺をすするほうがずっと好きだけどね！
* pull「(麺を引っ張って) 持ち上げる」　hot broth「熱いスープ」

異文化交流 ★★★

STEP 3

— 313 —

STEP 3　　日本語訳を見ながらスキットを演じてみよう。　　CD 3-30

F :

日本人は麺類が大好きなの！ ラーメン、うどん、そば、そうめんとかね。

M : Well, noodles are great! We Americans have to have our pasta!

F :

日本人もパスタ好きだよ！ でも、ほとんどのアジアの麺料理は麺をスープに入れて出すのよ。

M : Yes, so yummy! I love ramen too.

F :

アメリカ人はなにかの食べ物を似たように気に入っているのかな？

M : Well, there's pasta. And I guess I would say bread. We have many kinds, like bagels, sourdough bread, etc. And pizza, which is basically bread with sauce on top.

F :

そうね！ ピザの皮が上手に焼けると、おいしいパンを食べている感じよね。

M : Exactly! And freshly baked!

F :

そうよね。でも、私は熱々のスープからおいしい麺をすするほうがずっと好きだけどね！

Unit 151 Favorite Foods of Kids 子どもの好きな食べ物

STEP 1 　各センテンスをシャドーイングしよう。　　CD 3-31

STEP 2 　テキストを見ながらスキットを演じてみよう。　　CD 3-31

F : What kind of food do American kids like to eat the most?
アメリカの子どもたちはどんな食べ物がいちばん好きなの？

M : You mean for meals? Hmmm. Probably pizza and hamburgers.
食事っていう意味でかな？　うーん。おそらくピザとハンバーガーだね。

F : For meals? Aren't those just basically snack foods?
食事に？　それって基本的にはただのスナックなんじゃないの？

M : Not at all. Pizza and salad is a meal. Same with a hamburger, fries and a salad.
全然。ピザとサラダで食事になるよ。ハンバーガーとポテト・フライとサラダもそうだよ。
* same with ... 「…も同じ」

F : A lot of Japanese kids like those too.
日本の子どもたちの多くもピザとハンバーガーは好きだよ。

M : So what do Japanese kids love the most?
で、日本の子どもたちはなにがいちばん好きなの？

F : Curry rice! Kids want to have it at least once a week. They also like 'hamburg.'
カレーライスね！　子どもは週に1回は食べたがるわ。ハンバーグも好きだよ。

M : You mean hamburgers, just like we have?
アメリカで食べるような、ハンバーガーのこと？

F : It's different. We serve a ground beef patty with gravy and a lot of rice.
違うわ。牛挽肉のパティーをグレイビー・ソースとたくさんのご飯といっしょに出すの。
* ground beef「牛挽肉」　patty「挽肉などを平たく丸く焼いたもの」　gravy「グレイビー・ソース」

M : So Japanese kids want to have rice with each dinner?
で、日本の子どもは毎食ご飯を食べたがるんだね？

F : Almost. Another favorite is ramen.
ほとんどね。子どもは、ほかにもラーメンも大好きなのよ。

異文化交流 ★★★

— 315 —

STEP 3 　日本語訳を見ながらスキットを演じてみよう。　CD 3-31

F :

アメリカの子どもたちはどんな食べ物がいちばん好きなの？

M : You mean for meals? Hmmm. Probably pizza and hamburgers.

F :

食事に？ それって基本的にはただのスナックなんじゃないの？

M : Not at all. Pizza and salad is a meal. Same with a hamburger, fries and a salad.

F :

日本の子どもたちの多くもピザとハンバーガーは好きだよ。

M : So what do Japanese kids love the most?

F :

カレーライスね！ 子どもは週に1回は食べたがるわよ。ハンバーグも好きだよ。

M : You mean hamburgers, just like we have?

F :

違うわ。牛挽肉のパティーをグレイビー・ソースとたくさんのご飯といっしょに出すの。

M : So Japanese kids want to have rice with each dinner?

F :

ほとんどね。子どもは、ほかにもラーメンも大好きなのよ。

Unit 152 Obesity 肥満

STEP 1 各センテンスをシャドーイングしよう。 CD 3-32

STEP 2 テキストを見ながらスキットを演じてみよう。 CD 3-32

F: America really has a problem with obesity, doesn't it?
アメリカはホントにひどい肥満の問題を抱えているよね？
* obesity「肥満」

M: Yes, it does, and it's getting worse. It's happening at younger ages, and people are getting bigger.
うん、そうだね。それにさらに悪化しているよ。さらに若い年齢から起こっているし、どんどんみんなのカラダが巨大化してるんだよね。

F: Yes, the last time I was there, I noticed how huge some of the kids are. What's happening?
ええ、前にアメリカにいたとき、すごく大きな子どもたちがいるのに気づいたわ。どうなってるの？
* I noticed how huge ... are「…がどれほど大きいかに気づいた」

M: I think it's basically our food choices. We eat too much fried food, too much junk food.
基本的には、食べ物の選択だと思うよ。揚げ物やジャンク・フードを食べすぎてるしね。

F: Those types of foods have really caught on in Japan, too. We have an obesity problem too, but much smaller.
そういう食べ物は日本でもすごく流行しているわ。日本にも肥満の問題があるんだけど、ずっと小さいわ。
* catch on in ...「…で流行する」 smaller「より小さな」

M: Yeah, most Japanese keep so slim. What's your secret?
うん、ほとんどの日本人はずっとスリムだよね。なにか秘訣があるの？

F: It's the traditional diet, of fish, rice, miso, etc. It is one of the healthiest in the world. We are pretty proud of that.
魚やお米、味噌なんかの伝統的な食事だよ。世界中でももっとも健康な食事なのよ。日本人の誇りね。
* traditional diet「伝統的な食事・食餌」 healthiest「もっとも健康な」

M: You should be!
誇りに思って当然だよ！

異文化交流 ★★★

317

STEP 3 　日本語訳を見ながらスキットを演じてみよう。　CD 3-32

F :

アメリカはホントにひどい肥満の問題を抱えているよね？

M : Yes, it does, and it's getting worse. It's happening at younger ages, and people are getting bigger.

F :

ええ、前にアメリカにいたとき、すごく大きな子どもたちがいるのに気づいたわ。どうなってるの？

M : I think it's basically our food choices. We eat too much fried food, too much junk food.

F :

そういう食べ物は日本でもすごく流行しているわ。日本にも肥満の問題があるんだけど、ずっと小さいわ。

M : Yeah, most Japanese keep so slim. What's your secret?

F :

魚やお米、味噌なんかの伝統的な食事だよ。世界中でももっとも健康な食事なのよ。日本人の誇りね。

M : You should be!

Unit 153 ファミレス
Family Restaurants

STEP 1 >> 各センテンスをシャドーイングしよう。　CD 3-33

STEP 2 >> テキストを見ながらスキットを演じてみよう。　CD 3-33

F: In American family restaurants, the same person always comes to your table, right?
アメリカのファミレスでは、必ず同じ人がテーブルに来るんでしょ？

M: Well ... yes! Don't they in Japan?
えーと、そうだね！ 日本では来ないの？

F: No, in Japanese family restaurants it is different.
うん、日本のファミレスでは、違うわね。

M: Then how do you know who to tip? Oh, wait, no tipping in Japan, right?
じゃあ、だれにチップをあげればいいか、どうやったらわかるのさ？ ああ、待って、日本にはチップはないよね？
＊ no tipping「チップをあげることはない」

F: That's right. Oh, I see. So you tip your waitress even in family restaurants?
そうなのよ。そうか。ということは、アメリカ人はファミレスでもウェイトレスさんにチップをあげるのね？

M: Yeah, we sure do! They hardly make anything in wages and depend on tips.
うん、もちろん！ 彼女たちは賃金ではほとんど稼げなくて、チップに頼ってるんだよ。
＊ in wage「賃金として」　depend on ...「…に頼る」

F: So they must be very friendly and give good service!
だから、フレンドリーにして、いいサービスをしなければならないのね！

M: Hmmm ... most of the time. Sometimes you get somebody who is rude. I never leave a big tip then.
うーん…ほとんどの場合はね。たまに失礼な人もいるにはいるよ。そういう場合はチップを減らすんだ。

F: In Japan we don't tip, but we still get great service.
日本ではチップはあげないけど、サービスはいいわよ。

M: Wow, that sounds super!
へえ、それは最高だね！

異文化交流 ★★★

STEP 3 　日本語訳を見ながらスキットを演じてみよう。　CD 3-33

F :

アメリカのファミレスでは、必ず同じ人がテーブルに来るんでしょ？

M : Well ... yes! Don't they in Japan?

F :

うん、日本のファミレスでは、違うわね。

M : Then how do you know who to tip? Oh, wait, no tipping in Japan, right?

F :

そうなのよ。そうか。ということは、アメリカ人はファミレスでもウェイトレスさんにチップをあげるのね？

M : Yeah, we sure do! They hardly make anything in wages and depend on tips.

F :

だから、フレンドリーにして、いいサービスをしなければならないのね！

M : Hmmm ... most of the time. Sometimes you get somebody who is rude. I never leave a big tip then.

F :

日本ではチップはあげないけど、サービスはいいわよ。

M : Wow, that sounds super!

Unit 154 Service Standards サービスのレベル

STEP 1 各センテンスをシャドーイングしよう。　CD 3-34

STEP 2 テキストを見ながらスキットを演じてみよう。　CD 3-34

M: Japanese store workers are so courteous and helpful!
日本の店員さんたちは、とてもていねいに手伝ってくれるよね！
* courteous 「ていねいな；礼儀正しい」

F: Yes, it's a point of our business culture. The customer is king!
ええ、それが日本のビジネス文化のポイントなのよ。お客さまは神様なの！

M: It must be a shock for Japanese to go abroad and be treated rudely in stores.
日本人が外国に行って、お店で失礼な扱いを受けたらショックだろうね。
* must be ... 「…に違いない」　rudely 「失礼に；不躾に」

F: Yes, pretty shocking. Often people act like they don't want to help you.
うん、かなりショックよ。手伝いなんかしたくないって感じで振る舞う人がよくいるわよね。

M: Ha, ha, they probably don't! They are paid very low wages for that kind of work.
ハハ、おそらく手伝いたくないんだよ！ああいった仕事はとても給料が低いからね。

F: But still, if a store loses customers it can't do business.
でも、お店が顧客を失ったら、商売にならないじゃないの。

M: True, but some people just have a bad attitude.
そうだけど、態度が悪い人はいるんだよ。

F: I think that's strange though, because American companies are the most successful in the world.
それでも変だと思うわ。だって、アメリカの会社は世界でももっとも成功してるでしょ。

M: NOT because of the customer service they provide. I WISH it was better, but I don't see it changing.
企業が提供している顧客サービスが (成功の) 理由ではないよ。もっとよかったらいいんだけど、変わるとは思わないね。
* don't see it changing 「変わるとは思わない」

異文化交流 ★★★

STEP 3 》 日本語訳を見ながらスキットを演じてみよう。 CD 3-34

M: Japanese store workers are so courteous and helpful!

F:

ええ、それが日本のビジネス文化のポイントなのよ。お客さまは神様なの！

M: It must be a shock for Japanese to go abroad and be treated rudely in stores.

F:

うん、かなりショックよ。手伝いなんかしたくないって感じで振る舞う人がよくいるわよね。

M: Ha, ha, they probably don't! They are paid very low wages for that kind of work.

F:

でも、お店が顧客を失ったら、商売にならないじゃないの。

M: True, but some people just have a bad attitude.

F:

それでも変だと思うわ。だって、アメリカの会社は世界でももっとも成功してるでしょ。

M: NOT because of the customer service they provide. I WISH it was better, but I don't see it changing.

Unit 155　Public Toilets and Restrooms 公衆トイレ

STEP 1 　各センテンスをシャドーイングしよう。　CD 3-35

STEP 2 　テキストを見ながらスキットを演じてみよう。　CD 3-35

M: I went into a restroom in Tokyo and the toilet had so many buttons!
東京のレストランでお手洗いに入ったんだけど、トイレにものすごい数のボタンがついてたよ！

F: Yes, many homes have that kind of toilet as well. Very hi-tech!
うん、多くの家にも同じようなトイレがあるのよ。すごくハイテクなのよ！

M: I was too afraid to try! I imagined water splashing all over the place!
恐ろしくて使えなかったよ！ 水がそこいら中に飛び散るのを想像しちゃってさ！
* splash「(水や泥などが) 飛び散る；跳ねる」 all over the place「辺り一面に」

F: Ha ha! Next time you definitely should. So you don't have them in America, huh?
ハハ！ 次は絶対に試すべきよ。ということは、アメリカにはそういうのはないのね？

M: I've never seen one. Public restrooms in America are very simple things.
見たこともないよ。アメリカの公衆トイレはとてもシンプルなものだよ。
* public restroom「公衆便所」 simple thing「シンプルなもの」

F: Is it true that some public toilets don't even have doors? Like in stadiums?
トイレによっては、ドアもないってホントなの？ スタジアムのトイレみたいに。

M: No, no; they have doors! But the doors don't go all the way down to the floor.
いや、いや、ドアはあるよ！ でも、ドアが床までずっとは降りてないんだけどね。
* all the way down to ...「ずっと…まで下に」

F: Yikes! I don't think I could use one, then. It would be humiliating to show my legs when I'm ... you know ...
ゲッ！ じゃあ、私には使えないかも。足を見せながらなんて屈辱だわよ、あのときに…ってわかるでしょ…
* Yikes!「ゲッ！；うわっ！」嫌悪や苦痛の表現。

異文化交流 ★★★

323

STEP 3　日本語訳を見ながらスキットを演じてみよう。　CD 3-35

M: I went into a restroom in Tokyo and the toilet had so many buttons!

F:

うん、多くの家にも同じようなトイレがあるのよ。すごくハイテクなのよ！

M: I was too afraid to try! I imagined water splashing all over the place!

F:

ハハ！ 次は絶対に試すべきよ。ということは、アメリカにはそういうのはないのね？

M: I've never seen one. Public restrooms in America are very simple things.

F:

トイレによっては、ドアもないってホントなの？ スタジアムのトイレみたいに。

M: No, no; they have doors! But the doors don't go all the way down to the floor.

F:

ゲッ！ じゃあ、私には使えないかも。足を見せながらなんて屈辱だわよ、あのときに…ってわかるでしょ…

Unit 156 Tipping / チップ

STEP 1 各センテンスをシャドーイングしよう。 CD 3-36

STEP 2 テキストを見ながらスキットを演じてみよう。 CD 3-36

F: Tipping is one of the things about America I just don't understand!
チップは、アメリカに関して私にわからないことのひとつなのよね！

M: Ha ha! I can imagine!
ハハ！ 想像はつくよ！

F: In America, I never know who to tip, or how much.
アメリカで、だれにどれだけのチップをあげたらいいのかわからないの。

M: Let me help. We tip taxi drivers. We tip people who do our hair. We tip waiters, and we tip people who help us at hotels.
僕が教えてあげるよ。タクシーの運転手にチップをあげて、美容師さんにもチップをあげるんだ。ウェイターやホテルで手伝ってくれる人にもね。

F: At hotels too!? Am I supposed to leave a tip when I check out?
ホテルでもなの？ チェック・アウトするときにもチップをあげるべきなの？
* check out「チェック・アウトする」

M: No, not then. But if someone does something nice for you like carrying your bags up or calling you a taxi, they probably expect a tip.
いや、そのときはいらないよ。バッグを運ぶとか、タクシーを呼ぶとか、だれかがなにかいいことをしてくれたら、その人たちはチップを期待しているよ。

F: Gosh, what a confusing system! Besides, it's those peoples' jobs to help you!
ああ、なんて紛らわしいシステムなの！ それに、手伝うのが、彼らの仕事でしょ！
* Gosh「ああ；まあ」驚きや不快を表す。 besides「その上；さらに」

M: Ha ha, you're right! But it's just our way.
ハハ、そのとおりだよ！ でも、それがアメリカ人のやり方のさ。
* way「やり方；方法」

異文化交流 ★★★

325

STEP 3 　日本語訳を見ながらスキットを演じてみよう。　CD 3-36

F :
　　　チップは、アメリカに関して私にわからないことのひとつなのよね！

M : Ha ha! I can imagine!

F :
　　　アメリカで、だれにどれだけのチップをあげたらいいのかわからないの。

M : Let me help. We tip taxi drivers. We tip people who do our hair. We tip waiters, and we tip people who help us at hotels.

F :
　　　ホテルでもなの？ チェック・アウトするときにもチップをあげるべきなの？

M : No, not then. But if someone does something nice for you like carrying your bags up or calling you a taxi, they probably expect a tip.

F :
　　　ああ、なんて紛らわしいシステムなの！ それに、手伝うのが、彼らの仕事でしょ！

M : Ha ha, you're right! But it's just our way.

Unit 157 ハグとお辞儀
Hugging and Bowing

STEP 1 各センテンスをシャドーイングしよう。　CD 3-37

STEP 2 テキストを見ながらスキットを演じてみよう。　CD 3-37

M: I think Americans don't know how to bow, but Japanese don't know how to hug!

アメリカ人はお辞儀の仕方がわからないけど、日本人はハグの仕方がわからないよね！

＊ how to bow/hug「お辞儀／ハグの仕方」

F: Ha, ha! You're right! The idea of hugging someone is really embarrassing to most of us.

ハハ！　そのとおりね！　だれかをハグするって考えは、私たちの多くにとってホントに恥ずかしいのよ。

＊ embarrassing「恥ずかしい」

M: We Americans love to hug! Well, most of us do. We hug friends and family. We even hug at work sometimes.

僕らアメリカ人はハグが大好きだよ！　ほとんどの人がハグをするんだ。友人や家族にハグをするし、時には仕事でもするよ。

F: In Japan, we don't even hug family members! We're really shy about displaying strong affection.

日本では、家族にさえハグはしないわよ！　強い愛情を表現するのがすごく照れくさいのよね。

＊ display「表現する；（感情などを）表す」　affection「愛情」

M: Well, I don't really understand bows. I guess they are meant to show respect, huh?

あのさ、僕はお辞儀がよくわからないよ。尊敬を表現するためのものなのかなあ？

F: Yes, but most people just do it out of habit. When someone walks into a room we bow as a greeting.

ええ、でも多くの人は習慣でやっているの。だれかが部屋に入ってきたら、あいさつとしてお辞儀をするのよ。

＊ out of habit「習慣から」　greeting「あいさつ」

M: You mean it's kind of like saying hi?

「やあ」ってあいさつしてる感じってこと？

F: In that case, yeah. But we also bow when we apologize. We bow very deeply then.

その場合はね。でも、日本人は謝るときにもお辞儀をするわ。そのときはとても深くね。

— 327 —

STEP 3 　日本語訳を見ながらスキットを演じてみよう。　CD 3-37

M: I think Americans don't know how to bow, but Japanese don't know how to hug!

F:

ハハ！　そのとおりね！　だれかをハグするって考えは、私たちの多くにとってホントに恥ずかしいのよ。

M: We Americans love to hug! Well, most of us do. We hug friends and family. We even hug at work sometimes.

F:

日本では、家族にさえハグはしないわよ！　強い愛情を表現するのがすごく照れくさいのよね。

M: Well, I don't really understand bows. I guess they are meant to show respect, huh?

F:

ええ、でも多くの人は習慣でやっているの。だれかが部屋に入ってきたら、あいさつとしてお辞儀をするのよ。

M: You mean it's kind of like saying hi?

F:

その場合はね。でも、日本人は謝るときにもお辞儀をするわ。そのときはとても深くね。

Unit 158 Shortened Phrases 1 略語 ①

STEP 1 各センテンスをシャドーイングしよう。　CD 3-38

STEP 2 テキストを見ながらスキットを演じてみよう。　CD 3-38

M: That's the second KFC I've seen today. They are popular here.
あそこで、今日見つけた 2 軒目の KFC だよ。こっちでは人気なんだね。
* KFC「ケンタッキーフライドチキン」

F: 'KFC?' Oh, you mean 'Kentucky'?
「KFC」？ ああ、「ケンタッキー」のことね？

M: Ha, ha. That's what you call it? Kentucky is a state, not a restaurant!
ハハ。日本ではそう呼んでいるの？ ケンタッキーは州でレストランじゃないよ！

F: Do you know what we call McDonald's? We call it just 'Mac.' Much easier to say!
日本人がマクドナルドをなんと呼んでいるか知ってる？ 単に「マック」って呼ぶのよ。言いやすいでしょ！
* what we call McDonald's「僕らがマクドナルドをどう呼ぶか」

M: That's true! But if you said you wanted to go to Mac in the U.S. nobody would know what you meant!
そうだね！ でも、アメリカでマックに行きたいって言っても、意味がわからないよ。

F: Do Americans shorten names in the same way?
アメリカ人も同じように名前を短くするのかな？
* shorten「短くする」　in the same way「同じように」

M: Hmm. Let me think. Well, some people call "McDonald's" "Micky D's."
うーん、そうだねー。えっとね、「マクドナルド」を「ミッキー・ディーズ」って呼ぶ人はいるよ。

F: Ha ha! In Japan people would think you were talking about the cartoon character!
ハハ！ 日本ではマンガのキャラクターの話をしているのかと思っちゃうわね！

M: I guess we have a lot. We call movies 'flicks' and BMWs 'Beemers.'
アメリカには、たくさんあるかもね。映画を「フリックス」と言ったり、BMW を「ビーマーズ」って言ったりするよ。
* flick「映画」　Beemer「BMW」いずれも俗語表現。

異文化交流 ★★★

STEP 3 日本語訳を見ながらスキットを演じてみよう。 CD 3-38

M: That's the second KFC I've seen today. They are popular here.

F:

「KFC」？ ああ、「ケンタッキー」のことね？

M: Ha, ha. That's what you call it? Kentucky is a state, not a restaurant!

F:

日本人がマクドナルドをなんと呼んでいるか知ってる？ 単に「マック」って呼ぶのよ。言いやすいでしょ！

M: That's true! But if you said you wanted to go to Mac in the U.S. nobody would know what you meant!

F:

アメリカ人も同じように名前を短くするのかな？

M: Hmm. Let me think. Well, some people call "McDonald's" "Micky D's."

F:

ハハ！ 日本ではマンガのキャラクターの話をしているのかと思っちゃうわね！

M: I guess we have a lot. We call movies 'flicks' and BMWs 'Beemers.'

Unit 159 　Shortened Phrases 2 　略語②

STEP 1 　各センテンスをシャドーイングしよう。　CD 3-39

STEP 2 　テキストを見ながらスキットを演じてみよう。　CD 3-39

F: What does 'Pokemon' mean in Japanese?
日本語の「ポケモン」ってどういう意味なの？

M: You didn't know? It's short for 'Pocket Monster!'
知らなかったの？「ポケットモンスター」を短くしたものだよ！
＊ short「省略」

F: Wow! I never even thought of that. That's clever!
へえ！ それは考えたことさえなかったわ。うまいわね！
＊ clever「巧みな；巧妙な」

M: In Japan, we shorten things like that a lot. For example, people's names.
日本では、そういうのを、たくさん短くするんだよね。例えば、人名とかね。
＊ things like that「そういったもの」

F: We do that too, of course. For example, I'm Sally, but people call me 'Sal.'
それは、アメリカ人も、もちろんやるわ。例えば私はサリーだけど、みんなは「サル」って呼ぶの。

M: One of our most popular TV stars is 'Kimutaku.' It's short for 'Kimura Takuya.'
日本の有名なテレビ・スターは「キムタク」だけど、それって「キムラタクヤ」を短くしたものなんだ。

F: Is this a recent trend or something?
それって最近のトレンドかなにかなの？
＊ ... or something「…かなにか」

M: It has become more popular. Young people even say "AkeOme" instead of "Akemashite Omedetou" as a New Year's greeting.
ずいぶん多くなってきてるよ。若者は、お正月のあいさつで、「明けましておめでとう」の代わりに「あけおめ」って言ったりさえするよ。

F: Our young people do something similar. For example, they use 'YOLO' to mean 'you only live once' and say 'sup?' instead of 'what's up?'
アメリカの若者も似たようなことをするわ。例えば、'you only live once'（人生は一度きりしかない）の代わりに 'YOLO' を使ったり、'what's up?'（どうしてる？）の代わりに 'sup?' と言ったりするのよね。

異文化交流 ★★★

STEP 3 　日本語訳を見ながらスキットを演じてみよう。　CD 3-39

F: What does 'Pokemon' mean in Japanese?

M:

知らなかったの？「ポケットモンスター」を短くしたものだよ！

F: Wow! I never even thought of that. That's clever!

M:

日本では、そういうのを、たくさん短くするんだよね。例えば、人名とかね。

F: We do that too, of course. For example, I'm Sally, but people call me 'Sal.'

M:

日本の有名なテレビ・スターは「キムタク」だけど、それって「キムラタクヤ」を短くしたものなんだ。

F: Is this a recent trend or something?

M:

ずいぶん多くなってきてるよ。若者は、お正月のあいさつで、「明けましておめでとう」の代わりに「あけおめ」って言ったりさえするよ。

F: Our young people do something similar. For example, they use 'YOLO' to mean 'you only live once' and say 'sup?' instead of 'what's up?'

Unit 160 Getting Words Wrong 言葉の間違い

STEP 1 各センテンスをシャドーイングしよう。 CD 3-40

STEP 2 テキストを見ながらスキットを演じてみよう。 CD 3-40

M: A Japanese friend of mine said that I was 'high tension.' It sounded terrible, but she said it wasn't bad.

僕の友人の日本人が、僕のことを「ハイ・テンション」だって言うんだよ。僕にはひどいことに聞こえたんだけど、彼女は、それは悪いことじゃないって言ってたんだよね。

* tension「緊張；緊迫状態」 terrible「ひどく悪い」

F: Really? Why? What does it mean in English?

そうなの？ どうして？ 英語ではどういう意味なの？

M: Well, first of all, it's not used to describe people. But it refers to a tense situation.

うん、まず、人を描写するのには使わないんだけどね。緊迫した状況に言及する言葉なんだよ。

* first of all「まず第一に」 refer to ...「…に言及する」 situation「状況」

F: Oh, that's almost the opposite of what it means here!

ああ、それは日本語での意味とは、ほぼ真逆ね！

* opposite「正反対（の物事）」 what it means here「ここでそれが意味すること」

M: She also called me 'energish,' and I had no idea what she meant! Ha ha!

僕のことを「エネルギッシュ」だとも言ってたけど、なんのことだかさっぱりわからなかったよ！ ハハ！

* have no idea「さっぱりわからない」

F: That isn't English? I always thought it was.

それって英語じゃないの？ ずっと英語だと思ってたけど。

M: Well, the word we use is 'energetic.'

うん、僕らが使う単語は「エナジェティック」だよ。

F: Still, it's embarrassing that we use so many words wrongly. Do Americans do the same thing?

それにしても、日本人がたくさんの単語を間違って使っているのは恥ずかしいわ。アメリカ人も同じことをするのかなあ？

M: A lot of Americans don't know the difference between sushi and sashimi. They think sashimi is sushi!

多くのアメリカ人が、すしと刺身の違いを知らないよ。みんな、刺身とすしが同じだと思ってるよ。

異文化交流 ★★★

— 333 —

STEP 3 　日本語訳を見ながらスキットを演じてみよう。　CD 3-40

M: A Japanese friend of mine said that I was 'high tension.' It sounded terrible, but she said it wasn't bad.

F:

そうなの？ どうして？ 英語ではどういう意味なの？

M: Well, first of all, it's not used to describe people. But it refers to a tense situation.

F:

ああ、それは日本語での意味とは、ほぼ真逆ね！

M: She also called me 'energish,' and I had no idea what she meant! Ha ha!

F:

それって英語じゃないの？ ずっと英語だと思ってたけど。

M: Well, the word we use is 'energetic.'

F:

それにしても、日本人がたくさんの単語を間違って使っているのは恥ずかしいわ。アメリカ人も同じことをするのかなあ？

M: A lot of Americans don't know the difference between sushi and sashimi. They think sashimi is sushi!

■ 著者略歴

長尾 和夫（Kazuo Nagao）
福岡県出身。南雲堂出版、アスク講談社、NOVA などで、大学英語教科書や語学系書籍・CD-ROM・Web サイトなどの編集・制作・執筆に携わる。現在、語学書籍の出版プロデュース・執筆・編集・翻訳などを行うアルファ・プラス・カフェ（www.alphapluscafe.com）を主宰。『絶対「英語の耳」になる！』シリーズ全 13 点（三修社）、『日常生活を英語でドンドン説明してみよう』（アスク出版）、『英会話 見たまま練習帳』（DHC）、『ビジネス英会話 高速変換トレーニング』（アルク）、『英語で自分をアピールできますか？』『英語でケンカができますか？』（角川グループパブリッシング）、『書き込み式・英語で自分を説明できる本』（日本経済新聞出版社）ほか、著訳書・編集は 250 点を超える。

アンディ・バーガー（Andy Boerger）
米国出身。オハイオ州立大学で BFA を取得。横浜国立大学講師。サイマルアカデミー CTC（Simul Academy Corporate Training Center）、アルク、タイムライフなどでの英会話講師経験を活かし、A+Café（アルファ・プラス・カフェ）の主要メンバーとして、多岐にわたる語学書籍の執筆に活躍中。主著に、『絶対「英語の口」になる！ 中学英語で基礎から鍛えるシャドーイング大特訓 50』『絶対「英語の耳」になる！ リスニング 50 のルール』（三修社）、『聴こえる！話せる！ネイティヴ英語発音の法則』（DHC）、『英語で返事ができますか？』（角川グループパブリッシング）などがある。

トーマス・マーティン（Thomas Martin）
米国在住、オハイオ州出身。南山大学卒業。日本語・日本史専攻。株式会社 NOVA での豊富な英語指導経験を活かし、同社出版局に移籍。雑誌『NOVA Station（ノヴァ・ステーション）』、語学書籍シリーズ『NOVA Books』をはじめ、数多くの英語・異文化交流関連出版物の編集・執筆・翻訳等に携わる。98 年に独立後も、語学書籍の執筆・編集、知的財産権関連の翻訳などでマルチに活躍中。著書に『つぶやき英語ビジネス編』（アスク出版）、『絶対「英語の耳」になる！ 音声変化リスニング・パーフェクト・ディクショナリー』（三修社）、『説明するためのビジネス英語表現練習帳』（DHC）などがある。

しゃべって身につく
英会話 スキット・トレーニング160

2014 年 11 月 10 日　第 1 刷発行

著　者	長尾和夫　アンディ・バーガー　トーマス・マーティン
発行者	前田俊秀
発行所	株式会社三修社

〒 150-0001　東京都渋谷区神宮前 2-2-22
TEL 03-3405-4511　FAX 03-3405-4522
振替 00190-9-72758
http://www.sanshusha.co.jp/
編集担当　北村英治

印刷・製本　壮光舎印刷株式会社

©2014 A+Café　Printed in Japan
ISBN978-4-384-04620-5 C2082

®〈日本複製権センター委託出版物〉
本書を無断で複写複製（コピー）することは、著作権法上の例外を除き、禁じられています。
本書をコピーされる場合は、事前に日本複製権センター（JRRC）の許諾を受けてください。
JRRC〈http://www.jrrc.or.jp　e-mail：info@jrrc.or.jp　電話：03-3401-2382〉